NOT JUST DES

NOT JUST DESERTS

A Republican Theory of Criminal Justice

JOHN BRAITHWAITE
and
PHILIP PETTIT

CLARENDON PRESS · OXFORD

Oxford University Press, Great Clarendon Street, Oxford OX2 6DP
Oxford New York
Athens Auckland Bangkok Bogota Bombay Buenos Aires
Calcutta Cape Town Dar es Salaam Delhi Florence Hong Kong Istanbul
Karachi Kuala Lumpur Madras Madrid Melbourne Mexico City
Nairobi Paris Singapore Taipei Tokyo Toronto Warsaw
and associated companies in
Berlin Ibadan

Oxford is a registered trade mark of Oxford University Press

Published in the United States
by Oxford University Press Inc., New York

Reprinted 1998

ISBN 0–19–824056–2

Printed in Great Britain
by Biddles Short Run Books
King's Lynn

For Joyce Braithwaite
and the memory of Dick;

for Anto Pettit
and the memory of Chris

Preface

Although this book is equally the product of the two authors, it goes back to an exchange which John Braithwaite had with Andrew von Hirsch and Ernest van den Haag in the *Journal of Criminal Law and Criminology* in 1982. A good bit of that attack on retributivism appears in Chapter 9 of the book, though some of the views in the 1982 contribution have been substantially modified in the present work. During that debate, von Hirsch accused Braithwaite, fairly we think, of being a destructive critic of just deserts without offering a coherent theoretical alternative. It has taken eight years to think through a response to this challenge. True to von Hirsch's prediction, the discipline of doing so has modified Braithwaite's views considerably.

The book connects with Philip Pettit's work in a different way. He had been concerned to identify values whose consequentialist promotion looked attractive and appealing: in particular, looked likely to sustain a natural respect for rights, deserts, and such constraints (Pettit and Brennan 1986). He had identified dominion as a political goal whose institutional promotion could guarantee respect for certain rights of individuals and he had come to recognize this as a goal of a republican stamp (Pettit 1988a, b). Dominion amounts to freedom in the social sense of full citizenship—elsewhere he describes it as 'franchise'—and a focus on that goal is distinctive of the republican tradition which dominated Western political thinking from Machiavelli down to the end of the eighteenth century.

There is also a complementarity between Braithwaite's *Crime, Shame and Reintegration*, an explanatory theory of crime, and the present normative theory of criminal justice. The explanatory theory book contends that crime will be less in societies which shame offenders without stigmatizing them, which denounce and reason with offenders over their crimes while maintaining bonds of community and respect. Low-crime societies are those that foster a sequence of shaming, forgiveness, and repentance: they are societies that give relatively more prominence to moralizing social control over punitive social control. The republican theory of the present book finds virtue in those forms of social control which involve such a response to crimes: that sort of response serves to foster a greater enjoyment of dominion overall.

Braithwaite is a criminologist, Pettit a philosopher, though both sometimes describe themselves as social and political theorists. The difference of discipline is reflected in the structure of the book: some chapters are equally the work of both, but Pettit bears primary responsibility for those that connect particularly with the philosophical literature (3, 4, 5), Braithwaite for those that connect particularly with the criminological (6, 7, 9). Though primary responsibility is distributed in this way, the book is genuinely the product of interdisciplinary collaboration. Countless hours of discussion, drafting, and revision have meant that every claim has been touched by both pairs of hands. Such collaboration would have been impossible for us were it not for the opportunities afforded by the Research School of Social Sciences at the Australian National University. There can hardly be a better place in the world for pursuing our sort of project.

We would like to thank Beverly Bullpitt, Loraine Hugh, Louise O'Connor, and Anne Robinson, for assistance with typing and David Bennett, Michele Robertson, Jan Robinson, and Ann Smith for help with library research. We are also grateful to a large number of academic colleagues who have offered us comments on aspects of the text or ideas it contains. We should mention in particular Paul Bourke, Andrew Brien, Tom Campbell, Kathleen Daly, Jerry Dworkin, Paul Finn, Brent Fisse, Robert Goodin, Alan Hamlin, Russell Hardin, Andrew von Hirsch, Frank Jackson, Martin Krygier, Norval Morris, and David Neale. Geoffrey Brennan deserves special mention. He has been a tireless discussant of many of the ideas in the book and, sharing our enthusiasm for at least some aspects of republicanism, he has been a great source of encouragement. Finally, we should thank the anonymous referees for Oxford University Press, who gave us many useful suggestions.

Canberra J.B.
1989 P.P.

Contents

Introduction

The core debate throughout the history of criminology has been between theories of punishment. The aim of this book is to transcend this debate with a comprehensive theory: a theory, not only of punishment, but of criminal justice generally. Theories of punishment are dubious guides to public policy, because they funnel our thinking about human conflict and harm-doing into criminal stereotypes; these stereotypes invoke judgements about what is the right punishment to inflict. In shifting from theories of punishment to the theory of criminal justice more generally, we open up for analysis the presumption that punishment is the pre-eminent way of dealing with crime.

John Braithwaite and Philip Pettit are good friends, but they argue a lot about social theory. One night over a few beers such an argument becomes heated and Braithwaite hits Pettit over the head with a half-full bottle of lager. Pettit could respond to this by putting Braithwaite into the master status 'criminal' and calling the police. But this is only one of many characterizations available to Pettit. He might respond by characterizing Braithwaite as a 'violent bastard', a 'terrible drunk', an 'unscholarly wretch', and leaving it at that; or he might come to interpret the incident as an aberration arising from unusual personal problems.

Knowing Braithwaite and Pettit as well as we do, we suspect that the invocation of the criminal label would be one of the least likely results and indeed one of the least sensible ways of dealing with such an incident. After he cleaned up the blood we trust that Pettit would come to view Braithwaite's assault as an immoral and clumsy attempt to say something; thus, in Christie's (1981: 11) words, he would let the crime 'become a starting point for real dialogue, and not for an equally clumsy answer in the form of a spoonful of pain.'

Consider another example. A factory inspector investigates an accident in which a worker slipped on a wet floor into the jaws of a machine which devoured his leg. The investigation reveals that management of the factory had failed to respond to previous slipping incidents either by redesigning the work space or by adding extra guards to the machinery. Now in law the inspector might be justified in defining the factory manager as a corporate criminal and laying charges; but equally she might find that a better way to protect the workers would be to eschew such labelling, sit down with a stunned and shame-faced manager, and try to iron out the sloppiness in his safety management system.

Most human action which fits criminal categories is best dealt with by refraining from invoking a punitive response. This is not to say that we think assaults, for example, should never be punished. It is to say that we need a theory of criminal justice which allows us to respond in the best way to harmful conduct, where responding in that way sometimes will, and more often will not, entail punishment.

Our aspiration then, is for a theory of criminal justice that does not impel us to think about harmful conduct in terms of crime and punishment. But before we begin to develop such a theory, we must provide a brief summary of the state of the art in criminal justice scholarship. And that means that we must look at some theories which are primarily theories of punishment.

The Resurgence of Retributivism

Until the 1970s retributivism—the idea that criminals should be punished because they deserve it—was something of a dead letter in criminology; there were a few scholars in jurisprudence and philosophy who continued to dabble with retributive theories but they did so in ways that had little impact on public policy. During and since the Victorian era retributivism had become increasingly disreputable, probably unfairly, as an unscientific indulgence of emotions of revenge.

In that period a descendant of utilitarianism dominated criminal justice policy-making. This is the theory we call 'preventionism'. Preventionist criminologists were motivated by the search for ways of sentencing criminals that would incapacitate them from continuing to offend (as by locking them away from potential victims), that would give the healing and helping professions opportunities to rehabilitate them, and that would deter both those convicted (specific deterrence) and others who became aware of the punishment (general deterrence).

In that same period, ironically, positive criminology accumulated masses of evidence testifying to the failures of such utilitarian doctrines. All manner of rehabilitation programmes for offenders were tried without any producing consistent evidence that they reduce reoffending rates. The deterrence literature also failed to produce the expected evidence that more police, more prisons, and more certain and severe punishment made a significant difference to the crime rate (e.g. Blumstein *et al.* 1978). Since the literature we are referring to here is massive, and the conclusion we reach fairly uncontroversial within criminology, we will not delay the reader by reviewing it.

The evidence on incapacitation, as distinct from rehabilitation or deterrence, was not so clear. There is no doubt that we can prevent bank robbers from robbing banks by incarcerating or executing them. However, we cannot rely on incarceration to prevent assaulters or rapists from committing their type of offence; nor by such measures can we stop drug dealers from selling drugs or organized crime figures from running criminal empires. And while there is a minority of criminologists who think that if we can lock up enough of the right offenders for long enough we can have a substantial impact on the crime rate (James Q. Wilson 1975; Greenwood 1972; Mark H. Moore *et al.* 1984; Janus 1985), most evidence suggests that with the best techniques available we are wrong about twice as often as we are right in predicting serious reoffending (Cocozza and Steadman 1978; M. L. Cohen and Groth 1978; Dinitz and Conrad 1978; Schlesinger 1978; Monahan 1981; cf. Monahan 1984). The evidence is that we can never catch enough criminals to reduce crime substantially through incapacitation, or at least that the costs of locking up enough criminals to make a real difference to crime is beyond the fiscal capacities of even the wealthiest countries in the world (Conrad and Dinitz 1977; Van Dine *et al.* 1979). Moreover, there are questions about whether imprisonment does not actually worsen the problem in some ways: the convict often learns new illegal skills in 'schools for crime' and criminal groups may recruit new members to fill the gap while colleagues are incarcerated (Reiss 1980).

The flight to retributivism was not only fuelled by the realization that utilitarian and preventionist criminology had failed to deliver on its promises. There was also growing documentation of the injustices perpetrated in the name of preventionist criminal justice. Indeterminate sentences, on the grounds of rehabilitation or incapacitation, allowed offenders to be locked up until they were 'safe' to be returned to the community. Many offenders were locked up for extremely long periods for minor crimes; others got very short terms for serious crimes, thanks to their acting skills in feigning rehabilitation. This disparity was often the product of genuine but misguided utilitarian beliefs that certain minor offenders could be prevented from a downward spiral into more serious crime if only psychologists had long enough to work on their rehabilitation. But it also happened that rehabilitation and incapacitation were used to excuse locking up indefinitely some minor offenders who were regarded as subversive or insolent (Wald 1980). At the other extreme, bribes were sometimes paid to secure the early release of serious offenders, ostensibly on grounds of their remarkable rehabilitation.

These indeed were good reasons for the retributivists to reject utilitarianism and preventionism. Furthermore, the new retributivists rightly accused preventionists of denying the human dignity of offenders by treating them as determined creatures whose behaviour could not be accounted for by their own choices to break the law. Preventionists tended to back off from blaming offenders; instead of holding them responsible for their wrongdoing, they sought to manipulate them by curing their sickness (rehabilitation), changing the reward–cost calculations that determined their offending (deterrence), and keeping them away from criminal opportunities (incapacitation). The retributivists were struck by the injustice, not to mention the futility, of this. So they called for punishment of offenders in proportion to their desert; mostly this meant in proportion to the harmfulness and blameworthiness of their actions. Criminals should get what they deserve—no more, no less.

By and large, then, the new retributivists who gained the ascendency in the punishment debate during the 1970s (von Hirsch 1976; Twentieth-Century Fund Task Force 1976; Singer 1979) were responding to what they correctly identified as the failures, the excesses, the injustices, and the denigration of human agency of utilitarianism and preventionism. The retributivists, we will argue, were moved by the right reasons but took the wrong turn. In particular, they turned too sharply away from the positive, caring strands in the utilitarian and preventionist traditions (Cullen and Gilbert 1982). Tony Bottoms (1980: 21) made the point well when he remarked: 'The rehabilitative ethic, and perhaps still more the liberal reformism which preceded it, was an ethic of coercive caring, but at least there was caring.'

Why the Debate Matters

For most of its history criminology has played a significant role in legitimating state intrusions into the lives and liberties of citizens. In the 1990s it is now playing this role again, thanks in part to the revival of retributivism. Yet in the 1960s and 1970s mainstream criminology began to delegitimate punitive crime control and intrusive police powers. It did this because by then criminology had shown that increased investment in deterrence, rehabilitation, and incapacitation made little or no difference to the crime rate and cost the taxpayer a fortune. The conventional wisdom of criminology was that imprisonment was a discredited institution and the less we had of it the better, that police were necessary but that attempts to give them more powers and resources should be resisted because it could not be demonstrated that doing this would reduce crime.

In some crucial respects criminologists still play this role. In Australia, for example, public opinion polls consistently show a community where those who support capital punishment outnumber those who oppose it. Most expert criminological opinion sits on the side of the opponents, from time to time trotting out evidence in public debates that where capital punishment has been reintroduced crime rates have not fallen. If expert opinion shifted to support for the view that crime could be reduced by capital punishment, the balance in the debate would probably tip, and the noose return.

But this is a vestige of the 1960s and 1970s when mainstream criminology was more consistently delegitimating of punishment. Instead of continuing to contribute to a healthy scepticism about the rationality of punishment, many of the brightest and best criminologists have now begun to cast around for alternative justifications for maintaining punishment as the pre-eminent response to crime. Retributivism serves them well, for the community can be assured that it matters not whether acts of punishment protect them from crime; we do right when we punish because we give people their just deserts. Even scholars who are anything but law and order conservatives have caught the enthusiasm: 'There is a feeling of a Kantian imperative behind the word "deserts". Certain things are simply wrong and ought to be punished. And this we do believe.' (Gaylin and Rothman 1976: xxxix).

It follows from the theory we defend, which we will summarize in a moment, that it is good when societies feel uncomfortable about punishment, when people see punishment as a necessary evil rather than a good in itself. Just as it is healthy for citizens to be uncomfortable rather than morally smug about the rightness of killing others in war, so too with punishing criminals. Wilkins (1984: 76) reminds us that: 'if freedom is to be protected, it must be protected at its frontiers', by which he means that if we are to respect freedom, we must be particularly watchful for the freedom of those who seem least deserving of our concern. A society which feels morally comfortable about sending thousands of terrified young men and women to institutions in which they are bashed, raped, and brutalized, stripped of human dignity, denied freedom of speech and movement, has a doubtful commitment to freedom. A theory which assures us that any human being can deserve these things is subversive of that commitment.

In contending that the new retributivism has provided this assurance, we are not accusing its adherents of necessarily wanting to increase the oppressiveness of the criminal justice system. A good number of the new retributivists, especially some of the more influential among them, are liberals, even radicals, and they see the punishments deserved as much less than those currently administered by criminal justice systems. But liberal versions of just deserts inevitably reduce, in the realities of table-thumping politics, to a strategy of 'getting tough' (Cullen and Gilbert 1982; Cohen 1985).

When you play the game of criminal justice on the field of retribution, you play it on the home ground of conservative law-and-order politicians. You give full rein to those who play to the sense of normality of the majority, urging them to tyrannize the minority. Once all the players agree that retribution, or giving people what they deserve, is the rationale for punishment, the genteel visions of liberal retributivists count for nought. Some of the left retributivists now concede that they may have been co-opted into playing on the conservatives' home ground (Greenberg and Humphries 1980; see also Cohen 1985). Complicated notions like the balancing of benefits and burdens which can underpin liberal egalitarian versions of retributivism (e.g. Sadurski 1985) are quickly discarded by law-and-order politicians who find that their press releases are most likely to get a run by appealing to simple-minded vengeance. The long-term effect of the new retributivism in criminal justice theory will be to make the community feel more comfortable with punishment, encouraging prisons which are even more overcrowded and more brutal than at present (Orland 1978; Cullen and Gilbert 1982).

None of this proves that retributivism is wrong or inadequate as a theory. It is perhaps just another illustration of Thorsten Sellin's dictum on criminal justice reform that 'beautiful theories have a way of turning into ugly practices' (quoted in Cullen and Gilbert 1982: 151). All we have wanted to show in this section is that the debate is one that matters. Whether for good or ill, whether in the way they would have wanted or not, the new retributivists have certainly changed both the punishment debate and criminal justice policy. The long list of American states that have shifted to 'flat', 'determinate', or 'presumptive' sentencing codes since the mid-1970s—Illinois, California, Connecticut, Colorado, Alaska, Arizona, Maine, Indiana, Minnesota, and others—is sufficient testimony to that.

A Consequentialist Republican Theory: A Summary

Chapter 2 argues that we should seek a comprehensive theory of criminal justice, not just a theory of punishment or a theory of police powers or a theory of prosecutorial discretion. There are serious flaws in theories limited to sub-systems of the criminal justice system, arising from the fact that the sub-systems are closely connected and are in constant interaction. This linkage means, for example, that a prescription to limit discretion in the sentencing sub-system would be defeated by a shift of that discretion to the prosecutorial sub-system. Sub-system theories are necessary and desirable but they should be open to consideration of the consequences of any recommendations for other subsystems; ideally they should be guided by a general theory of the whole system.

The contention of Chapter 3 is that in addition to being comprehensive, it is best that the theory be consequentialist, setting a target by which to judge the criminal justice system. The alternative is a deontological theory which imposes a constraint that the system must satisfy, independent of any target to which it is directed. Retributivism is a deontological theory, the relevant constraints having to do with giving offenders deserved punishments. We find formal reasons, specifically reasons of methodological simplicity, for a presumption in favour of a consequentialist theory. First, we suggest that if retributivists are to offer a comprehensive theory of criminal justice, they will have to supplement the constraints they invoke by one or more consequentialist targets. Consequentialism scores, then, by being comparatively simple: it involves only targets in its foundation; it does not have to appeal to constraints as well. Second, we argue that not only does retributivism have to admit values in two different roles, some as constraints, some as targets; it also offends against simplicity, in so far as it fails to provide an account of why some values suit the one role, some the other. And third, we show that consequentialism is a simpler sort of theory because, unlike retributivism or indeed any deontological approach, it allows us to take a unified view of the demands of rationality and morality. These are reasons that make for a presumption in favour of a consequentialist theory, though they provide no guarantee that an adequate consequentialist theory can be constructed.

Chapter 4 looks at the challenge of defining an appropriate target for a comprehensive, consequentialist theory. Three desiderata for such a target are developed and it is shown that the standard consequentialist theories fail the test of satisfying these desiderata. The theories considered are preventionism, utilitarianism, and a theory which hails the satisfaction of retributivist constraints as the appropriate target; we describe this as target-retributivism.

Chapter 5 introduces the target which we propose ourselves: that of maximizing dominion. Dominion is freedom, holistically conceived: not the liberal conception of freedom as the condition of the atomistic individual, but a republican conception of freedom as freedom of the city, freedom in a social world. Dominion is constituted by the enjoyment of certain rights and by the infrastructure of capacity and power which this involves. Crucially, it has a subjective element: to enjoy dominion you must know that you enjoy all that it otherwise involves (the rights, etc.) and this indeed must be a matter of common knowledge. Dominion is nothing more nor less than the republican conception of full citizenship.

We argue that the promotion of dominion looks like a target which satisfies the relevant desiderata. A part of its attraction as a target for the criminal justice system is that its promotion enjoins respect for the key spheres we expect the criminal justice system to protect—our persons, property, and province. The promotion of dominion enjoins respect for these spheres, moreover, not just among the potential and actual victims of crime, but also among those affected by the criminal process itself: the defendants, witnesses, taxpayers, and others it involves. Thus, the promotion of dominion requires us to weigh the losses of crime victims against the losses of those affected by the criminal justice process.

Chapter 6 is a long chapter with only a little to say about a great many things. Incredible but true, it sets out to show that our republican theory has something useful to say about all of the key dilemmas of criminal justice policy. Furthermore, it tries to give some feel for how these solutions differ from preventionist and retributivist solutions. Informed readers will be dissatisfied that we have not come to grips with the intricacies of any of the policy dilemmas considered. The most we claim of Chapter 6 is that it establishes a research agenda for republican criminology.

The chapter begins with a derivation of four presumptions from our republican theory. These are presumptions in favour, respectively, of parsimony, the checking of power, reprobation, and the reintegration of victims and offenders. Parsimony means that the onus of proof must always be on the side of justifying criminal justice intrusions, not on the side of justifying their removal. The checking of power means the protection of citizens against the abuse of power by giving them rights against the powerful and by subjecting the powerful to accountability restraints. The pursuit of reprobation means that criminal justice practices should be designed to expose offenders in a constructive way to community disapproval. And the pursuit of reintegration means that there should be systematic efforts to restore the victims of crime to the full enjoyment of dominion, as also those offenders who have been convicted. With the help of these presumptions, we derive a number of lessons for how the criminal justice system should be organized if it is to promote dominion.

Among a host of other things, we suggest that the theory supports a codification of rights (some crucial ones are specified); opposes the notions of crimes of offence or consensual crimes but accommodates certain types of strict liability crimes; supports a right to protection from punishments against the person (capital, corporal punishment) and a presumption in favour of punishments against the property of offenders (fines, restitution) over punishments against province (imprisonment); supports some principles about how to distribute resources between different parts of the system (police, courts, prisons, etc.), and some principles for rendering police surveillance of suspects more accountable and for targeting investigations and prosecutions; supports a right to a fair trial and principles of sentencing that give prominence to denunciation and moral reasoning; and promises, finally, to support parole, work release, and remission of sentence for good behaviour. The book is a bargain at the price!

Chapter 7 is the crucial one for the practical import of the theory. We argue that theories that can only provide a blueprint for a package of compatible reforms for all sub-systems of a system are not very useful to practitioners and reformers. Theories are useful only when they can be applied to the world of incremental, politically realistic policy change, a world wherein unintended consequences are the rule rather than the exception. We show that our republican theory is capable of this sort of practical application. At the same time, we argue that atheoretical incrementalism is also folly. Our approach is theoretical, even if the theory is capable of incremental application, and this is one of its great merits.

In a nutshell, the theory supports repeated decrements to all layers of criminal justice intervention—less criminal law, less police surveillance, less prosecution, less punishment—until solid evidence emerges that crime increases as a result. We believe that empirical criminology instructs us that the process of repeated decrements could go quite a long way without clearly causing an increase in crime, but we think that the political realities of law-and-order politics would not allow decremental change to proceed to this point. If this did happen, if scientifically credible research showed the accumulated decrements to have increased crime, then a question of great import would arise. Weighing the dominion loss from increased crime against the dominion loss from higher taxes and a more intrusive or punitive state, we would have to decide whether to return to a higher level of criminal justice activity.

In Chapter 7 we argued in passing that, ironically, retributivism cannot tell us what is the deserved level of punishment, though it can rank crimes according to how severely they ought to be punished. This is only the beginning. In Chapter 8 we show, more generally, that unlike our republican theory, retributivism cannot provide a satisfactory set of answers to the key questions about sentencing and punishment—'Why punish?', 'Who to punish?', and 'How to punish?' This means that retributivism fails, even on its own terms; by contrast with republicanism, it is an inherently inadequate theory.

Chapter 9 addresses the difficulties of applying retributivism in any real or sociologically possible world. We contend that a variety of considerations, mainly considerations related to white-collar crime, means that it would not be possible or desirable to apply a retributivist policy consistently. More than that, we argue that such a policy would do worse than republican theory in bringing about justice as equality in the criminal justice system. This is a nice result, since retributivists like to claim a special degree of concern for justice as equality.

2

For a Comprehensive Theory

In Chapter 1 some initial reservations were expressed about how narrow theories of punishment foster an inclination to view punishment as the only appropriate response to crime. In this chapter we will argue that what is needed to address this, and a number of additional problems, is a comprehensive normative theory of the criminal justice system. By 'comprehensive' we mean a theory which will give an integrated account of what ought to be done by the legislature, the judiciary, and the executive in regard to the key policy questions raised by the criminal justice system. Here we identify ten such questions; there are others we might have considered as well but these are the most salient. After each question we will briefly suggest some of the issues and institutions implicated in answering the question.

The Main Issues of Criminal Justice

1. *What Kinds of Behaviours Should be Criminalized by the System?*

Should those things which are the greatest evils in the society be those that are criminalized? Should we criminalize victimless crimes (e.g. drug use), crimes in which the victim consents (e.g. selling drugs), and crimes of offence (e.g. offensive language) as opposed to harm? Should we always require intention or knowledge, or at least negligence or recklessness, for an act to be a crime? How should we judge the relevant actions of individuals when a given sort of corporate act is criminalized?

2. *What Sorts of Sentences Should be Permitted or Enjoined?*

Should there be certain types of punishment (e.g. capital punishment) that are forbidden? Should there be maximum and/or minimum penalties which judges must recognize in deciding sentences? How binding should precedents be in sentencing?

3. How Should Resources be Allocated to the System, Among Different Parts Within the System, and Within a Single Part or Sub-System (e.g. the Police)?

Should the criminal justice system get more money from the government? Should police get some of the money currently spent on making life more comfortable for prisoners? How should the police decide whether to spend more on patrol cars or training?

4. What Kind and Intensity of Surveillance Should be Tolerated?

Should phone tapping be allowed, and if so, on what kinds of suspects? How do we get the police to strike the right balance between civil liberties and crime prevention? To what extent should police vacate a domain of surveillance, leaving this domain to the private security industry?

5. What Cases Should be Targeted for Criminal Investigation and How Should These Investigations be Conducted?

Should computerized information systems be used to target dangerous offenders? To what extent should the police be reactive to complaints, or be proactive investigators who use intelligence to seek new suspects? Should there be a place for commissions of inquiry into certain areas of crime or for authorities with a mix of investigative and prosecutorial powers designed to bolster the police?

6. What Cases Should be Selected for Prosecution?

Should there be prosecution guidelines on the kinds of cases prosecutors must take to court, or must decline to prosecute? What considerations should the prosecutor take into account in deciding how to exercise discretion?

7. *How Should Pre-Trial Decisions be Made—Decisions About Charge and Plea Bargaining, Full and Partial Immunities, Bail or Pre-Trial Detention?*

Should we allow the practice of bargaining for a plea of guilty to less-serious charges in return for dropping more-serious charges? Should we compel suspects to answer questions even if the answers are incriminating? If we do so, should we grant the suspect full immunity from prosecution or immunity from prosecutions relating only to what they reveal? What kinds of suspects should be held in custody while awaiting trial? Should every suspect have the right to counsel, if necessary counsel provided at public expense? Should we allow pre-trial diversion into alternatives to punishment?

8. *What Adjudication Procedures Should be Used to Determine Guilt?*

Should the practice, found in most countries, of perfunctory lower court bench trials (without a jury) be tolerated? Is the expense of jury trials unjustified for all but the most-serious crimes? When is administrative or civil adjudication superior to the criminal trial? Should proceedings be adversarial or inquisitorial? What rules of evidence ought to apply? What defences ought to be available against different charges? What appeal procedures should apply?

9. *Within the Discretionary Limits Set, What Sentences Should Courts Impose on Those Found Guilty?*

Should judges be influenced by considerations of retribution, rehabilitation, deterrence, incapacitation, moral education, by considerations of compensation or restitution, or by some combination of these, in passing sentence? Is it wrong for judges to allow the guilty to go unpunished? When should the judge choose a fine rather than imprisonment or probation as a sentence? What compensation, if any, should be ordered for victims?

10. How Should the Sentence be Administered by Prison, Probation, and Parole Authorities?

Should prisons be run to maximize rehabilitation or should they be made as unpleasant as possible to maximize deterrence? Or should they simply aspire to being secure and decent? Should post-trial variation of sentence (amnesty, pardon, parole, remission of sentence for good behaviour, work release, compassionate leave) be forbidden because it undermines the integrity of judicial deliberations? Should prisoners be let out early if they are rehabilitated while in prison?

Most theories of punishment are limited to saying things about the setting and administering of criminal sentences. At best, they address questions 2, 9, and 10 on our list. This book will not supply definitive answers to all these questions. What it will do is show the need to address them within a comprehensive theoretical framework, and begin to show how to go about answering them.

Defining Comprehensiveness

A comprehensive theory of criminal justice must be capable of generating a set of answers to policy questions which is complete, coherent, and systemic. A comprehensive theory is complete in so far as it provides answers at least to all ten key questions listed above. Note that it may be complete without being a unitary theory that applies the same yardstick to each question. A number of yardsticks can be applied and weighted differently in answering different questions. A comprehensive theory is coherent in so far as the answers provided are consistent with one another. The prescriptions provided in answer to one question must not negate the prescriptions supplied in answer to another.

A theory might be complete and coherent without being systemic; hence a third requirement on a comprehensive theory. It is hardly enough to go down the list of questions satisfying the minimal condition that each answer be given in a way that does not compromise other answers. If we wish to theorize about a system, we should try to do so holistically rather than by dealing separately with each of the questions raised. It may be that the set of separately supplied answers will be inferior as a whole to a set derived in a process of continuing comparison and adjustment. A theory is systemic to the extent that it is designed so as to ensure that the set of answers as a whole is better than any other set; it is guided by desiderata and exposed to tests that promote the likelihood that the answers have that global superiority.

Thus, the ideal of a comprehensive theory is obtained when a *complete* and *coherent* set of answers is provided to the key questions under a *systemic* answering strategy.

The quest for coherent answers, systemically approached, does not mean that we should pursue a theory that aims for maximum interdependence in the criminal justice system. We can have a theory of house design which considers design of the plumbing in terms of how it will interface with the configuration of living, cooking, and cleaning spaces, but in which the plumbing is also designed so that it can be changed without triggering consequential changes to other parts of the system: without tearing the house apart (Alexander 1971). Equally, through being mindful of the systemic properties of our project, we might prescribe policies to maximize the independence of a sub-system from other parts of the system. For example, being mindful of the pressures judges are placed under from other parts of the system—from politicians, police, prosecutors—we might prescribe policies to preserve the independence of the judiciary from these systemic pressures.

Why Comprehensiveness?

Perhaps only Bentham could be characterized as having genuinely taken up the challenge of comprehensive theorizing on criminal justice. The tendency has been for theories of punishment, of sentencing, and of police discretion to be developed without articulating them in a general theory of criminal justice. Why should we seek a theory that systemically selects a complete and coherent set of answers to all our key questions? In particular, since the other features are self-vindicating, why should we seek a theory which simultaneously provides a complete set of answers?

The reason derives from a general methodological observation. If we are concerned with how far certain closely connected systems manifest some desired features or produce some desired results then the very connection between the systems means that it is going to be a bad idea to concentrate on one of them to the neglect of others. Such a concentration runs a double risk: first, a risk of inefficiency and second, a risk of counterproductivity. If we concentrate on the design of one of the systems in isolation, then we may prescribe arrangements there to achieve an effect that would be more efficiently realized by arrangements in another system. Worse still, if we pursue our system design in this isolated fashion, we may make a change to the system under examination which causes uncharted changes in other systems, changes that make the intervention counterproductive. The intervention is designed to promote a certain result, let us say, but its influence on other systems is such that the desired result is less well achieved than before.

In so far as the criminal justice system in any society is required simultaneously to resolve the different sorts of policy issues distinguished, we can represent it as a network of highly connected sub-systems. It is divided traditionally into sub-systems such as those associated with law-making, policing, prosecution, sentencing, probation, imprisonment, and so on. Such sub-systems pursue distinct functions and tend to be semi-autonomous (Sally Falk Moore 1978). They have often been supplemented in recent years by hybrid institutions, also enjoying a certain autonomy, which combine previously separate functions: strike forces of police and prosecutors, crime commissions, independent commissions of inquiry into corruption, business regulatory commissions, grand juries, and the like. Criminal justice sub-systems, traditional and hybrid, can be variously taxonomized, and variously mapped on to our ten key issues. The point which we want to stress, however, is that under any representation of them, they are closely connected with one another. What the legislators criminalize is affected by their expectations in regard to the agents in other sub-systems: their expectation, for example, that the police will be able to identify those who break the laws enacted, and that prosecutors will be able to make a case against them. What the police investigate is a function of what they think the prosecutors will prosecute, the juries be convinced about, and the judges sentence. What variations in sentence parole boards are prepared to contemplate is influenced, and should be influenced, by their assumptions as to the basis on which the initial sentence was fixed by the judge. And so on.

The fact that the criminal justice system is articulated in this way, involving a set of highly connected sub-systems, means that our general methodological observation is relevant to policy-making on matters of criminal justice. Such policy-making is always guided by the desire to see certain features or results realized, whether the relevant policy is utilitarian, retributivist, or whatever. If the policy-making is pursued in concentration on an isolated sub-system, say with a focus exclusively on sentencing, then it is exposed to the double risk mentioned. The measures recommended for that sub-system may be relatively inefficient ways of promoting the object desired, there being adjustments possible in other sub-systems that would better realize that end. Or, worse again, the measures recommended may be counter-productive, having unforeseen effects in other systems, which mean that ultimately the end is less well realized than before.

The upshot is that in our normative thinking about criminal justice, we ought to look for a comprehensive theory. We ought to have an eye to all the different sub-systems involved, looking for a complete, coherent, and systemically developed set of answers to questions like the ten distinguished earlier. We can have nothing to do with a strategy which identifies one sub-system or issue, or even one small set of sub-systems or issues, as the relevant concern, dismissing others as business for another desk or another day.

Our commitment to comprehensive theorizing about criminal justice calls for two qualifying comments. First of all, the commitment is compatible with detailed policy-driven studies of particular sub-systems, studies of the kind that often represent the cutting edge of criminology. It would be self-defeating to denounce detailed studies of this concentrated sort, since practical limitations may rule out any other kind. What our commitment requires is not that such studies cease but, first, that they be pursued with at least a minimal sensitivity to the larger system in which the sub-system under investigation is placed; and, second, that any normative claims supported by the studies be regarded as conditional on the availability of reinforcing support from studies of other sub-systems.

The second comment we want to make on that commitment bears on its significance, not for research on components of the criminal justice system, but for research on other systems altogether: systems such as those constituted by the civil law, by non-criminal systems of public law, and by extra-legal systems of community norms. Our commitment to thinking comprehensively about the criminal justice system is premissed on the assumption that its sub-systems are particularly closely connected. But the system as a whole is also connected, if not so closely, to the other systems mentioned. And so the very motive for going comprehensive within the criminal justice system also provides a motive for not complacently focusing on that system alone. We should always remain alert to the possibility that some result we want the criminal justice system to produce may be better achieved elsewhere. Even more important, we should be constantly on the watch for the possibility that the criminal justice measures advocated will have counterproductive effects in other areas of legal and social life. Here we should take on board the lesson stressed by legal pluralists, that certain important phenomena arise from the interaction between private and public systems of justice, between custom and law (Pospisil 1971; Sally Falk Moore 1978; Henry 1983). If our perspective on criminal justice matters is that of systems theory, it is associated with open systems theory in particular (Katz and Kahn 1978).

The picture emerging from our considerations is this. The criminal justice sub-systems are so closely connected that it is bad practice to concentrate on any one of them in policy recommendations, without at least remaining sensitive to the impact on other sub-systems. But the criminal justice system as a whole is not entirely disconnected from other systems in the legal and social order. And so the commitment to thinking comprehensively about that system should be paired with a willingness to contemplate the relevance of those systems for the achievement of criminal justice goals. Our ideal theorist will keep a steady focus on the criminal justice system as a whole, even when she pursues more or less concentrated research programmes. But she will always keep an eye open for relevant opportunities and effects in other systems, turning to examine them whenever they become particularly salient.

Squeezing the Toothpaste of Discretion

Our discussion so far has been excessively abstract and in concluding this Chapter we will consider a particular issue in policy-making which brings out the interconnected nature of criminal justice sub-systems. The issue is how far the legislature should allow discretion to various agents in the system. It turns out that a policy on the discretion to be allowed in any particular sub-system will often have effects on the discretion available in other sub-systems. This demonstrates that if we are concerned to reduce discretion, for example, then we cannot hope to satisfy that concern by a policy for one sub-system which is developed without attention to others. If we go for such a policy, the intervention we recommend risks being counterproductive.

Discretion in the criminal justice system makes possible the unequal treatment of equal offenders, offenders who have done equal wrong. One of the thrusts of the new retributivists has been to guard against this by urging limitations on the discretion of judges and parole boards to vary presumptive or determinate sentences. There is a real question, however, as to whether attempts to destroy discretion in one or two sub-systems of the criminal justice system simply displaces it to other sub-systems.

For example, determinate sentencing reforms that narrow the discretion of judges may enhance the discretion of prosecutors. This is because bargaining over charges ultimately has more effect on sentences in determinate systems than in indeterminate systems. Under indeterminate sentencing, the respective sentences imposed for, say, 'premeditated killing' versus 'intentional killing' are a matter for the judge; under determinate sentencing the prosecutor can hold out the prospect of ten years to the defendant if she charges him with premeditated killing, five if he accepts the bargain of a charge of intentional killing (Zimring 1976). A Rand study of determinate sentencing reform in California found that judges and trial attorneys agreed in interviews that the power of prosecutors increased because of the availability of 'enhancements' as a bargaining counter (Lipson and Peterson

1980). Instead of the judge taking into account, say, the perceived viciousness of a particular offender in sentence, it may now be prosecutors who do more of this by decisions to seek or not to seek an enhancement of sentence on grounds such as use of a weapon, or injury to the victim.

There are good reasons for greater concern over prosecutorial discretion than judicial discretion because judges are more publicly accountable than prosecutors. Moreover, as Zimring points out, giving more leverage to prosecutors exacerbates discretionary unequal treatment at the very point in the system where the problem is worst:

> The *prosecutor* is not normally thought of as an official who has, or exercises, the power to determine punishment. In practice, however, the prosecutor is the most important institutional determinant of a criminal sentence. He has the legal authority to drop criminal charges, thus ending the possibility of punishment. He has the legal authority in most systems to determine the specific offense for which a person is to be prosecuted, and this ability to select a charge can also broaden or narrow the range of sentences that can be imposed upon conviction. In congested urban court systems (and elsewhere) he has the absolute power to reduce charges in exchange for guilty pleas and to recommend particular sentences to the court as a part of a 'plea bargain'; rarely will his recommendation for a lenient sentence be refused in an adversary system in which he is supposed to represent the punitive interests of the state. (Zimring 1976: 13)

Cullen and Gilbert (1982: 168–70) argue that one of the unintended consequences of determinate sentencing reforms to abolish parole boards is that there is no longer any way to even out disparities in the way different institutions revoke remission for good behaviour. Institutions with more punitive administrative styles can be four times more likely than other institutions to cancel good-behaviour remissions that would otherwise automatically come off the sentence.

> Formerly, when an inmate lost good time days, it meant only that the date on which (s)he would become eligible for parole would be delayed. However, under fixed-term statutes where parole-release no longer occurs, when a day of good time is subtracted, it means that an inmate will actually spend an extra day in prison. A general consequence of determinacy, then, is that prison personnel in effect acquire sentencing powers. According to Paul Bigman of the John Howard Association,

'Now your release date is not dependent on your parole board but on the guards and warden in your prison, because every time [they] take away a day of good time, what they are really doing is sentencing you to a day in prison.' In light of this new 'sentencing power' at their disposal and the fact that staffs at the various state penitentiaries differ in their inclination to revoke good time, the institution to which an inmate is sentenced can now directly and significantly affect an inmate's tenure behind bars. (Cullen and Gilbert 1982: 169)

An extreme form of displacing discretion from judges to prison administrators occurs with mass early release of offenders from overcrowded prisons. Illinois is one US state which introduced a 'get tough' determinate sentencing policy. The Illinois adult prison population increased from less than 6,000 in 1974 to over 10,500 when determinate sentencing was implemented in 1978 (Hepburn and Goodstein 1985), and to 20,000 in 1988 (figure supplied by Illinois Department of Corrections. See Lane 1986). Overcrowded prisons became powder-kegs of unconstitutional mistreatment of prisoners. In an effort to forestall the explosion, the head of the Illinois Department of Corrections ordered the early release of 21,000 prisoners between 1980 and 1983. The application of pressure on the legislative and judicial sentencing sub-systems (questions 2 and 9) created problems for the executive which surfaced in the prison sub-system (question 10): the result was that a prison administrator could arrogate to himself authority for a virtual mass amnesty.

Examples of the displacement of discretion can also be found in the area of business regulation. A long-standing concern of critics of business regulatory agencies 'captured' by the industries they regulate is that the agencies fail to prosecute when they discover offences. A solution advocated has been obligatory enforcement action against every violation detected by the agency. The Mine Safety and Health Act in the United States, for example, has taken up this call by mandating at least a civil penalty (a fine) for every violation of the Act. One result is that inspectors, who bear the brunt of the paperwork burden of mandatory enforcement action, exercise more discretion in what they write up and in what offences they ignore (Braithwaite 1985).

Non-discretionary regulatory enforcement policies can also be self-defeating because they look for solutions in the prosecution process, a part of the system which is a litigation game, ignoring effects on the bargaining game of day-to-day regulation. Enforcing the law against wealthy corporations and their executives is a more difficult business than it is with common criminals. Corporate defendants have a capacity to employ top counsel who can exploit loopholes in the law (Mann 1985). The result is that laws or policies to mandate litigation by a regulatory agency will often force them into defeats they would otherwise avoid. In regulation as a bargaining game the agency uses the prospect of litigation as one of a number of bargaining counters to secure agreement from the corporation to spend money on measures which will prevent a recurrence, often much more money than a court would have imposed by way of a fine. Moreover, it is common in these bargaining games for the regulatory agency to secure compliance with a standard of, say, pollution control well in excess of that mandated by the law (see e.g. Winter 1985; Hawkins 1984; Braithwaite 1985). Thus, the belief that more potent deterrence can be achieved by limiting the discretion of the agency not to prosecute can paradoxically achieve weaker rather than tougher regulation by forcing the agency to swap bartering at the border of its authority for defeat in the court.

Thus, in any highly interconnected system where discretion is exercised at different points in the system, policies to change the way discretion is exercised at one point are always susceptible to discretionary changes elsewhere to reassert the old equilibrium. This happens because so often discretion is exercised to deal with environmental pressures (like crowded prisons) that just cannot be ignored. The disapproved way of exercising discretion often manifests values shared by personnel at points in the system beyond those where the new policy fetters discretion. If we stop actors in one sub-system from exercising discretion to implement such values, we leave it to actors in other sub-systems who share these same values to compensate by exercising their discretion to the same end. Hence, if the problem of judges who are soft on drinking and driving is dealt with by mandatory prison terms or mandatory licence suspension, police officers who are equally soft on drunk drivers may exercise their discretion to arrest fewer of them. When judges are forced to sentence murderers to death, psychiatrists who can show that murderers are 'mentally ill' may be given more influence in the system. When a Speedy Trial Act imposes a difficult deadline in complex cases, prosecutors may delay the request for indictment, so that preparation normally done after indictment is done before indictment (Mann 1985: 239).

We are not suggesting an iron law that any attempt to control discretion in one sub-system will result in a displacement of the discretion to another sub-system. Often it will not (see, for example, Miethe 1987). But the shifting of discretion happens regularly enough (for further examples see Feeley 1983: 126–38) for closed sub-system theories to be a serious folly.

Conclusion

Most theories of criminal justice encompass only a couple of our ten key questions of criminal justice policy. There has not been a serious attempt at a general normative theory of criminal justice; indeed the literature has made a virtue of different theories for different parts of the system. We have argued against this that theorizing only for parts of a system may undermine attainment of the goals set by the theorist for the system as a whole. Theorizing will naturally concentrate on parts of the system but it should always be sensitive to the ramifications for other parts and, ideally, it should be informed by a general theory of the whole.

We can reconceptualize in this light our claims in Chapter 1 that punishment is not an efficacious way of dealing with most violations of law. We said there that the trouble with theories of sentencing or punishment is that they funnel our thinking into whether or not, and how, to punish. Because of this narrow view, we are led to sub-optimize on a goal like that of controlling crime; thus, we do not ponder the possibilities of moving certain types of cases out of the punishment funnel altogether. To optimize we must consider the benefit of such shifts, not only for the crime control efficacy of the sentencing sub-system, but also for the efficacy of other sub-systems.

3
For a Consequentialist Theory

The upshot of the last chapter is that we ought to have a normative theory which will tell us how all the various matters that are settled by a criminal justice system should be determined. We ought to have a comprehensive theory for assessing issues as widespread as what ought to be criminalized, what ought to be policed, what ought to be investigated, and what ought to be brought before the courts.

A normative theory of the criminal justice system must be able to select the best system or subset of systems from among any set of options. It will meet this requirement most naturally if it can rank alternative systems in an order of merit (Sen 1982*a*: 285–6). But we should not expect it to consist simply in an enumeration and ordering of the different possible systems of criminal justice. What we will look for in the theory is, rather, a criterion by which such a ranking can be developed, given appropriate empirical information.

Our concern in this chapter is with the nature of the criterion which our theory of criminal justice ought to deploy. There are two very different sorts of criteria that it might try to use, one consequentialist or teleological, the other deontological. We wish to argue that the criterion ideally ought to be consequentialist. We wish to make the case for a consequentialist theory of criminal justice.

Distinguishing between normative theories on the basis of the criterion they supply is only one way of taxonomizing them (Hamlin and Pettit 1989). Another common basis is the mode of argument employed in the theory: this generates distinctions such as that between contractualist theories that appeal to what people would endorse under certain ideal conditions and other, more direct approaches.[1] Yet another basis of taxonomy is the

[1] We assume that contractualism is not an alternative on a par with teleological and deontological approaches to ethics. The contractualist device identifies the

interventionist effect of the theory, which introduces divides along the spectrum between minimalist and maximalist doctrines. Our theory is grounded in relatively direct intuitions, as we shall see in the next chapter, where we support it on the basis that it satisfies certain intuitive desiderata. Our theory is on the minimal end of the intervention spectrum, as we shall see in Chapter 5, when we look at its practical policy implications. But these features are of secondary importance for our purposes. The first and most significant property of the theory is that it is consequentialist.

A consequentialist criterion of criminal justice defines a target for the criminal justice system; a deontological criterion defines a constraint. Our plan in the chapter is first to introduce the distinction between constraints and targets; then to make some connections between constraints, rights, and deserts; next to look at the two sorts of theory of criminal justice; and finally to present our reasons for preferring a consequentialist theory.

Constraints and Targets

Before distinguishing constraints and targets, one preliminary point has to be made. This is that any theory which proposes a criterion of criminal justice, or more generally any theory which proposes a criterion of right action, invokes as valuable a property that does not involve a particular individual or setting essentially. It invokes a universal value that is capable of being realized here or there, with this individual or that. Suppose the theory prescribes that this or that offender ought to be justly punished. Can it be restricted to such particular judgements? Surely not. In consistency, the theory must be prepared to abstract from the identities involved—these are presumably not relevant—and hail as valuable the universal property of having any such offenders punished in that way. The commitment of every

property of being contractually satisfactory, a property which may be regarded as indicative or actually definitive of desirability (see Scanlon 1982; Pettit 1982). But contractualism, as such, still faces the question on which teleologists and deontologists will divide. This is the question of whether contractual satisfactoriness presents a target or a constraint; see below and Pettit 1988c.

normative theory to a universal value of this kind is an important assumption in our discussion. The difference between constraining and targeting theories, theories of a deontological and consequentialist cast, is represented in this discussion as a difference in how the two sorts of theories deploy the universal values they countenance: whether as constraints or targets. Constraints and targets, as understood here, are universal values which differ in the role they are made to play. Indeed, one and the same value, one and the same valued property, may be invoked in one theory as a target, in another as a constraint.

The best way to introduce the distinction between constraints and targets is by example. If we take a value like truth or justice, peace or happiness, we can use it to define a target or a constraint. Abstracting for the moment from risk and uncertainty, the value defines a target if the agent is required to promote in some sense—typically to maximize—truth or justice, peace or happiness. It defines a constraint if the agent is instructed to choose an option which exemplifies that value in a distinctive way: he is instructed to tell the whole truth, not to offend against justice, to behave peacefully, or not to be the direct cause of unhappiness to another (Pettit, forthcoming *b*).

Whenever a criterion is proposed for the assessment of an agent's performance, the assumption is that he faces a set of options between which he can and must choose; the criterion invokes a certain valued characteristic then to determine which choice is right or best. That the criterion is a constraint means, we may take it, that the agent is required to choose one of those options which exemplify the valued characteristic: they involve telling the whole truth, acting peacefully, or whatever. That the criterion is a target means that the agent is enjoined to choose one option over another according to how well it promotes the valued characteristic, the implication being that he should seek out the option which does best by that property; for example, he should maximize truth or peace or whatever, even if that means that he must tell a lie or be violent.

The essential difference between a constraint and a target comes out in the sort of information you require to try to satisfy them. To try to satisfy a constraint you need information relevant to how far the different options exemplify the value in question: information on whether this or that option involves telling the truth—or, say, telling the truth to a non-malevolent person—keeping a promise, or whatever. To try to satisfy a target you need much richer data: information, not just on the valued properties that different options will exemplify, but also information on the properties realized through the consequences of the different options. Putting the difference in shorthand, the constraint requires only information necessary to determine how to keep your own hands clean, the target requires the information necessary to determine how to have the world maximally realize the value in question.

In this account of constraints and targets, we have abstracted from risk and uncertainty. Those who invoke a value as a target—consequentialists—recognize that there is no telling for sure what the consequences of each option will be and so they identify the best option as that which promises in some sense to realize the value maximally; to promote the value will then be to go for that option. Usually they equate the option which promises to realize the value maximally with the option which a rational and well-informed gambler who was concerned with the value would choose. This is the option which maximizes the expectation of the value, as decision theory has it, under a reasonable assignment of probabilities (Pettit and Brennan 1986: 438). Those who invoke a value as a constraint—deontologists—do not pay the same heed to uncertainty, probably because it is often easy to say whether a given option will display the sort of valued characteristic with which they are mostly concerned: whether it will be truthful, faithful, loyal, or whatever. This neglect of uncertainty is almost a hallmark of deontological thinking. Indeed deontological theory is probably best regarded as undefined for properties whose exemplification is a matter of significant risk or uncertainty. Some deontological claims may embed issues of risk and uncertainty, like the claims that an army at war ought not to put civilian lives at 'significant' risk. But even this move is unusual. All familiar deontological theories presume that risk and uncertainty are irrelevant and require the endorsement, without further qualification, of options with the valued properties.

This point about uncertainty and risk will prove relevant in later discussion. The belief in just deserts is naturally taken as a deontological belief that the system of criminal justice should be constrained, in its various aspects, to provide offenders with the punishment due to them. But were it taken in this way, then the theory would be bedevilled by the uncertainties associated with the actions of police and prosecutors. Hence it may be no accident that in practice the theory is usually applied only to sentencing; we discuss this restriction later in this chapter.

Constraints, Rights, and Deserts

As we have defined them, constraints may be entirely abstract or impersonal. An example would be the requirement that the criminal justice system should conform at every point to the dictates of natural law. But the constraints which are more often invoked in discussions of criminal justice are person-centred, not requirements of such an abstract sort.

A person-centred constraint is one that dictates how a system —or, again, any agent or agency—ought to deal with individual people. With regard to each person, or each person satisfying a certain condition, it ordains that the system ought to treat him in a certain way. Such a constraint is imposed on the system of criminal justice when it is said that no person known to be innocent ought to be charged with a crime, that no one ought to be convicted without the possibility of appeal, that no offender ought to be given an indeterminate sentence, and the like.

Whenever a person-centred constraint is imposed on a system then persons—individual or corporate—are invested with the capacity, in appropriate circumstances, to trigger the sort of treatment required. Let the system be constrained to treat any person who satisfies condition C in manner *M*. It follows then that every person has a warrant to treatment *M* in circumstance *C*. That warrant is simply the other side of the constraint.

Warrants often serve to protect a person's interests in his dealings with the system and in such a case we usually speak of them as rights (Pettit 1987). That any person convicted for a crime warrants the opportunity of appeal means that everyone has the right of appeal. And so on in other cases where warrants play a protective role.

But not all warrants involve what we would usually describe as rights. The outstanding example arises with the constraint which many retributivists impose on the criminal justice system, that it ought to impose due punishment on every convicted offender. If the system is constrained in this way, that means that every convicted offender warrants punishment. But the warrant, not serving a protective role, can scarcely be described as a right (but see Hegel 1942 ed.; Herbert Morris 1968). We would normally say that the offender deserves punishment, not that he has a right to it.

The observation suggests a generalization. This is that the warrants associated with constraints constitute rights whenever they serve to protect the interests of a person; and that in so far as they do something else or something more they constitute deserts (cf. Feinberg 1970: chap. 4). The desert may be negative, as in the case of deserving punishment. But equally it may be positive, as in the case where the winner of a race is said to deserve the prize. The winner's warrant to the prize involves a protective element, and so we may also say that he has a right to receive it. The warrant is not exhausted by that element, however, serving as it does to go further and mark the exclusiveness of the winner's claim. And so we find it natural to describe the warrant as a desert (on the variety of desert claims see Sher 1987).

Whether they constitute rights or deserts, the important feature of warrants is that they correlate with constraints. This means that if a person warrants treatment *M* in circumstances *C*, then the system is required to provide that treatment in *C*, regardless of the consequences. The circumstances may be specified, so that certain consequences are not put at risk by the warrant; it may be required for example, that satisfaction of the warrant does not put national security at risk. But not all consequences can be quarantined in this way and so a warrant inevitably involves a very strict sort of requirement.

Let us make the point in the abstract first. The reason not all consequences can be quarantined in this way is that a warrant on someone's part to treatment of kind *M* must be fulfilled whatever are the consequences for others receiving treatment *M* at the hands of others. The warrant is supposed to mean that you, the relevant agent, are constrained to provide treatment *M* for that person. If the *M*-property is a constraint and not a target from your point of view, then his warrant to *M* binds you independently of the consequences of your honouring it for the honouring of that sort of warrant overall. The demand on you is to provide the *M*-treatment and not concern yourself with those consequences. Constraints are quite different sorts of things from targets; they do not give you bearings, but serve rather to bind your hands (Nozick 1974: 28–30; Pettit 1987).

The point will benefit from illustration. Suppose a judge believes that by breaching desert constraints, say by imposing an exemplary sentence beyond a particular offender's desert, she can reduce crime and thereby ensure that just deserts are better achieved overall: this, because with fewer offenders, a higher proportion of those deserving it will be identified, convicted, and punished. So she is led to ponder whether she should breach the just deserts constraint in this instance, ignoring the claim of the offender before her, in order to maximize satisfaction of the constraint overall. But she should not ponder long. If she really accepts desert as a constraint, she cannot contemplate the breach. She is not set on a target of doing all she can to maximize desert; rather, she is committed to honouring the constraint involved, giving every offender before her his just deserts, no less and certainly no more.

Two Criteria of Criminal Justice

After this discussion of the difference between constraints and targets, it is time to see how they can serve as criteria for ranking systems of criminal justice. The distinctions that they generate help to map the boundaries between familiar positions in the area.

The most straightforward sort of criterion for assessing systems of criminal justice would define a target—a valued characteristic—which such systems are meant to promote and would select that system which does so most effectively. Any theory that embodies such a criterion is teleological or consequentialist. It proposes that the best system is that which promises to leave the world best off in its wake, at least in so far as the relevant characteristic goes; that which promises the best consequences or the most good.

Consequentialist theories divide on the question of what it is for a system or agent to promise more of a value than alternatives. But we need not concern ourselves with this division. We shall assume, in line with earlier comments, that a system promises more good than alternatives if and only if it is the option which a rational gambler, who is concerned with the relevant value, would choose. A more significant distinction between consequentialist theories of criminal justice turns on a difference in the accounts offered of the good, the accounts offered of the value relevant in assessing criminal justice systems. The simplest account of the good with which a system of criminal justice ought to be concerned identifies that good as the happiness of those affected by the system, where the happiness of each counts equally into the total sum; this is known nowadays as welfarism (Sen 1979). The marriage of consequentialism and welfarism says that the best criminal justice system—indeed the best option among any set of alternatives—is that which promises maximum happiness. This is the classical form of utilitarianism defended by Jeremy Bentham (1970 edn.).

But consequentialism can also be wedded to less-encompassing accounts of the relevant good. The dominant tradition in consequentialist criminology replaces the target of happiness with the more restricted goal of crime prevention. The marriage of consequentialism and this account of the good can be usefully described as preventionism. There are also more specific accounts of the target of the criminal justice system; in particular, more specific forms of preventionism. Some preventionists restrict attention to the incapacitation and deterrence of proven offenders; others to their rehabilitation; others to the deterrence of all potential offenders; others to a combination of these goals. In each case a quite specific target is hailed as the ultimate yardstick of evaluation. This is said to be what matters and the best system is identified as that which promises the most of that good, that which promotes that value.

Although consequentialist theories ultimately refer all questions of assessment back to the imputed target of the system, they must make a place for constraints at some less fundamental level, if they are to be credible. Any plausible system of criminal justice, and therefore any system which a consequentialist theory should support, will prescribe constraints on how agents within the system conduct themselves. Rules will be laid down for how police officers and prosecutors, judges and juries, should make the decisions that fall to them and many of those rules will have the form of constraints. Police officers will be enjoined to respect the privacy of innocent parties in pursuing their investigations; jurors will be required to consider only the evidence of guilt in determining whether someone should be convicted of a crime; and so on (Rawls 1955).

It is clearly vital for a consequentialist theory to be able to give constraints this derived status, for no one can be attracted by the prospect of a system in which agents are unconstrained. But it is worth noting that there is a problem often raised in this connection for consequentialism. Under a consequentialist theory, it appears that agents can never regard the reasons on which they are expected to act—that this person has the right to go free, that that person deserves punishment—as motivationally ultimate considerations. They will always be tempted to ask whether the target of the system, the ultimate motivational force, is really best served in this particular instance by honouring that sort of reason. And such temptation, so it is said, is bound to produce some instances of consequentially motivated trespass; the agents will take the target, and the law, into their own hands. The problem then is whether a consequentialist theory can ever give constraints sufficient weight to guard against that temptation. We shall address this problem in the next two chapters.

So much for theories of the targeting or consequentialist kind. A deontological theory will differ from such approaches by giving an axiomatic, underived status to some constraint or set of constraints. It will assess systems of criminal justice by reference to whether or not they satisfy those ultimate demands. That the constraints are axiomatic means that the requirement to satisfy them is a prime; it does not turn on the assumption that satisfaction promotes some independent target.

If utilitarianism and preventionism are the standard consequentialist theories of criminal justice, retributivism is the standard deontological theory. But retributivism is a loosely defined body of doctrine and we shall have to be somewhat stipulative in setting it up. We discuss retributivism at many points later in the book and it is important that we get clear about what it involves. Here we offer an account of retributivism proper, retributivism in the sense in which it invokes constraints. In the next Chapter we shall distinguish such constraint-retributivism from a version of the doctrine that we describe as target-retributivism. This version hails as targets for maximal realization, by whatever means, conditions that retributivism proper regards as constraints.

The core retributivist idea is that those guilty of certain sorts of acts—at least the sorts, whatever they are, which ought to be criminalized in a society—deserve to be punished appropriately; those innocent of such acts deserve not to be punished. Some retributivist thinkers take this idea as a bedrock intuition, others as an intuition that can be made plausible by analysis (Murphy and Hampton 1989: 112). All agree, however, that it dictates important constraints that a criminal justice system should satisfy.

Looking at the idea, it might seem that the constraints indicated bear on the system as a whole, requiring it to take such actions, whether actions involving police, prosecutors, judges, or prison authorities, as ensure that just deserts are delivered, the guilty being punished duly, the innocent left alone. But retributivists do not generally endorse comprehensive constraints of this kind. One reason may well be that such constraints involve risk and uncertainty and, in view of our earlier remarks, are beyond the grasp of deontological thinking. Another is certainly that the financial cost of having the system seriously try to honour comprehensive constraints would be prohibitive. In practice retributivists mostly use their guiding idea, not to generate constraints on the system as a whole, but only constraints on the sentencing sub-system. The constraints require that those (duly) found guilty of a crime be proportionately punished, those not found guilty not punished; and this, in all normal circumstances, whatever the costs.

Spelt out fully, there are four distinct constraints on offer. The first pair deal with who should be punished; the second with how large the punishment should be.

1. No one other than a person found to be guilty of a crime may be punished for it.
2. Anyone found to be guilty of a crime must be punished for it.
3. Punishment must not be more than of a degree commensurate with the nature of the crime and the culpability of the criminal.
4. Punishment must not be less than of a degree commensurate with the nature of the crime and the culpability of the criminal.

We need not pronounce on which of these constraints are strictly required for retributivism but we can make some useful distinctions. We will define negative retributivism as a theory that supports constraints 1 and 3 (Mackie 1982), positive retributivism as a theory that supports constraints 2 and 4, and full retributivism as a theory that endorses the lot. The negative retributivist is concerned that punishment should not be imposed on the wrong people or be imposed too harshly. The positive retributivist is concerned that it should be imposed on the right people and be imposed at a level that is harsh enough. The full retributivist embraces both concerns.

In passing, we make one observation on the fourth constraint. Full or positive retributivists differ on what is the best administrative or legislative policy for assuring that the punishment is no less than of a degree commensurate with the nature of the crime and the culpability of the criminal. The simplest full retributivist policy is a mandatory minimum and maximum punishment for each type of crime, with a narrow range between the two: armed robbery should attract not more than ten but not less than six years of imprisonment. Other full retributivists think that the best way to ensure that the deserved punishment is delivered is to set a presumptive sentence: armed robbers are presumptively sentenced to eight years of prison. Then retributivists will differ on what sort of considerations (e.g. duress, unusual harm being caused by the offence) should allow the presumption to be overridden, and how wide a deviation from the presumptive sentence should be allowed in such cases. For simplicity throughout the book, we will concentrate on the simple full retributivist policy of a minimum and maximum punishment. But what we say about such full retributivists will also generally be true of full retributivists who seek to use presumptive sentencing to guarantee that offenders get no less than they deserve.

In spite of such distinctions, notice that if any or all of the constraints are built into the criterion for assessing systems of criminal justice, then the theory put forward is a properly deontological one. Its deontological character comes out in the fact that the criminal justice system is required to satisfy the criterion, regardless of the effect on other, even other related, goals. Suppose that all the constraints are honoured by a system in respect of those who come before the courts. One result may be that juries are less willing than otherwise to convict; another that prosecutors are less inclined to charge; yet another that offenders are given less incentive to reveal the identities of fellow criminals. But none of these consequences will worry the retributivist. He will not be worried even if a result is that there is less overall satisfaction of the very requirements involved in his constraints: that is, fewer convicted criminals get their just deserts. The system is required always to satisfy the relevant constraints, not to do whatever is likely to increase such satisfaction overall. It is required to exemplify constraint-satisfaction, not to maximize it.

However retributivism is defined, one feature must be marked. This is that the constraints are not enough, even in combination, to constitute a criterion for the comprehensive assessment of a criminal justice system. They do not offer guidance on what is to be criminalized, on what is to be policed, on what offences are to be investigated, or even on what offences are to be prosecuted. They may be the makings of a theory of sentencing but they are not the stuff of which a comprehensive theory of criminal justice is made. We shall return to this matter in Chapter 8.

If the retributivist wishes to provide a comprehensive theory of criminal justice, then he will have to supplement his preferred constraints with an account of what the system otherwise ought to be trying to achieve. The complete account will inevitably bring a target into play. It will propose that while it is a first requirement on a system that retributivist constraints should be satisfied, systems which satisfy those constraints equally should be further ranked according to how well they promote some favoured goal: this may be happiness, crime-prevention, or whatever (Murphy 1985).

The observation about the need to supplement retributivist constraints is not meant to make an original point. Most retributivists are interested in more than sentencing issues, even if they are not given to seeking comprehensive theories of criminal justice. In practice most of them appeal therefore to a target as well as to a set of constraints. They may argue, for example, that the primary job of the system of criminal justice is to honour those constraints but that a further task to be considered when that job is done is how well the system promotes the target which they assign to it (see Ezorsky 1972: chap. 2, Pt. 3; Ten 1987: chap. 4).

Against Retributivism; For Consequentialism

There are at least three reasons, all of them considerations of simplicity, why we should be predisposed towards consequentialism in thinking about criminal justice. These are not conclusive considerations and should certainly be overridden if we cannot identify a satisfactory theory; in the next chapter we say what is required for a theory to be satisfactory. The considerations provide a reason to look first for a suitable consequentialist theory and to explore the prospects for a retributivist substitute only if we fail. They do not provide a reason for being consequentialist, come what may.

It is often remarked that retributivism, in particular the new retributivism of the last fifteen years, has its roots in despair over the possibility of building a suitable utilitarian or preventionist theory (Bedau 1978: 601). That observation fits with the case we want to make for consequentialism. The considerations we mention suggest that a theory of the consequentialist type is clearly the most desirable kind to have. The only question is whether we can devise a satisfactory theory of that type; that is the challenge for remaining Chapters.

The first consideration is one of simplicity. If you go the retributivist way in setting up a criterion of criminal justice, then, as we saw in the last section, you will have to supplement your formulation of the constraints on a system of criminal justice with an account of the target which the system ought otherwise to pursue. This means that a comprehensive retributivist theory will have to combine both sorts of evaluative criteria in the role of ultimate measure, where a consequentialist theory would employ only one. Simplicity suggests then that we ought to see if a satisfactory consequentialist theory is available before we begin to look at the prospects for a retributivist candidate (cf. Quine and Ullian 1978: 71).

The second consideration is also one of simplicity. If you go the retributivist way, admitting two sorts of values, constraining and targeting, then simplicity in the structure of the theory requires that there should be a natural basis for distinguishing between those two sorts of values. But in fact no such basis is in the offing. The retributivist says that the valued property of having convicted offenders justly punished should be honoured—that is the constraint which defines her theory—while admitting that a valued property like that of preventing crime should be promoted. She may admit the latter so far as she would condone the action of police in allowing an offender to commit a crime—say, a theft—in order to see who he reports to as his boss. But why should the value of just punishment call to be honoured, the value of crime prevention to be promoted? It seems *ad hoc* of the retributivist to draw the relevant distinction where she does.

The third consideration in favour of consequentialism is also one of simplicity. Contemporary views of rationality, say rationality in pursuit of personally beneficial goals, cast it as instrumental rather than expressive. Given a property in the realization of which rationality is relevant—say, the property of having a profit—we all expect the rational agent to promote it. This will come as no surprise to the consequentialist who thinks that the proper way for an agent to respond to the universal values that he countenances is also to promote them in this fashion. But the retributivist, and more generally the deontologist, must find the fact somewhat embarrassing. For what it makes clear is that the retributivist has to see the moral agent as responding to the values he countenances in a manner not endorsed by the generally accepted theory of rationality. She has to see him as slavishly honouring the values in his actions, even if this does not promote them. The retributivist has one theory of response in matters moral, another in matters beyond the moral realm. Here again consequentialism proves to be the simpler doctrine, offering a unified theory of response—a unified theory of rationality—for all areas.[2]

It is worth noting that just as a general methodological observation enabled us to argue in the last Chapter for the attractions of a comprehensive theory of criminal justice, so the methodological virtue of simplicity is invoked here to make our case for the merits

[2] A reply the deontologist may make is that in counselling the honouring of a universal value like that of offenders being justly punished, she counsels the promotion by every relevant agent of the non-universal value of *his* punishing justly those offenders *he* has to sentence. But the question, raised in the preliminary point mentioned at the beginning of the discussion of constraints and targets, is how that non-universal value can be endorsed independently of a commitment to the universal value of, say, such offenders being justly punished in general. There are tricky matters here but they need not concern us in this discussion (see Pettit 1988*b*).

of a consequentialist theory. It is good that we can base our approach on such solid and uncontested foundations, though our arguments so far are meant to establish relatively little. They show only that there ought to be a presumption in favour of a comprehensive, consequentialist theory of criminal justice. Whether that presumption is justified depends on whether we can identify a satisfactory example of such a theory. We begin to take up that latter task in the next chapter.

Before leaving this chapter, however, it may be worth stressing that while the considerations we have mentioned offer only presumptive reasons in favour of consequentialism, the reasons are still of great importance. The consequentialist and the deontologist may agree, as we have seen, in hailing certain properties as values or goods. Where they differ is on the question of how goodness determines rightness. The deontologist says that the right action or the right system is that which exemplifies the goods embraced. The consequentialist says that it is that action or system which produces the goods. All that the considerations of simplicity do is bring out how much more natural it is to look in the moral area for what produces the goods than for what exemplifies them. If we go the deontological way and worry about exemplification rather than production in the moral area, then we shall have to recognize that there are two irreducibly different sorts of practical concern; we shall have to acknowledge the difficulty of explaining why one is relevant in moral matters, another in non-moral; and we shall have to admit that the notion of rationality that applies in the non-moral area does not carry over to the moral. In short, we shall be stuck with a monster of a theory.

As against this claim, it may be said that what we see as monstrosity is nothing more nor less than the degree of complexity required of a theory that is designed to cope with the real world. Postmodernist scholars who relish complexity may espouse deontological thinking then for the very feature that makes us recoil. And even social scientists who scorn such fashions may join them in arguing that the simplicity which we prize in normative theory may be a disabling characteristic rather than a virtue.

It goes without saying that an explanatory or normative theory must be complex enough to deal as it is intended to deal with the real world. What simplicity requires is that it is not more complex than necessary. The charge against us therefore is that the complexity introduced by the deontologist is complexity of a kind that is needed in normative theory. So what then can be said against that?

What can be said against it is something we have already emphasized a number of times, that whether the complexity is needed depends on how far a consequentialist theory meets the desiderata of a satisfactory approach. We are returned to the claim that in any area of normative theory we should look first to the possibility of finding a satisfactory consequentialist account and seek refuge in a deontological story only as a last resort. Consequentialism represents the rest-position in normative thinking.

Summary

However they are otherwise taxonomized, a crucial divide among comprehensive theories of criminal justice will turn on whether they employ a consequentialist or a deontological criterion: a criterion that sets up a target for the criminal justice system or a criterion which constrains it. We looked at the difference between constraints and targets and examined the connections between constraints, rights, and deserts. We saw how targeting theories of criminal justice have assumed a variety of forms, utilitarian and preventionist, and how constraining theories deploy some subset of the four retributivist constraints that we distinguished. Finally, we mentioned three considerations which strongly suggest that we should go the consequentialist way and view retributivism only as a last resort. They show that the consequentialist option enjoys greater simplicity than the retributivist and they create a natural presumption in its favour.

4

Identifying a Comprehensive, Consequentialist Target

We have found relatively formal methodological reasons for preferring a comprehensive, consequentialist theory of criminal justice. The question now is whether we can identify a comprehensive, consequentialist theory that is materially satisfactory. If we cannot then we shall have to explore the pathways of retributivism in search of something better.

In the next chapter we offer a first, abstract account of the theory we defend. In later chapters we develop a more concrete —though still a sketchy—image. Whether the theory is satisfactory or not depends, ultimately, not just on its formal merits, but on whether it sits easily, perhaps after some accommodation, with the considered judgements of criminal justice on which we can expect to attain some consensus within relevant communities. If it can be made to sit easily with those judgements, then the theory enjoys what John Rawls describes as reflective equilibrium (Rawls 1971: chap. 1; Pettit 1980: chap. 4). Reflective equilibrium is to normative theory what empirical confirmation is to positive theory.

We are obviously not in a position to argue that the theory we sketch in this book enjoys reflective equilibrium; we cannot develop the theory sufficiently for such a judgement to be securely made. But we believe that it is possible to isolate the most important desiderata in any theory that is likely to attain reflective equilibrium. And we are in a position to argue that our theory exemplifies those qualities. We design the theory, in particular we define the target deployed by the theory, so as to ensure that the desiderata are satisfied. That will become clear in the next chapter.

In this chapter we shall lay the ground for the presentation and defence of our own theory. First we identify three desiderata which every consequentialist theory of criminal justice, in particular every consequentialist target, ought to exemplify. Then we examine some candidate targets in the light of those desiderata. We reject utilitarian and preventionist approaches as well as an approach that we describe as target-retributivism: this casts the maximum satisfaction of the requirements which proper retributivists take as constraints in the role of a target for the criminal justice system.

First Desideratum

A first and minimal feature that we ought to look for in any candidate target is that it is relatively uncontroversial in relevant communities. What are the communities relevant for our purposes? Avoiding universalist pretensions, we stipulate the Western-style democracies of the modern world. We require of any candidate target for the criminal justice system that it be the sort of thing that can be fairly naturally assigned the role of directing the criminal justice system in such societies. Unless it satisfies this basic desideratum then the candidate is unlikely to generate a secure equilibrium with our considered judgements; it will raise misgivings about the very foundations of the theory. Thus we would not take seriously any candidate which appeals to a conception of the good—say, a religious view of the point of life—that is radically incapable of commanding consensus in a pluralist society.

The second and third desiderata are tailored rather more specifically to the demands of a theory of criminal justice. They are as obvious and as unobjectionable as the first but, as we shall see, they have been rather more often ignored. We owe a debt to recent retributivist writing for drawing attention to the two desiderata, for the retributivist critique of utilitarian and preventionist theory invokes them prominently.

Second Desideratum

The second desideratum is that the target invoked should not only be uncontroversial in itself, it should generate a stable allocation of the rights which are uncontroversial in relevant communities, in the area of criminal justice. These rights include the right of a party known to be innocent not to be penalized for a crime, the right of a person charged with a crime to a fair trial, and the like.

In our discussion we shall focus on the right of the innocent not to be victimized but the points made bear on all rights in the area that are genuinely uncontroversial. The right not to be victimized is so deeply entrenched that some regard it as definitional of punishment that it is imposed only on those thought to be guilty; Sadurski provides a useful review and critique of the position (1985: 233–7). We do not think that this definitional point is of much interest, since those who would allow the punishment of the innocent can always call it by another name. But it serves to mark the extent to which this right of the innocent is uncontroversial.

Our second desideratum is well grounded: no theory which countenanced something like the victimization of the innocent could be taken seriously. However, it is important to notice that what is required of a target is that it motivates not just the allocation of uncontroversial rights but their stable allocation. This feature needs some explanation if its rationale is to be obvious.

A target would motivate an unstable allocation of rights if it provided a reason for establishing the rights in law, but failed to provide a reason why the criminal justice authorities, or indeed any other agents, should take the rights seriously. Suppose that a goal *X* is furthered if people are each given legal rights to *A*. An agent will not be given reason by *X* to take *A*-rights seriously if, despite the legal sanctions, it remains that the best way to promote *X* is by always considering what that goal requires, honouring *A*-rights when honouring is best, offending against them when offending is best. It is often said, for example, that while the utilitarian target of maximizing happiness overall may be advanced by giving people certain legal rights—this will protect them against evil-doers—still the goal does not give reason to agents concerned with such happiness to take the rights seriously. Those agents will respect the rights when respect promises to maximize happiness; they will offend against them when, despite the legal sanctions in play, offending promises to maximize happiness. The rights are not given any autonomous or moral force by the goal (Lyons 1982). Agents concerned with the goal only have reason to honour the rights in those circumstances where doing so promotes the goal. They do not have reason to honour the rights in circumstances generally, without explicit regard to whether doing so is optimal.

A common charge against consequentialist theories, as against utilitarianism in particular, is that they only allow unstable allocations of criminal justice rights. The charge is that even if a consequentialist theory motivates a legal allocation of such rights, it fails to provide the criminal justice authorities with reason to take the rights seriously, attaching moral as well as legal force to them. Thus, we are offered the spectre of the sheriff whose zeal in pursuit of law and order leads him to try to play judge and jury as well as policeman. In order to placate the mob, it leads him, say, to be willing to frame and hang an innocent person.

Our response to this charge is built into the second desideratum. We agree that a consequentialist theory, in particular a consequentialist target, will only be attractive if it can motivate a stable allocation of uncontroversial rights: an allocation that is not highly vulnerable in the presence of zealous agents who identify with the overall target. Emphasizing the stability component, we shall describe the desideratum henceforth as the requirement that the target be a stabilizing one.

Third Desideratum

A stable allocation of uncontroversial rights will serve to protect people individually by constraining other agents, in particular agents of the state, to treat them suitably. But consistently with honouring such individually protective rights, a system of criminal justice might still offend against the considered judgements of most people in Western-style democracies. It will do so if the practices of the system transgress certain uncontroversial limits in a way which does not offend directly against any individual's uncontroversial rights. It will transgress such limits, for example, if it puts a police officer on every corner, prosecutes on the basis of possible rather than probable guilt, imposes punishments that mutilate or deform, and the like. Transgressing such limits may breach certain uncontroversial rights but even if it does not do so, it is still clearly objectionable.

The third desideratum is that not only should the target be uncontroversial itself; and not only should it generate a stable allocation of uncontroversial rights; it should also motivate respect for uncontroversial limits on the powers associated with the criminal justice system. It should not make voracious demands on the system, demands which put the limits at risk; it should be, as we shall say, a satiable goal.

We said that in considering whether various targets satisfy the second desideratum we would focus on the uncontroversial right of a person not to be victimized. Similarly, in applying the third desideratum we will focus on the limit which prohibits the imposition of what is described in the US Constitution as 'cruel and unusual punishment'. It is clear that if a theory offends against that limit then it will stand little chance of attaining reflective equilibrium with the considered judgements which most of us would defend.

If we can identify a target that is uncontroversial, stabilizing, and satiable, then we shall have gone a good way towards constructing a satisfactory consequentialist theory of criminal justice. We think we can identify such a target but before we introduce it, in the next chapter, we would like to show that the targets usually proposed as criteria of criminal justice fail to meet these tests of desirability.

A Preventionist Target

The goal most frequently ascribed to the criminal justice system is crime-prevention. This goal is usually broken down into one or more sub-goals: the incapacitation or rehabilitation of actual offenders, for example, or the deterrence of potential offenders. These preventionist targets have probably appealed for their lack of vagueness and for the fact, which we are prepared to concede, that they look reasonably uncontroversial. It is ironic, however, that they have prevailed, for they are outrageously destabilizing and insatiable objectives.

They will be destabilizing goals if they do not motivate the allocation of uncontroversial rights or if they do not motivate a stable allocation of such claims. In fact the preventionist targets fail on both counts. They do not give reason for legally allocating such criminal justice rights and, even if they did, they would not provide the criminal justice authorities with reason to take those rights seriously: to invest them with moral as well as legal force. The point can be made by considering their capacity to justify penalization of the innocent.

All of the preventionist aims are individually capable of motivating punishment of the innocent. If there is reason to incapacitate or rehabilitate an actual offender, there is equal reason to provide such treatment for anyone who is judged likely to offend. And if there is deterrent reason to penalize an actual offender, so there may be reason to penalize any party—in particular, any potential offender—who is widely believed to be guilty of a crime, or who can be made into a credible scapegoat. Crime prevention is in flagrant breach of our second desideratum.

Equally, it is in conflict with the third desideratum, being an inherently insatiable objective. No matter how hard the system is driven to promote crime prevention or one of the associated sub-goals, there will always be more that can in principle be achieved. And so the target is bound to make demands which press the system beyond the currently uncontroversial limits on its practices. The target is a voracious and consuming goal.

The point is obvious when we consider what it is capable of requiring in the area of punishment of the guilty. All the preventionist aims are as likely to motivate excessive penalties as they are to encourage intuitively acceptable ones. If there is reason to incapacitate an offender for a limited period, why not incapacitate her so long as she remains a potential nuisance? If there is reason to rehabilitate her, why not keep her under treatment for as long as the job requires? If there is reason to deter potential offenders by punishing actual ones, why not let the punishment increase to create an ever more effective deterrent? Boiling oil for bicycle thieves.

Although it is the dominant variety of consequentialist criminology, it is clear that preventionism has absolutely no chance of attaining reflective equilibrium. It may invoke a target that looks uncontroversial itself but the target fails to vindicate the uncontroversial rights and limits that are widely recognized in the area of criminal justice. The target is at open war with our second and third desiderata.

But while preventionism encounters problems like these, it does have other attractions and they probably explain its popularity. Preventionism goes well with the liberal presumption that the most important social value is people's negative liberty: their freedom from the harmful and culpable intrusions of others. The only activities which ought to be criminalized, according to standard liberal doctrine, are such harmful intrusions (Feinberg 1986). And so the minimization of crime is a natural policy for liberals to impose on the criminal justice system, at least so far as liberals see liberty as a target to be promoted, not as a constraint to be honoured.

Mention of the liberal connection prompts a further comment on preventionism. This is that there would seem to be no reason for the preventionist not to focus on the minimization of the sort of harm associated with crime, rather than on the narrower goal of just minimizing crime itself. This move would still leave the preventionist with a destabilizing goal, since our earlier comments would continue to apply. But it would make for a goal that is less obviously insatiable.

There is no crime involved in raising the severity of punishment and so crime reduction can press us towards controversial sorts of punishment. But there is harm done in taking this route—harm to the person punished—and so harm reduction may not press us so far. The shift of goal would still allow controversial levels of punishment if the harm done in excessively punishing one thief is easily outweighed by the harm avoided through preventing ten further thefts. Besides, moving from crime reduction to harm reduction is not likely, on any standard account of harm, to stop the criminal justice system breaching uncontroversial limits in areas other than punishment, such as surveillance. But at least the problem would not be as acute as under crime preventionism.

Preventionists do not as a matter of fact focus on harm reduction rather than crime reduction. We note the possibility of doing so here, for two reasons. First, harm preventionism would seem to fit better with liberalism than the standard kind. And second, as we shall see in the next chapter, the idea behind the harm prevention proposal foreshadows the idea driving the proposal which we defend.

A 'Retributivist' Target

But however dominant preventionism has been, there are at least two other sorts of consequentialist theory which are worth examining. One is a consequentialist version of retributivism, the other is utilitarianism in its classical form. These have a marginal currency in criminology and we must see how they match up against our desiderata.

Although retributivists have been to the fore in the criticism of consequentialist theories, it is a curious feature of their writing that sometimes they themselves move into a consequentialist mode of thinking. They do this, for example, when they offer a rationale for retributive constraints on sentencing and then focus on the rationale as if it involved a goal to be realized by the sentencing sub-system, and even by the system as a whole. We shall be reviewing some of the rationales offered in Chapter 8. They include claims of the kind that honouring the retributive constraints communicates to offenders the evil of what they have done, gives expression to the community's denunciation of the activities in question, and re-establishes a balance in the benefits and burdens enjoyed by different people under a regime of mutual constraint. Once retributivist thinkers begin to focus on such communication or denunciation or balancing as the important achievement of the criminal justice system, it is not clear how they can avoid thinking of those features as values to be promoted (see Hampton 1984: 215–16; Ten 1987: 60). The phrases used in framing the rationales bear the mark of retributivist concerns but what we are being offered may still be a consequentialist theory.

Take the theory which holds up the achievement of an equilibrium between benefits and burdens as the point of the system. 'The punishment—by imposing a counterbalancing disadvantage on the violator—restores the equilibrium: after having undergone the punishment, the violator ceases to be at advantage over his non-violating fellows' (von Hirsch, 1976: 47). For all that this sort of characterization tells us, the theory fits a consequentialist mould just as comfortably as a deontological one. The balancing task prescribed in the theory may be variously construed, so that what is required is an equilibrium between all the benefits and burdens enjoyed by different members of a community; or an equilibrium between the benefits and burdens associated in particular with mutual non-interference; or whatever. No matter how it is construed, however, the criterion proposed as a basis for assessing a criminal justice system can be naturally read as a target rather than a constraint. Consider, again, this remark from Wojciech Sadurski: 'The general justification of punishment is analogous to that of rewards: it is a method of restoring an overall balance of benefits and burdens' (1985: 225). Or consider this comment from Jeffrie Murphy: 'Justice —that is punishing such individuals—restores the equilibrium of benefits and burdens' (1970: 109). Like the original quotation from von Hirsch, such remarks are quite naturally read as statements of a consequentialist position, according to which the penal system should be organized so as to achieve a certain end, not so as to honour a certain constraint.

Taken at the letter of the proposal, and without regard to the retributive sentiments of those who make it, the idea can be construed as follows. The system is required, not, for example, to match the benefit of every convicted offender's crime with a penal burden, but rather to take whatever steps are required for the promotion of an optimal balance overall. Strictly speaking, those steps may include the toleration of a local imbalance which a retributivist proper might be expected to condemn. The imbalance may come of too little or too much punishment for a convicted offender, or even of the imposition of a penalty on someone known to be innocent. Just as we can conceive of circumstances where preventionism would justify punishment of the innocent, so there can be circumstances where the preventive effects of punishing an innocent person would generate a better balance of benefits and burdens overall.

We do not say that those whose wont is to speak of goals like the balancing of benefits and burdens are always explicitly committed to a consequentialist theory. We claim only that the position they outline can be taken as a consequentialist theory, involving consequentialist modes of argument. Such a theory we shall describe as a form of target-retributivism; it is a theory of the kind that Robert Nozick (1981: 374) calls 'teleological retributivism'. But though there are not many explicit target-retributivists, there are some. George Sher argues for the balancing of suitable benefits and burdens as the point of punishment and then makes clear that the balancing in question is to be seen as a value to be promoted, not a value that constrains; his arguments, as he puts it, 'appeal not to any obligation to rectify deviations from independent standards, but instead to the superior value of the rectification of such deviations' (1987: 198). In similar vein, while arguing that the retributivist ought to see the point of punishment as that of defeating the offender and reasserting the value against which he has offended, Jean Hampton freely admits that this is to make goals of those desiderata (Murphy and Hampton 1989: 122).

So much by way of introducing the notion of a target-retributivist goal for the criminal justice system. We turn now to consider how such a goal is likely to do on our three criteria. We shall only consider the version of target-retributivism which hails the balancing of benefits and burdens as the value to be promoted, as the points to be made in relation to it suggest similar observations on other target-retributivist candidates.

Is the balancing of benefits and burdens inherently controversial as a target for the criminal justice system? Perhaps not, understood as an objective for the sentencing of convicted criminals; at least not, if it is charitably granted that we can identify the sort of punishment that balances the benefit procured by crime: on this difficulty see Chapter 8. But this is not to say that the target is an uncontroversial goal for the system of criminal justice as a whole. It may be thought objectionable on at least one count. Suppose, however unrealistically, that we had two systems which promised to balance benefits and burdens equally but which differed so far as one was likely to cause a higher level of crime than the other; it would compensate for this, maintaining the same balance of benefits and burdens, by producing a higher level of punishment. The target of balancing benefits and burdens would not give us reason to prefer the system involving the lower level of crime and to many that will seem a ground for complaint.

Even if it is thought uncontroversial, however, the target of balancing benefits and burdens can hardly be said to be stabilizing. It may motivate the allocation of uncontroversial rights but it certainly does not provide a reason for agents of the system to take those rights seriously. Rather, it is capable on occasion of providing those agents with reason to exercise illegal initiative and infringe on such rights. Consider a case where the imposition of a penalty on someone known to be innocent but generally supposed to be guilty will increase the overall balance of benefits and burdens; it may promise to reduce the level of crime or to generate more effective detection and prosecution. In such a case the goal of balancing benefits and burdens would provide a powerful reason for a zealous agent of the system to look at possibilities of an effective frame-up. The same problem arises with reprobation or any other retributivist target.

The count on which the target of balancing benefits and burdens is strongest is that of satiability. Insatiability arises with crime prevention, because the imposition of horrible punishments—or some other transgression of uncontroversial limits on criminal justice practice—can produce a benefit in terms of the target—can reduce crime—without incurring any corresponding cost in those terms—without being a crime. Now, the imposition of such penalties may produce an improvement in the balance of benefits and burdens by reducing the level of crime but it would simultaneously incur a cost: that of imposing penalties so severe in degree or kind as to be out of proportion to the offences committed. The balancing of benefits and burdens resembles the goal of harm reduction in this regard. The involvement of the balancing target on the cost as well as on the benefit side of any putative transgression of uncontroversial limits suggests that, in regard to penalties, the target may be attractively satiable.

But the reassurance offered is limited, as with harm reduction, for two reasons. First, the cost of creating a local imbalance for the sake of greater balance overall may be easily outweighed by the latter benefit. If the excessive punishment of one thief prevents ten thefts then the imbalance created by the excessive punishment would have to be very great to be ten times the imbalance prevented in the other cases. Second, there may be no such cost to be counted in the target-retributivist's book for transgression of uncontroversial limits in non-penal areas of the criminal justice system; the police may be allowed, for example, to practise quite intolerable forms of surveillance. Both considerations argue that the goal may be not just controversial and destabilizing but also insatiable.

There are other possible forms of target-retributivism apart from that associated with improving the balance of benefits and burdens. For example, there is a target-retributivism corresponding to the view that the rationale of punishment is to deliver community reprobation: more on this, and other variations, in Chapter 8. We hope it is clear that the same failings are likely to beset any other form of the doctrine as affect the balancing version. Target-retributivism is no more attractive than preventionism.

A Utilitarian Target

Apart from preventionism and target-retributivism, we also have to take notice of the most classical of all forms of consequentialist theory: utilitarianism. This, as we know, sets the maximization of the happiness of those affected by the criminal justice system as its proper goal.

The utilitarian target looks uncontroversial but that may only be because it is so vaguely defined. Two hundred years after the formulation of the utilitarian doctrine, there is a continuing debate about what exactly happiness connotes (Griffin 1986; Pettit 1980: chap. 11; Dworkin 1981). It is probably the vagueness of the goal which accounts for the fact that within consequentialist criminology utilitarianism has given way to preventionism.

But whether or not it is uncontroversial, the utilitarian target is likely to be stabilizing only if a contestable empirical claim is conceded by the agents of the system and is known to be conceded by them. We may grant that the target will motivate the legal allocation of uncontroversial rights. But we cannot have any confidence that it will motivate a stable allocation, for it seems perfectly possible that on occasion the penalization of an innocent person will promise to maximize overall happiness in the calculations of the zealous agent of the system. A zealous agent will identify strongly with the system goal of maximizing overall happiness. If victimization does not promise to maximize happiness in certain circumstances—say, when a mob needs pacifying—then that can only be because the agent happens to believe that the unease created in those who will suspect what he has done weighs heavily in the happiness stakes. And that belief, however plausible, is not necessarily going to prevail. Thus, the agent, be she police officer, prosecutor, or judge, may be motivated to offend against the right of the innocent person not to be punished.

Apart from the possibility of being destabilizing, the utilitarian target is likely to be insatiable. Any practice that exceeds uncontroversial limits—any horrible penalty, for example—may seem to incur a cost in the happiness of the person punished, whatever the benefit in overall happiness it produces. But that is not necessarily so. A penalty could breach those limits without incurring any utilitarian cost: say, if it involved extended imprisonment with drugs administered regularly to ensure euphoria. And so the utilitarian target may make demands voracious enough to license a breach of currently uncontroversial limits on criminal justice practice.

Conclusion

It is clear from this quick review of consequentialist theories that if consequentialism is to be vindicated, then we need a very different account of the target which the criminal justice system ought to promote. Preventionism, target-retributivism, and utilitarianism are unsatisfactory consequentialist theories when evaluated against our three desiderata. In the next chapter we offer our own account and try to show that the target proposed is at once an uncontroversial, a stabilizing, and a satiable objective.

5

The Republican Idea

We mentioned in the last Chapter that the dominant consequentialist approach to criminal justice, preventionism, ties up closely with liberalism. Especially in the form of harm-preventionism, it is the sort of policy we might expect to be endorsed by thinkers concerned with maximizing negative liberty, as liberalism conceives of such liberty. The approach which we shall be defending in this chapter has certain parallels with preventionism. It is also a policy which we might expect to be endorsed by thinkers concerned with maximizing negative liberty. The difference is, however, that any thinkers likely to endorse it would conceive of negative liberty in a republican rather than a liberal fashion.

As a self-conscious tradition, liberalism goes back no more than two hundred years (Arblaster 1984; Gray 1986). But for three centuries or so before that, the dominant political tradition in Europe and America had stressed the importance of liberty, and indeed negative liberty, just as much as liberals have ever done. This is the republican tradition, modelled on the civic humanism of ancient Rome, which is charted in J. G. A. Pocock's now classic study, *The Machiavellian Moment: Florentine Political Theory and the Atlantic Republican Tradition* (Pocock, 1975).

In this chapter we shall first of all try to characterize the republican notion of liberty. Then we shall offer a definition of the target we propose for the criminal justice system, which is designed to reflect most aspects of that notion. Because the word 'liberty' belongs now to liberalism, we shall describe the target as the maximization of the dominion of individual people. Having identified this target we shall then argue that it promises to be an uncontroversial, stabilizing, and satiable goal for the criminal justice system: a goal which satisfies the three desiderata distinguished in the last chapter. This will put us in a position to consider, in the two chapters following, what a republican criminal justice system would mean in practice and how it might begin to be implemented. But before turning to those tasks we shall add one further section to this chapter: a discussion of the institutional possibilities which a republican who is attached to dominion should find attractive. This will serve to connect the chapter with the more practice-orientated discussions that follow.

Republican Liberty

In order to identify the republican notion of liberty or freedom it may be useful to situate it, and other notions, in relation to some important distinctions. Political values in general divide first into those that are properties of individuals—e.g. happiness, self-reliance—and those that are properties of larger groups—e.g. cohesiveness, solidarity. Individual-centred values divide in turn into those which belong to individuals *qua* agents—say, independence—and those that belong to individuals *qua* centres of experience—say, happiness. We assume that in any version that concerns us, liberty is an individual-centred agency value and we shall not discuss the relevant distinctions further. That is to say that we are interested in personal liberty rather than, for example, the liberty of groups or nations.

But an individual-centred agency value like liberty can still go either way on further distinctions. First there is the distinction between liberty in a negative sense and liberty under some more positive construal. Negative liberty involves, roughly, the absence of interference by others, or at least of interference that is sufficiently intentional, negligent, reckless, or indifferent to count as blameworthy or culpable; we may leave open for the moment the notion of what constitutes interference. Positive liberty involves something more in addition. What more is required varies from one account to another. It may be the absence of physical inability, psychological incapacity, personal ignorance, or something of that kind; in such a case, people often speak of liberty as autonomy (Feinberg 1973: 12–13; Lindley 1986; Young 1986; Dworkin 1988). It may be the exercise of the liberty in a morally suitable way, say in pursuit of fitting ends (Baldwin 1984). It may even be the exercise of the liberty in a political manner, by participation in democratic collective decision-making.

As we understand it, the notion of republican liberty, like the standard liberal one, is negative rather than positive. To be free in the sense in question does not by definition require the sort of extra factor envisaged by positive theorists. This means that the value we hail in this book, the value we describe as that of 'dominion', should be distinguished for example, from the now commonly invoked value of autonomy. More on this later.

The essential difference between the liberal and the republican notions of freedom or liberty only becomes clear when we turn to a final distinction among political values. This is the asocial–social distinction: the distinction between values such that an individual can enjoy them, in principle, outside a social context and values of which this is not true (Hamlin and Pettit 1989). Happiness in this sense is an asocial value, whereas equality with others—at least as naturally construed—is not. It turns out that negative liberty, liberty in the sense in which it does not by definition require any of the extras mentioned, can be interpreted in an asocial or a social way. The asocial construal is the liberal one, the social construal the republican.

The asocial concept of freedom is probably derived in its more recent manifestations from Hobbes. The first thing that Hobbes insists on is that freedom, as we would say, is negative. 'A free-man, is he, that in those things, which by his strength and wit he is able to do, is not hindred to do what he has a will to do' (Hobbes 1968 edn.: 262–4). But here Hobbes is not to be distinguished from republicans, at least of the Machiavellian stripe (Skinner 1983), or indeed of the Roman (Wirszubski 1968: 30). The second thing he insists on is what marks him off. This is that a person can enjoy liberty in the state of nature, when cut off from other human beings, and that if he enjoys it in society, it makes no difference to the liberty he enjoys that it comes to him under one set of laws or another: for example, under a tyrannical or constitutional regime. 'Whether a Commonwealth be Monarchicall, or Popular, the Freedome is still the same' (Hobbes 1968 edn.: 266).

The view that freedom can be enjoyed outside society as well as within, and can be enjoyed as well under one sort of law as under another, became central to the classical liberal tradition of thinking. What the view comes down to essentially is that social convention and law is just one means whereby freedom can be achieved and that the nature of the means does not matter so long as in the end people have the space for choice which freedom requires (see Benn and Peters 1959: 213). In the tradition of those who describe themselves as liberals, there have been some exceptional figures who have argued that liberty involves a socio-legal condition essentially: see, for example, Green (1889). But in our view these figures are best seen as covert republicans. The overwhelming consensus among liberals, even indeed non-classical liberals who go for more positive conceptions of liberty, has been that the law is merely an instrument for promoting liberty, not a part of what it involves.

Negative liberty, by all accounts, requires the minimization or elimination of interference by others. Under the Hobbesian and classical liberal interpretation the condition required is this: that it is not the case that there are others who interfere. That means that if we ask what perfect liberty consists in, if we seek a regulative interpretation of the requirements of liberty, then the answer that naturally suggests itself is: the solitary condition, the condition of being the only person around, so that there are no others who can possibly interfere. This may explain the asocial character of negative liberty, as it is interpreted in the liberal tradition.

The key to understanding the rival republican tradition of interpretation is to see that there is an alternative way of characterizing the condition of non-interference. The condition, under the republican interpretation, is this: that there are others around, and they do not interfere. The place of the negation operator is different in this characterization, for it is now required that there are others around who do not interfere; it is not enough if there are no others available to interfere. Thus we are pointed towards a different account of the ideal requirements of liberty. We cannot say that perfect liberty is exemplified by the solitary condition. What republicans generally say is that it is exemplified by the condition of citizenship in a free society, a condition under which each is properly safeguarded by the law against the predations of others. The regulative interpretation of liberty, the interpretation which guides us on what liberty requires, equates freedom not with being left alone, but with being given equal protection before a suitable law.

It is important to be clear on why this republican conception is an interpretation of the negative conception of liberty, not just another positive conception. There are two questions that arise with an ideal of liberty. One is: what is the best definition, abstracting as far as possible from detail? The other is: what does the ideal require in any relevant circumstances; how is it best interpreted as an ideal to regulate the arrangements we make in social life? Republicans differ from those who adopt positive conceptions of liberty in going for the negative definition as the most appropriate abstract analysis; in this they agree with classical liberals. Republicans differ from classical liberals on the other hand in arguing for a different interpretation of what the ideal of negative liberty is more or less bound to involve. According to the classical liberal interpretation, the sort of condition required is that of being left alone, a condition exemplified *par excellence* in the solitary individual. According to the republican interpretation, it is the condition of citizenship or equality before the law. The classical liberal might think that liberty in his sense is promoted in such and such circumstances by equality before the law. The republican interprets liberty in such a way that the linkage with equality before the law is not contingent in that way; there is no relevant possibility of their coming apart.[1]

A parallel may help to shed further light on the difference between liberals and republicans on freedom. Consider the notion of poverty and assume that a fair characterization is this: poverty is the condition under which someone is unable to provide for his material needs. Such a notion might be interpreted asocially by asking what would produce poverty in a solitary state. Thus the regulative interpretation of poverty would be a condition of lacking the means of subsistence. But equally the notion might be interpreted under the assumption that everyone belongs to a society. And under such an approach poverty would be taken as exemplified, not just in a condition of lacking the means of subsistence, but more generally in any condition of lacking the material requirements for functioning in the society —say in Adam Smith's phrase, for living without shame (Sen 1982*b*). Just as theorists who share the original definition of poverty may have rather different regulative interpretations of what constitutes it, so our claim is that liberal and republican

[1] Quentin Skinner argues for what is probably best seen as a similar sort of linkage, within the republican tradition, between liberty and virtue (e.g. 1984: 217).

theorists can share a negative definition of liberty and interpret the ideal requirements of liberty in quite different ways. An extra feature in the liberty case of course is that the liberal–republican difference derives from the different readings to which the characterization of non-interference lends itself.

The republican notion of freedom goes back at least to the days of the Roman republic. The Romans did not think that the simple fact of not suffering interference constituted liberty: you could be a *servus sine domino*, a slave without a master, and still not be free. To be free, as they saw it, was to be a full and equal party to the rule of Roman law, someone protected as well as any other by that law, someone incorporated as a citizen into the body politic.

At Rome and with regard to Romans full *libertas* is coterminous with *civitas*. A Roman's *libertas* and his *civitas* both denote the same thing, only that each does it from a different point of view and with emphasis on a different aspect: *libertas* signifies in the first place the status of an individual as such, whereas *civitas* denotes primarily the status of an individual in relation to the community. Only a Roman citizen enjoys all the rights, personal and political, that constitute *libertas*. (Wirszubski, 1968: 3–4)

This Roman view of freedom remained at the centre of the republican tradition established after the Renaissance in Europe. It is present in the works of Machiavelli and in those of the many thinkers who followed his lead in the following centuries (Skinner 1983). Thus it is no surprise to find James Harrington, Machiavelli's seventeenth-century English disciple, mock the asocial idea of freedom which Hobbes put forward. In particular he mocks the Hobbesian claim that the citizen of republican Lucca may have no more freedom than the inhabitant of despotic Constantinople. He may have no more freedom *from* the law, says Harrington, but he certainly has more freedom *by* the law.

The mountain hath brought forth, and we have a little equivocation! For to say that a Lucchese hath no more liberty or immunity *from* the laws of Lucca than a Turk hath from those of Constantinople, and to say that a Lucchese hath no more liberty or immunity *by* the laws of Lucca than a Turk hath by those of Constantinople, are pretty different speeches. (Harrington 1977 edn.: 170)

The republican notion of liberty as citizenship, which we find in Harrington, may have had other sources than the Roman idea of *libertas*. The medieval terms 'freedom' and 'franchise' held connotations of citizenship for different reasons. C. S. Lewis (1967: 125), although he is surely wrong about the ancient languages, says this about those words.

The medieval words nearly always refer . . . to the guaranteed freedoms or immunities (from royal or baronial interference) of a corporate entity which cuts across states, like the Church, or which exists within the state, like a city or guild . . . This led to a development unparalleled, I believe, in the ancient languages. By becoming a member of any corporation which enjoys such freedom or franchise you of course come to share that *freedom* or *franchise*. You become a *freeman* of, or receive the *freedom* of, that city . . . These are familiar. But a further development along this line is more startling. *Freedom* can mean simply 'citizenship' . . . This meaning is fossilized in the surviving English use of *franchise* to mean the power of voting, conceived as the essential mark of full citizenship.

We propose now to take the republican rather than the liberal notion of freedom and consider how well the promotion of freedom in this sense might serve as a target for the criminal justice system. We shall not generally describe the target as liberty or freedom, since these terms have been captured by the liberal traditions. Instead we shall introduce the word 'dominion' to describe what we have in mind, usually deploying the word 'liberty' in the ordinary liberal way. We hope that the term has the connotations required to suggest that the bearer of dominion has control in a certain area, being free from the interference of others, but has that control in virtue of the recognition of others and the protection of the law. In short, we hope that it can suggest to modern ears what *libertas* must have suggested to the Romans, 'franchise' to the medievals.

The rest of the chapter falls into three major sections. First we shall try to set out more exactly what dominion involves. Then we shall try to show that it represents a satisfactory target for the criminal justice system. And finally we shall look at the institutions that someone attached to dominion would naturally favour; here we find a further contrast between liberals and republicans.

Before moving on from historical matters, however, we would like to link our enterprise with an important precedent. One of the most significant thinkers in the republican tradition, broadly conceived, is the eighteenth-century French writer, the Baron de Montesquieu. Like all republicans Montesquieu associates liberty essentially with law. 'Liberty is the right of doing whatever the laws permit' (Montesquieu 1977 ed.: 200). But he pays an unusual degree of attention to matters of criminal law, on the following grounds. 'Political liberty consists in security, or at least in the opinion we have of security. This security is never more dangerously attacked than in public or private accusations. It is therefore on the goodness of criminal laws that the liberty of the subject principally depends' (Montesquieu 1977 edn.: 217).

Montesquieu's recommendations in regard to criminal justice, motivated as they are by republican concerns, foreshadow much that we will be arguing in this book. He argues, as we do, for restricting and carefully defining the range of activities criminalized, for reducing the severity of punishments commonly practised, for focusing as much on the protection of the innocent as on the punishment of the guilty, and for putting constitutional constraints on the agents of the criminal justice system. More generally, he highlights a theme which is a constant motif in the pages following. 'One thread runs through all of Montesquieu's reflections on crime and punishment: how to lessen the burden of fear in the minds of ordinary citizens' (Shklar 1987: 91). Without endorsing all the details, we see in Montesquieu's work a tradition sustained in our own.

Dominion

An agent enjoys negative liberty, by all accounts, if and only if he is exempt from the constraints imposed by the intentional or at least the blameworthy actions of others in choosing certain options. Which options? Hobbes specifies those things 'which by his strength and wit he is able to do'. We prefer to standardize and say: those options which the normal agent is capable of realizing in normal conditions without the special collaboration of colleagues or circumstances. Where ∅-ing is such an option, the liberty to ∅ means in our view that you are not prevented from ∅-ing; that your choice of ∅-ing is not frustrated—say, by punishment; and that you are not coerced into not ∅-ing by a credible threat of prevention or frustration (for a defence of this conception see Pettit 1989*b*). More generally, it means that others do not deliberately or culpably worsen your situation so that the choice of the options in question ceases to be possible or at least 'eligible' (Benn and Weinstein 1971). It means that you enjoy the standard liberties of expression, movement, and association and, at least in some spheres, the usual privileges of ownership.

Our task now is to specify a conception of negative liberty derived under the assumption that there are always going to be other people in the community of a free agent, in particular to specify a conception which belongs to the republican family. We may approach the task of deriving an appropriate specification by asking first how an atomist, content to entertain the notion of the totally isolated agent, might specify the ideal of negative freedom, and then how the holist would differ from him. In doing so we follow Pettit (1989*a*). The atomist derivation ought to correspond to the liberal approach, given our earlier remarks, the holist to the republican. The difference between atomistic and holistic views of society—the difference between views which make the notion of the totally isolated agent coherent and those which in some way deny it coherence—is of great importance, not just in the present debate but more generally. If this has not been widely recognized, that may be because the 'horizontal' question of whether the notion of the solitary agent is coherent has been continually confused with the 'vertical' question of whether the institutional forces in a society preclude or pre-empt individual initiative (Pettit 1985–6; Pettit forthcoming *a*).

If you take an atomistic view of society, then there will be at least some temptation to provide a quick and easy answer to the question of what would ensure perfect liberty. The quick and easy answer is: the condition of the solitary individual. You will be tempted to say that someone perfectly enjoys liberty if and only if there are no other people around to get in his way: no other people to prevent or frustrate his choices; no other people to threaten prevention or frustration. You will be tempted in other words to take perfect freedom as an asocial condition that is always compromised, no matter how trivially, by the presence of other people. If you do take that line of course then you will have classic liberalism on your side. That may be because the atomism which legitimates your account of perfect liberty is an important part of that liberal tradition.

But suppose that instead of taking an atomistic view of society, you adopt the holistic perspective; or suppose that you decide for other reasons that the notion of the solitary individual is not appropriately invoked in this context. In that case the quick and easy answer to our question will no longer be available, for you will have to define the condition of perfect liberty in such a way that it is available to someone in society. You will have to think of it, not as an asocial condition compromised in any political arrangement, but as a certain sort of social status. Perfect liberty will be a condition enjoyed so far and only so far as a person relates to other people, and to the institutions of his society, in a way which gives him a certain sort of power.

Three things naturally follow if the condition of perfect liberty is a social status. The first thing is that whether someone perfectly enjoys liberty will depend not just on how he fares in himself but on how he fares comparatively with others in his society. No one can perfectly enjoy liberty under a given culture—for example, no one can perfectly enjoy an exemption from suitable constraints—if he is subject to more constraints than some others. Perfect liberty is no longer to be defined on an intrinsic basis as the absence, for example, of any sort of prevention, frustration, or coercion; it is to be defined comparatively or relationally.

The second thing that follows if perfect liberty is a social status is that it must require, not just as much exemption as anyone else from relevant constraints, but also some assurance, and indeed as much assurance as anyone else, of that exemption. If perfect liberty is defined as the condition of the solitary person, then not only are the constraints absent; their absence is also assured. This is not so if the condition required for perfect liberty is assumed to be a social status. A person might just have the good luck not to suffer any more invasion than anyone else in the society but we would hardly say that she therefore enjoyed liberty to the same extent as others. Certainly we would not say this if the others had the advantage over her of enjoying some assurance against invasion. If perfect liberty is cast as a social status then it must be made explicit that it requires a suitable assurance of the absence of constraint as well as the absence itself.

Finally, the third thing that follows if perfect liberty is a social status is that it must require, not just a suitably assured absence of constraint, but a knowledge of that assured absence. Under the atomistic explication a person could not enjoy liberty perfectly without being in a position to know that he enjoyed it; all that he would have to observe is that there is no one around to get in his way. Under the holist explication a person could enjoy the absence of invasion involved in perfect liberty without being in such a position; he might think that he was subject to more constraints than others, for example, when in fact he was not. Thus the enjoyment of perfect freedom requires, not just a suitably assured absence of invasion, but also an extra factor: the awareness of that assured absence.

But more than that, under the holistic explication the perfect enjoyment of liberty would also seem to require that the awareness in question be shared by a person with others in the community, so that it is common knowledge that he enjoys a suitably assured absence of constraint. This is because the assurance of exemption from constraint will be increased if everyone knows that the person is provided with such assurance, if everyone knows that the person himself knows that he is provided with it, and so on. Common knowledge would underwrite the assurance required for perfect liberty.

The consequence of these three implications is that if it is understood holistically then perfect liberty, like dignity or authority, is going to be a condition that a person can enjoy only so far as she has a certain standing *vis-à-vis* others. It is going to require freedom in the sense of the freedom of the city: that is, full citizenship or, as it used to be called, franchise. The freedom of the city stands in nice contrast to the freedom of the heath and it is hardly unfair to say that where the holist inevitably construes freedom as the former value, the atomist is easily led into taking it for the latter (Ignatieff 1984).

When we name dominion as the value that ought to be protected against invasion by the criminal justice system, it is this civic freedom, this franchise or citizenship, that we have in mind. We are now in a position to mention the important components of dominion from the point of view of our investigation. There are three conditions in particular which require highlighting.

A person enjoys full dominion, we say, if and only if:

1. she enjoys no less a prospect of liberty than is available to other citizens.
2. it is common knowledge among citizens that this condition obtains, so that she and nearly everyone else knows that she

enjoys the prospect mentioned, she and nearly everyone else knows that the others generally know this too, and so on.[2]

3. she enjoys no less a prospect of liberty than the best that is compatible with the same prospect for all citizens.[3]

These conditions are designed to catch the implications of construing the requirements of perfect liberty holistically. The comparative requirement is satisfied by the reference to others in the first and last clauses. The assurance requirement is honoured by the mention of the prospect of liberty in those clauses: the prospect of liberty enjoyed by a person is determined by the extent of the liberty on offer and the degree of assurance available that that liberty will not be violated. Finally, the common knowledge requirement mentioned in our holistic explication of perfect liberty is embodied in the second clause of the definition.

The definition of dominion calls for a number of further comments. A first is that the ideal in question is formally but not maximally egalitarian.[4] It is formally egalitarian, because if we are trying to maximize the realization of dominion then, assuming at least that the matter of common knowledge is fixed, the way to increase dominion at any point of inequality will be to improve equality in liberty-prospects with those who are best off. The claim should be obvious from the fact that someone who has a better prospect than others already has dominion in the fullest measure possible; it is logically impossible to give him more. Thus the only way to increase dominion in that society will be to put

[2] It is best to interpret such common knowledge negatively, so that what it requires is that everyone knows that the first two clauses obtain and at least no one knows or believes that the relevant conditions at higher levels do not obtain; this can be true without their positively knowing that the conditions do obtain.

[3] This is a revision of the definition in Pettit (1989*a*). The order of clauses 2 and 3 is reversed and the requirement of common knowledge that clause 3 obtains is thereby dropped. That requirement seems excessive and the revision puts the clauses in their natural order of importance.

[4] Notice, contrary to common assumptions, that there is no incoherence in the notion that an aggregative goal like the maximization of dominion may require a certain distributive pattern. Aggregation and distribution are not necessarily in competition.

him and others at the same level, or to reduce the difference between their levels.[5]

But though dominion is a formally egalitarian ideal, the equality required is not maximal. We understand the notion of equality in prospects as requiring, not that the bearers have the same actual prospects, but that they have the same prospects in the same suitably variable circumstances. Suppose that John is a dull and worthy citizen, James someone who likes to hang around in seedy establishments. The fact that actually their liberty-prospects differ—James is more likely to be mugged, for example—does not mean that their prospects are unequal in the sense that matters to us. The fact of hanging around in seedy establishments is plausibly seen as a variable circumstance, such that in that circumstance each would have the same prospect, and that is what we take to be important. There is a question of course about what should be seen for these purposes as a variable circumstance, what as a relevantly unvarying condition. We offer no judgement of a general kind on this; it may be something that resists theoretical adjudication. For the record, however, we think of a variable circumstance as one that is within the agent's control in some sense and we believe that being of a certain race or gender or religion, even being of a certain economic standing, should not be seen as a variable circumstance. Thus we would worry about differences in actual liberty-prospects across different racial groups or economic classes.

The fact that it is formally but not maximally egalitarian links the ideal of dominion with the Roman notion of *libertas* (Wirszubski 1968: 9–15). A second feature of the ideal may also connect with classical antecedents. This is the fact that though the ideal is egalitarian, it also has a quantitative dimension. Suppose that we find two societies, call them Athens and Sparta, in each of which the relevant citizens have equal prospects of liberty, but in

[5] This means that there will often be questions, for example, as to whether equality is best served by putting some of the worse off on the level of the best, leaving others in their original plight, or by raising in some measure the level of all the worse off. We ignore the problem, as it is common to all egalitarian projects. It might be resolved by having an index, such as the Gini index of economic inequality, which is sensitive both to the numbers at less than the best level and to the differences between levels. The Gini index focuses on the statistically expected difference in economic fortunes within a randomly chosen pair of people in a society.

one—Athens—those prospects are considerably larger than the other. The choice is between Athens with equal but higher liberty and Sparta with equal but lower liberty. The third clause in our definition of dominion rules that Athens ought to be preferred to Sparta, assuming that there is no difference between them in regard to the common knowledge mentioned in the second; it rules that it is only in Athens that citizens enjoy full dominion. We might describe the clause, for mnemonic purposes, as the Athens–Sparta principle.

The Athens–Sparta principle generalizes quite naturally to the case of two societies which, without providing perfect equality in liberty-prospects, provide the same degree of equality in prospects, and do not differ in common knowledge of these prospects. It says that as between two such societies, we should prefer that which provides the higher level of liberty-prospects. The Athens–Sparta principle is of significance for us in this book, so far as it underwrites the assumption we shall be making about taxation. We shall assume that as between two societies which do equally well or badly in securing equal prospects of liberty for all and in generating common knowledge of those prospects, if one of them taxes less than the other, we should prefer that which taxes less. We might call this the tax-tiebreaker principle.[6]

Finally, a third general comment on our definition of dominion. In discussing its egalitarian and quantitative aspects, we assumed that the matter of common knowledge did not arise as an issue. But we should recognize that one of the most common ways in which dominion can be reduced in a society is through subjective erosion: through people, even perhaps people who have reasonable liberty prospects, coming to lose faith in the prospects provided. Dominion, unlike the liberal ideal of freedom, can be reduced through psychological subversion. Here again the ideal belongs with the republican tradition. Montesquieu writes in suitable vein. 'The political liberty of the

[6] Every piece of taxation makes it more costly for someone to do things and so jeopardizes his liberty: it makes it more likely that his liberty will be frustrated. The extra taxation in the higher-taxing society affects someone's liberty-prospects adversely, then, without generating greater equality in prospects or improving the extent of common knowledge of those prospects. And so, in the comparison provided by the lower-taxing society that we prefer, we must see these acts as reductions of overall dominion.

subject is a tranquillity of mind, arising from the opinion each has of his safety. In order to have this liberty, it is requisite the government be so constituted as one man need not be afraid of another' (Montesquieu 1977 edn.: 202).

The consequence of these comments is to give us some guidance on what must be involved in promoting dominion in a society. Our view is that promoting dominion involves three ordered tasks. The first task must be to create as much equality as possible in liberty-prospects. This has precedence over the generation of common knowledge, since the best way of supporting knowledge that *p* is to make it the case that *p*. Equally it has precedence over the creation of maximum prospects, since that quantitative task is only relevant in so far as the egalitarian one is complete. Once we have created as much equality as possible in liberty-prospects, the next task must be to ensure as far as possible that these become and remain a matter of common knowledge. This task has precedence over the creation of maximum prospects because, as we see things, the value of equal liberty depends in great part on the knowledge, ideally knowledge shared with others, of having such liberty. The final task then in promoting dominion will be to maximize the liberty-prospects available consistently with the degree of equality and common knowledge that has been attained. The three tasks, corresponding to the three clauses in our definition of full dominion, are lexically ordered: the first is done as well as possible before the second is taken up, and the second is performed as well as possible before the third is assumed.

As it calls for various glosses, so our account of dominion raises a number of questions. To mention a few, the definition raises a question about how to define who is a citizen, considering age and mental competence; about how different liberties should be weighted against one another in estimating the prospects of liberty enjoyed by different people; and about how extent of liberty and degree of assurance combine in practice to determine such prospects of liberty. We shall not comment on the first two questions here: they are issues which our theory faces in common with others. But a brief comment on the third question may be useful.

Combining extent of liberty and degree of assurance in the notion of a prospect of liberty may cause anxiety on two counts.

First, it allows different levels of liberty, so long as they are balanced by different levels of assurance, to count for equality of prospects. And second, it allows low levels of liberty, so long as they are balanced by high levels of assurance, to constitute maximum prospects. But neither worry ought to be serious. The first should be reduced by the observation that the surest way to equalize prospects across people will be by equalizing both liberties and levels of assurance; the calculations otherwise required do not invite confidence. The second should be allayed by the observation that in maximizing prospects it is all too likely that we will find a ceiling on the levels of assurance available, in which case further enhancement of prospects can only come through the extension of people's liberties.

It remains now to argue that the promotion of dominion is an appropriate target to propose for the criminal justice system. What we shall attempt to show in this Chapter is that the target meets our three desiderata: unlike the competitors we have considered, it offers an uncontroversial, a stabilizing, and a satiable goal for the system.

An Uncontroversial Target

Promoting dominion—or minimizing the invasion of dominion—is an uncontroversial target for the criminal justice system, for the same sort of reason as minimizing the harm associated with crime is uncontroversial. The invasion of dominion is an evil associated with central cases of crime. The sort of cases we have in mind are murder, rape, assault, kidnap, harassment, extortion, burglary, theft and fraud (Feinberg 1986: 10–11). In such cases the offender trespasses against the victim's person (murder, rape), province (kidnap, harassment), or property (burglary, theft). Doing so, he invades the person's dominion, destroying or restricting her liberty in certain regards. Indeed he may also invade the dominion of others at the same time, inducing a loss of confidence in their prospect of avoiding similar intrusions, or actually lowering that prospect.

Not only is the invasion of dominion an evil associated with central cases of crime. It is also an evil such that if we minimize it we will also minimize other ills associated with crime. Protect someone's dominion and you will protect them in addition from the loss of life or health, happiness or security, that crime may inflict. Thus there is every reason to regard the promotion of dominion as an uncontroversial goal for the criminal justice system. It has all the attractions associated with the goal of minimizing the harm associated with crime.

But we go even further than this. We would argue that minimizing the invasion of dominion ought to be a more uncontroversial goal even than minimizing harm. A repressive authoritarian criminal justice system might do best in minimizing harm, as harm is normally understood, and yet such a system could leave in place a feeling of vulnerability similar to that which besets people in a crime-ridden world.[7] It is an important aspect of minimizing the invasion of dominion that it would not allow the creation of a system of that kind; it could not do so, since the system would erode the subjective component in people's dominion.

There are two reasons why someone might protest against the view that our preferred target is uncontroversial. One is that some of the things that are currently criminal are not likely to be criminalized under a system oriented by just that goal. And the other is that some of the things that are currently not criminal are likely to be criminalized under such a system.

Someone moved by the first consideration may cite crimes against children, since children are not full citizens of society. But this complaint is weak, for children can still enjoy dominion in significant measure; and certainly they can lose dominion through criminal invasion. Our opponent will be on firmer ground if he cites crimes against animals, crimes against the environment, and so-called victimless crimes, for the goal of promoting dominion may or may not give a reason for criminalizing such acts. That depends on how far the acts militate indirectly against human dominion and whether an analogue of dominion is recognized in animals. But even if the acts are not criminalized under a system orientated to the promotion of dominion, that does not mean that there will be no legal obstacle placed before

[7] If it be said that some conceptions of harm cast the causing of a feeling of vulnerability as harmful, we would reply that any such conception is congenial, for it represents harm as something close to the invasion of dominion.

them. They may still have to be cast as matters for regulation, as matters for educational campaigns, as torts (Drane and Neal 1980), or whatever. Criminalization is not the only way of inhibiting behaviour; indeed it is probably the most clumsy and intrusive means available to the state.

Someone moved by the second consideration worries that the promotion of dominion may require the criminal justice system to criminalize many acts that are not currently crimes and that no one would sensibly want to be crimes. He may say, for example, that since someone's dominion can be diminished by misinformation to the effect that others are institutionally better placed—the misinformation will undermine the subjective dimension of dominion—even that sort of deception should be criminalized. But this worry is premature. The fact that a certain kind of act diminishes or invades someone's dominion does not mean that it ought to be criminalized, for its criminalization may do more harm to dominion than good. We return to the point in the next chapter, when we consider the issue of what sorts of things ought to be subjected to criminal sanction.

A Stabilizing Target

If the promotion of dominion is agreed to be an uncontroversial target for the criminal justice system, then the next question is whether it is also a stabilizing one. Here there are two things to establish. First, that the target motivates a legal allocation of the uncontroversial rights in the domain of criminal justice. And second, that the allocation is stable: the target motivates the agents of the system to take those rights seriously.

It ought to be clear that the target will motivate a legal allocation of uncontroversial rights. If dominion is to be promoted by legal sanction, then certain negative liberties must certainly be legally protected. Their protection means that citizens will have a legal claim on the state to defend such liberties. More specifically, given how the law works, it means that they will have a claim which legally constrains the state rather than just providing it with a target: the state will not be able to excuse inaction on the grounds that this will better serve the defence of that sort of right overall, or the like. Thus there can be no doubt that if the promotion of dominion is the aim of the criminal justice system, then it is required that people be accorded certain legal rights.

As will become clear in the next chapter, it is not easy to derive the particular legal rights that are required for the promotion of dominion. But it seems certain that they will include what we have described as the uncontroversial rights associated with criminal justice: say, the right of someone charged with a crime to a fair trial or the right of an innocent person not to be punished. The liberties which such rights would protect are among those that everyone regards as basic.

But though the promotion of dominion would motivate the legal allocation of such uncontroversial rights, a question remains. This is whether the allocation would be stable. It will be unstable if the agents of the system are motivated by the target, if not collectively at least individually, to breach the legal rights on certain occasions: that is, if they are motivated by the target not to take the rights seriously, not to give them moral as well as legal force.

It may seem that the promotion of dominion is liable to motivate the occasional breach of such legal rights: say, the occasional imposition of penalties on the innocent. Won't rational agents of the criminal justice system be inclined to consider whether an offence of that kind may not occasionally promise more promotion of dominion overall? We think not. While it may be right for the preventionist sheriff to countenance the hanging of an innocent black in order to placate a white mob, it can never be right for the sheriff whose target is the promotion of dominion. We will argue at some length that concern to promote dominion requires the sheriff to internalize a commitment to promote the rights of the innocent and many other uncontroversial rights. The sheriff who takes the promotion of dominion seriously will deny himself the possibility of offending against such rights; furthermore, he will go to some pains to make it clear to others that he abides by such a self-denying ordinance.

Consider an analogy to the criminal justice enterprise of promoting dominion. This is the parental enterprise of conferring a sense of independence on a teenage child, an enterprise which most of us believe to have some importance. If you are in the parents' position then you might think of pursuing that goal directly or indirectly. To pursue it directly would be to take it into account, with an appropriate weighting, in every decision as to whether you should let your child do something. To pursue it indirectly would be to adopt some maxim or constraint on your decision-making which is designed to have the effect of giving your child a sense of independence. You might commit yourself to letting the child choose as he wishes on certain matters, however foolish the choice may seem to you.

Not much reflection is required to make it obvious that the indirect strategy is the only sensible one in parental enterprises of this kind. Direct pursuit of the goal would be a self-defeating procedure for, knowing that he was always subject to your veto, the child would know that any autonomy he seemed to have was illusory; he would have a sense of vassalage, not a sense of independence. If you are to realize your parental goal then there is only one thing for it. You must give the child authority to make his own decisions over a designated range of issues and, short of disaster situations, you must not withdraw that authority just because you believe he is making a mistake.

The parental goal requires this indirect sort of pursuit because if the child is to enjoy the condition desired then he must be aware that in a certain domain, however limited, he has more-or-less unconditional sovereignty. If you pursue the goal directly and if the child, as is inevitable, becomes aware of this, then he becomes aware precisely of not enjoying such control of his own affairs. Pursue the goal directly and you are bound to balance it against the other considerations that matter to you, in which case you will never cede the control that the child must be conscious of enjoying if he is to have a sense of being independent. With a goal of this elusive sort you can only promote it by tying your hands in a certain area, making a self-denying commitment, come what may, to behave in this or that fashion. Your only hope is that the goal will be realized as a by-product of that strategy of self-restriction (Pettit and Brennan 1986; Elster 1982: chap. 2).

We hold that the criminal justice goal of promoting dominion is significantly analogous to the parental objective considered. It is a goal whose promotion requires the agents of the system individually and collectively to tie their hands in regard to how individuals should be treated and to make it clear to people that this is what they are doing. Unless they make such a commitment then people generally will become aware that they are likely to have their personal dominion invaded if that is for the best overall; and since dominion has a subjective dimension, this means that people generally will find that their dominion is seriously compromised.

Assume, as seems only reasonable, that if the criminal justice authorities are guided by the target of promoting dominion, then it is occasionally going to seem desirable, even if the possibility is not announced, that some innocent party should be framed and penalized for a crime; it will at least seem desirable whenever such an individual trespass promises to maximize the overall promotion of dominion. Assume further that there is a chance that such state invasion of dominion—perhaps also its justification—will be suspected by many people and that if it occurs with any frequency, there is a near certainty of this. The conviction of the innocent is often manifest to the real offender, or her confidant, or a formerly silent witness.

We argue that under those minimal assumptions it does not make sense for the agents of the system of criminal justice to pursue the goal of promoting dominion in an exclusively direct fashion (Pettit 1988*a*). It will be as self-defeating to do this as it would be to pursue directly the goal of giving your child a sense of independence. The reason is that once it becomes a matter of common suspicion that the authorities use the promotion of overall dominion to justify particular invasions, then the dominion of ordinary people in the society is jeopardized. People will cease to believe that they have redress against all forms of interference with the liberties required for dominion; they will realize that far from enjoying equal assurance against interference they are, at least in some respects, at the mercy of the political authorities.

The consequence is that if the criminal justice authorities are bent on promoting dominion, then their responses must not always be determined by direct consideration of that target. If they pursue the promotion of dominion free of any constraints, then they will not promote it. Such a direct pursuit of the objective means open-mindedness about interfering with innocent individuals in order to promote it. And that means that ordinary people are denied awareness of the equal assurance against interference which is required for dominion. The promotion of dominion eludes direct pursuit in the same way as the parental goal considered earlier.

The self-defeating aspect of pursuing the goal is particularly salient given that it is the state that is involved. The state, as exemplified by the agents of criminal justice, is so powerful a presence that it constitutes perhaps the single greatest threat to the individual dominion of citizens. If it is disposed to invade the dominion of any ordinary citizen, and this is known or suspected, then it jeopardizes the dominion of all. No one outside the political élite can feel secure in the presence of such an unconstrained power. And this, no matter how fine or elevated the target in the name of which the power is exercised; no matter indeed whether the target is the promotion of dominion itself.

The lesson is that not only does the promotion of dominion require the legal recognition of the uncontroversial criminal justice rights. It also requires the criminal justice authorities to take those rights seriously, and show themselves to take the rights seriously, giving them moral as well as legal force in their own deliberations. The rights must have, and manifestly have, a deliberative impact on the sheriff who might hang an innocent person in order to placate a mob. And they must make a similar impression on rather less exotic figures too: the police inspector who is concerned about the effect of poor clear-up rates; the prosecutor who recognizes that someone is a past and potential offender, even though he is not guilty of the crime under investigation; and the judge who is worried about the possible consequences of not convicting someone who is widely believed to be guilty.

The point is worth labouring. A world in which police officers, prosecutors, and judges failed to forswear the framing of the innocent would be a world of insecure citizens whose dominion was extremely limited. Consider how dominion would be reduced in a world where police were thought to give speeding tickets solely with an eye to deterrent effects, and without regard to the guilt of the drivers stopped; the point is obvious when you think about the insecurity with which any driver would set out on the highway in such a society. The lesson becomes more pointed if you go on to think of states where general suspicion of the police and other officials extends also to matters of greater moment. Such considerations make it clear that for the agents of the state to fail to tie their hands by openly committing themselves to honour certain rights—to fail to abjure the possibility of expediently invading dominion—would be a serious error; or at least it would be an error if, as the hypothesis has it, they are zealously concerned with minimizing the overall invasion of dominion.

It may be instructive in connection with our claims to compare our target with the utilitarian one. We said that the utilitarian goal will be stabilizing only if the agents of the system believe that people's happiness is jeopardized by the unease created when they recognize that someone known to be innocent will be occasionally prosecuted. Our criticism of utilitarianism in this regard was that since the importance of such unease in the happiness stakes is a contingent empirical matter, there is little or no guarantee that agents will hold the required belief. Notice now that this criticism cannot be brought against our own position. It is true as a matter of how dominion is defined—it is part of the very concept of having dominion—that a person cannot enjoy dominion fully if she perceives or suspects that the agents of the state, or indeed any other powers in the land, will not be scrupulous in respecting her rights. Thus, any authorities who understand what dominion is are bound to recognize the importance of showing that they are scrupulous in their attention to her rights.

One question remains to be answered. We have argued that the promotion of dominion motivates a stable allocation of uncontroversial rights but we have said nothing on what other rights, if any, it will enshrine. Will it ensure the presumptive right of people not to have their phones tapped, for example? Or will it support any other alleged rights which are not beyond the bounds of controversy?

Our answer is that it all depends. It depends on whether the enshrining of such rights—their legal and moral recognition —promises to maximize overall dominion. People certainly suffer a loss of dominion if they know or suspect that they are liable to have their phones tapped. On the other hand some might argue that the invasion of dominion involved in phone tapping is compensated for by the overall improvement in dominion which phone tapping ensures through the prevention of crime. The issue is a matter for empirical debate and comes up again in the next chapter.

There is one right, however, which the promotion of dominion will certainly require us to recognize and this deserves special mention. It is the right of a victim to have the authorities apply the same criteria as with other victims in determining how far to investigate the offence, whether to prosecute, whether to convict and how to sentence. This right is required for the promotion of dominion. Without such a right a person does not have the same prospect of liberty as someone who is manifestly in a better position to ensure that any offence against him will occasion an official response; she will have less security against crime, for criminals are bound to realize that complaints from someone like her are less likely to be taken seriously. Besides, someone who has been the victim of a crime almost certainly requires reassurance about her liberty-prospects, if she is to regain her old level of dominion. One way for the system to reassure her will be by making clear that she has the right to the same official response as anyone else in her position would have. Notice, however, that the right is not a right to any particular level of response, only a right to have the response determined by certain criteria. The stronger right could not be guaranteed without the threat of an overall decrease in dominion: trying to give recognition to the right would entail the deployment of criminal justice resources without regard to the promise of a net return in overall dominion; for example, it might require a level of taxation or investigation which seriously compromised the dominion generally enjoyed in the society.

A right of the kind we ascribe to a victim is of particular importance because it enables us to rebut a common charge against consequentialism. The charge is that any consequentialist theory must have the authorities deal with a crime only for the forward-looking reason that how they deal with it may affect the likelihood of other crimes; it has them ignore the backward-looking reason, salient in the perceptions of ordinary people, that the victim has been wronged. With our right of the victim in place, the objection does not come off. Given the offence, the right of the victim constitutes a backward-looking consideration which ought to motivate the authorities to act. Our consequentialist theory does not remove backward-looking considerations from the scene; it only means that if they are allowed to remain in place, that is because of the forward-looking result that the promotion of dominion is thereby better served.

A Satiable Target

We have now shown that our target is both uncontroversial and stabilizing. The last question is whether it is also a satiable target for the criminal justice system: a target that is unlikely to make such voracious demands that it calls for the breach of uncontroversial limits on criminal justice practice: in particular, for the excessive punishment of the guilty.

In discussing the minimization of harm, the balancing of benefits and burdens, and the promotion of happiness, we conceded that these objectives had a structure which made for satiability. In each case the target was involved on the cost as well as the benefit side of any putative breach of uncontroversial limits. This concession did not amount to much in these cases. It applied to the minimization of harm and the balancing objective in regard to excessive punishment but not in regard to other breaches of uncontroversial limits; and then it applied in a way which did not promise to have much impact. And it failed to be true of the utilitarian target, so far as drugs make it possible to have horrible penalties which do not affect the happiness of prisoners. But it turns out that the promotion of dominion has a similar cost-benefit involvement in criminal justice practice and that this fact is not undermined by such considerations.

Consider any act of punishment which is justified by the fact that it promises to maximize dominion. The benefit in that case must exceed the cost of dominion involved in punishing the offender, in jeopardizing the security of those who are dependent on him for their upkeep or welfare, and in putting before people at large the prospect of suffering such punishment. And it will not do for the benefit barely to exceed the cost. It must be sufficiently greater than it to weigh against the fact that the cost is certain, the benefit a matter of probability. These considerations mean that it is unlikely that the promotion of dominion will motivate punishments that exceed uncontroversial limits in degree or kind. We think that on the contrary the punishments justified may be controversially light.

There is a clear contrast in this regard between dominion and the preventionist targets which dominate the consequentialist tradition. If your goal is crime prevention or a relevant sub-goal such as deterrence then you are not given any reason why you should not think of going beyond uncontroversial bounds in order to try the better to achieve your objective. If your goal is the promotion of dominion, you are. You must recognize that as you approach those bounds you will be inflicting a certain and grievous damage on dominion and that this is unlikely to be offset by an appropriately large increase in the benefit that must be promised in the level of overall dominion.

There is also a contrast in regard to satiability between dominion and harm reduction, or the balancing of benefits and burdens. There is a cost to both of those goals in excessive punishment but not a cost of the same dimensions: thus the psychological effect on people at large is irrelevant with those goals. And besides, where those goals are not usually relevant outside the area of punishment, dominion is. Thus the promotion of dominion supports limits that ought to be uncontroversial on the practices of police and prosecutors. It is an objective, unlike either of the other two, which promises to be satisfied well short of such limits.

One final and important comment on the satiability claim. The considerations mustered in its defence suggest that if the system of criminal justice is targeted on the promotion of dominion, then the onus of proof in the debate about appropriate punishments and other invasive practices is firmly placed on the side of those arguing for more rather than less or for some rather than none. Every act of punishment has the certain cost of diminishing someone's dominion and if we are concerned about dominion then every act of punishment will need positive justification. The rest-response will be mercy, the response that needs vindication punishment. More generally, the rest-response will be non-intervention, the response that requires justification will be intrusion.

This means that the promotion of dominion supports a principle of parsimony in punishment, and indeed in any state invasion of dominion which is held to be justified by overall promotion of that goal. The state should use those legislative, enforcement, and sentencing options which are minimally interventionist until the evidence is clear that more-intrusive practices are required to increase dominion. More than that, the state should actively search for alternative ways of promoting dominion to such interventionist policies as criminal punishment.

The principle of parsimony can be illustrated nicely with regard to corporate wrongdoing. It implies a presumption in favour of voluntary self-regulation by an industry rather than criminalization of business conduct. And if the evidence is clear that such self-regulation does not achieve maximum dominion, then parsimony counsels against any rapid escalation to full criminalization; it recommends a search for minimally coercive alternatives to see if they will do the job instead. Those alternatives include licensing, enforced self-regulation (Braithwaite 1982*c*), law reforms to facilitate control through civil litigation, and requirements to disclose the data necessary for the informed exercise of consumer choice.

Republican Institutions

A theory that takes the promotion of dominion as its target is reasonably described as republican, since dominion is a version of the republican notion of freedom. But there is also a second reason for describing our theory as republican. It bears, not on the sort of ideal invoked, but on the types of institutions which the theory is likely to explore as means to the realization of that ideal. It turns out that because of invoking a social concept of freedom, the theory is well disposed towards a type of institution which is an embarrassment, or at least a matter of ambivalence, for classical liberals.

Consider any circumstance where there is a public benefit to be wrung from individuals who are primarily directed to more private concerns. The situation may be the classic free-rider problem, where all are better off if some benefit is brought about rather than not, but where each reasons that he is best not contributing himself: if sufficient other people contribute then his contribution is superfluous; if sufficient other people fail to contribute then his contribution is in vain; and it is practically certain that he will not be the one to make the number of contributors just sufficient (Pettit 1986). In such a situation—and social life is a variation on situations of the kind—the problem is how to ensure that individuals behave so that the public benefit is actually produced; otherwise everyone is likely to be worse off.

Assume that there is no way of producing the public benefit other than via the actions of the individuals involved. That being so, there are two different institutional ways of ensuring that the benefit is realized. One is by establishing a market type of institution, the other by setting up an institution of a formative kind.

The market type of institution assumes that individuals will behave in a self-interested way and it arranges things in such a manner that self-interested actions of that kind will aggregate to produce the public benefit. The classical example is of course the perfectly competitive market in which, as if by an invisible hand, the good of all is allegedly served by the greed of each; the pursuit of individual advantage allegedly ensures competitive prices and, it is suggested, the optimum overall. But other examples might also be mentioned. The best known is the pluralist pattern of politics under which the lobbying effects of self-interested groups are said to affect government in such a proportional way that an overall balance is achieved in the satisfaction of interests.

Where the market institution purports to leave the psychology of individuals untouched, the formative institution is designed to affect people in such a way that they behave as if they were primarily concerned with the public benefit, not with their own particular interests. It does not try to gear up the actions of unreformed individuals so that they mesh to produce the common good. Rather, it seeks to shape those individuals themselves, inducing a more-or-less permanent shift in their behavioural dispositions or deliberative habits.

Formative institutions are of two major types, depending on whether they are designed to shift just the behavioural disposition or, as well, the deliberative habits of agents. The first sort is the coercive institution which introduces legal penalties—or perhaps rewards—such that agents who take those factors into account in their calculations will tend to behave as if they were primarily concerned with the public benefit in question. Such agents will display the behavioural disposition, at least in the rough, of virtuous citizens whose primary concern is with the public benefit. But they need not deliberate in the manner of such virtuous citizens. They may deliberate by reference to the costs and benefits to themselves.

The second type of formative institution seeks to change people's deliberative habits as well as their behavioural dispositions; it might be described as the socializing, as distinct from the coercive, institution. The socializing institution seeks to inculcate virtuous habits of deliberation by a combination of measures: by bringing home to people the admirable character of such deliberation, creating in them an appropriate sense of right and wrong; and by ensuring that if agents deliberate and act in a non-virtuous way, there is a good chance that they will be exposed before their peers and subjected to public disapproval (Lovejoy 1961: lecture 5).

Both types of formative institution contrast with the invisible hand of the market; they constitute what one of the authors has elsewhere described as the intangible hand (Pettit 1989*c*). But it is the socializing institution that is of particular importance in the area of criminal justice. If judges and jurors are not socialized against any consideration of their own self-interest in deliberating about guilt, defendants stand little chance of enjoying a right to a fair trial. Moreover, it is the socializing institution, and not any market or coercive arrangement, which affords the best protection for citizens against crime (Braithwaite 1989). Most of us refrain from fraud and theft and murder, not because we calculate that they are against our self-interest, but because these crimes are unthinkable for us. Socialization has developed in us a powerful sense of the evil of these crimes, and an equally powerful sense of the shame attendant on being found to contemplate them. It has influenced us to the point where calculation over such crimes is put right off our deliberative agenda.

So far as considerations of freedom go, no liberal or republican theory can have an objection in principle to the invisible hand of the market institution; there may be objections about its consequences for dominion in various contexts but these are too complex to consider here. The interesting thing, however, is that whereas our theory allows us to be equally enthusiastic about the intangible hand of formative institutions, there is a reason why liberals have not been able to muster a similar enthusiasm: their asocial concept of freedom creates an inhibition about endorsing such intrusive arrangements.

Suppose that you think of freedom, in the standard liberal fashion, as a condition which would be perfectly consummated in the isolation of the totally solitary individual. In that case you must view formative intrusions which are designed to stop a person ∅-ing as acts which deprive him of the liberty to ∅ or which put that liberty at risk. The point is obvious with penalty systems but it carries over also to reward structures and moralizing initiatives. The reward structure imposes at least comparative costs on someone who ∅s and the moralizing initiative runs the risk of coercing a person not to ∅ by holding up the spectre of social disapproval as a penalty for ∅-ing. The consequence is that if you think as a liberal about freedom, then you will see formative institutions as intrinsically questionable. You will see them as forms of restraint which are bad as such: as J. S. Mill (1910 edn.: 150) puts it, 'all restraint, *qua* restraint, is an evil' (see also Berlin 1958: 12; Feinberg 1973: 23–4; MacCallum 1967).

Of course even as a liberal you will have to tolerate the use of the formative institution, since there is no hope of organizing a society in which people enjoy liberty without recourse to coercive law; even to get a competitive market running, it may be necessary to surround it with legal bans against the formation of cartels, against misrepresentation, against failure to honour contracts, and the like. But the point is that you will only have recourse to the formative institution reluctantly.

The theory defended here suggests a different attitude. When freedom is construed as dominion, it is understood in such a way that there is no freedom without the creation of a system of mutual assurance of non-interference among the members of a society. Whatever is necessary to set up such a system of mutual assurance cannot be seen then as an invasion of people's freedom; it can scarcely be an invasion of something which does not pre-exist it. And so when freedom is construed as dominion, we are forced to take a different view of the formative institutions involved in creating a suitable system of mutual assurance. We are forced to see them in a positive light. Ironically, since he is one of the heroes invoked in later liberal thinking, Locke (1960 edn.) gives nice expression to the sentiment we must espouse: 'that ill deserves the name of confinement which hedges us in only from bogs and precipices . . . For in all the states of created beings capable of laws, where there is no law, there is no freedom' (p. 348).

This positive attitude to formative institutions need not be an incautious one. We can adopt it while recognizing that even when formative institutions promote dominion, they may still negatively affect liberties; that such institutions may pass the point of promoting overall dominion and actually reduce it; that if the institutions lead to punishment, then that punishment certainly reduces the offender's dominion; and that if the state proposes to introduce or intensify any formative institution then it incurs an obligation to justify doing so: the burden of proof is on its side. The important point is that the attitude is bound to generate an interest in exploring the full realm of possible formative institutions, whereas the negative attitude of the liberal is likely to kill any such interest.

It is an important feature of the theory that we are positively and unambivalently committed to exploring the varieties of formative institutions, in particular the varieties of socialization, whereby dominion may be promoted. This theme will come up at various points in later discussion. To anticipate a little, we might draw attention to our emphasis on procedures for making criminal justice authorities systematically answerable to other bodies and to each other; to our support for requiring businesses to establish codes and practices of self-regulation; and to our recurrent stress on the importance of having a culture for the integrative shaming of criminals (Braithwaite 1989).

This second feature of our theory links it as tightly to the republican tradition as its reliance on a social concept of freedom. Just as republicans emphasized the importance and value of citizenship, so they identified civic virtue among the citizenry as a prerequisite for the stable enjoyment of that condition; they argued that without widespread civic virtue the city would be taken over by an internal élite or an external enemy (Skinner 1983, 1984). Most republicans did not think that virtue came naturally to human beings. And so one of their recurrent concerns was with how to devise institutions—formative institutions—which would guard against corruption and induce citizens, particularly citizens in public office, to behave virtuously. Republicans were positively enthusiastic about formative institutions, where contemporary liberals are at best ambivalent about such structures. We associate ourselves with the republican tradition in adopting a view which is equally sanguine and uninhibited about the potential of formative institutions.

Summary

We have argued that the target of the criminal justice system should be to maximize dominion. Subject to one qualification, dominion is the social status you perfectly enjoy when you have no less a prospect of liberty than anyone else in your society and when it is common knowledge among you and others that this is so. The one qualification is that if you and your fellow-citizens are all equipped to enjoy dominion, being equal in relevant regards, you must have the largest prospects of liberty compatible with that equality; this is what we called the Athens–Sparta principle.

The proposal that dominion be our target amounts to a republican theory of criminal justice, for the dominion invoked is essentially a republican version of negative freedom. Moreover, the institutions appropriate for its promotion are of the formative kind with which republicans are particularly associated. We argued that this republican target was a satisfactory goal for the criminal justice system, so far as it could be held to satisfy our three desiderata, being at once an uncontroversial, a stabilizing, and a satiable objective.

The argument establishes clearly, we hope, that the promotion of dominion is an appealing target for the criminal justice system. If the system promotes dominion then it will certainly guard against the paradigm crimes constituted by offences against person, property, or province. And, something that is just as important, it will guard against those offences in a manner that is sensitive to the vulnerabilities of people in the face of the state; it will not do it, for example, by recourse to excessively intrusive and threatening practices. The promotion of dominion requires the state to take rights seriously and to subscribe to a principle of parsimony in the formulation of the punitive and other interventions associated with the criminal justice system.

6
Interpreting the Republican Theory

The task of this chapter is to show where the republican target of promoting dominion is likely to lead the criminal justice system. We do not mean to devise a republican blueprint for that system; space, if nothing else, makes that impossible. Our aim is to develop and communicate a sense of where republicanism is going. We see the theory sketched in the last chapter, not as a final, finished product, but rather as a research programme for normative thinking about criminal justice issues. Here we mean to provide an indication of the programme's drift. Our republican theory supplies a policy heuristic, though not a policy algorithm. As a heuristic, the theory suggests new ways of thinking about criminal justice and directs us to the kinds of questions the policy-maker should ask. Inevitably, the right answers to these questions will often be a historically and culturally contingent matter.

In the present chapter we will illustrate what the comprehensiveness requirement means in practical policy terms, looking at the key questions of criminal justice in a systemic way. In the space of one chapter we cannot provide a well-rounded analysis of any single policy question, let alone an analysis of all important criminal justice policies. Yet we do not want to shirk the responsibility of trying to show that our theory, unlike so many others, is capable of generating answers to the ten key questions of criminal justice listed in Chapter 2.

We will consider these ten questions in turn. Each is deserving of book-length treatment and our consideration must be very selective. The treatment we give the questions is determined by the need: (*a*) to show how the theory recommends different policies from its various better-known competitors—liberalism, retributivism, utilitarianism, preventionism; (*b*) to show how the theory recommends policies different from contemporary practice; and (*c*) to show the transformation in the research agenda of criminology required by the theory.

Before coming to the consideration of the ten questions, we will identify four general presumptions the republican stance supports. These presumptions serve as middle-range principles for interpreting the abstract goal endorsed by republicans: the promotion of dominion. In dealing with our questions we shall have to consider the goal directly but often the requirements of the goal will be highlighted by the presumptions. They are, respectively, presumptions in favour of parsimony, the checking of power, reprobation, and reintegration.

Parsimony

The presumption in favour of parsimony has already been introduced in our discussion of the satiable character of the republican target. That target is such that almost any criminal justice intervention involves initial, certain costs. Any act of criminalization, surveillance, investigation, or arrest, any prosecution or punishment, does immediate and unquestionable damage to someone's dominion. On the other hand, the benefits promised by the initiative are almost always of a distant and probabilistic character, as a glance at this same list makes obvious. Thus it is clear that the onus of proof ought to fall squarely on the side of justifying any such initiative, not on the side of justifying its absence or removal. The presumption ought to be in favour of less rather than more criminal justice activity.

Of the four presumptions, parsimony is the most important. Indeed, it is the master presumption, a presumption that applies as we address all of the ten questions. The other presumptions are of importance too but they are not relevant to the same range of issues.

Checking of Power

The presumption in favour of the checking of power is supported by our derivation of rights in the last Chapter and, more deeply, by the observation that dominion has a subjective dimension: a dimension which means that it can be undermined by the absence of a conscious assurance that one will receive suitable treatment. The presumption is that the power enjoyed by criminal justice authorities will always be subject to such checks and that people enjoy the assurance that the authorities will not be able to exercise prejudice or caprice in dealing with them. The most important way of subjecting the criminal justice authorities to appropriate checks is by the recognition of certain rights on the part of citizens: the right of the innocent not to be punished, the right to a fair trial, and so on. But even when authorities such as police, prosecutors, or judges are given discretion in certain matters, their power can still be subjected to checks which provide an assurance against prejudice or caprice. Mechanisms of appeal or complaint represent one sort of check; requirements on agents to answer for the exercise of their discretion represent another. Such mechanisms protect the subjective component in people's dominion. They provide an assurance for individuals that, even if they are treated differently in some way from others, the difference in treatment is justified by some publicly recognized feature in the circumstances; it is not the product of whim or malice. In short, the mechanisms can improve the assurance for individuals that in a crucial sense they are equal before the law, in particular equal before the criminal justice system.

Reprobation

The third presumption is that the criminal justice system be designed to ensure that criminality is subject to more-or-less effective reprobation or disapproval in the community. The argument for this presumption derives from our discussion of the formative institution on which republicans, unlike liberals, naturally look with favour. For liberals, being moralizing has generally negative connotations; for republicans, being moralizing about criminal threats to dominion has specifically positive connotations.

The formative institution comes in two major varieties: that of the coercive institution, which puts such penalties or rewards in place that people tend, if the institution is successful, to adopt the behavioural dispositions of the virtuous citizen; and that of the socializing institution, which seeks to bring home to people the shamefulness of crime and thereby induce in them, not just the behavioural dispositions, but the deliberative habits of the virtuous citizen. In bringing home to people the shamefulness of crime, the socializing institution will do two things at once: it will present crime as wrong and therefore as something of which people ought to be ashamed; and it will present it as a sort of activity actually disapproved of in the society and therefore as something of which people are likely to be made ashamed, if they choose it.

The criminal justice system clearly has to rely on one or other variety of the formative institution in its attempt to cope with those activities it designates as criminal. A republican theory of criminal justice will tend to favour reliance on the socializing variety and that is why it supports a presumption in favour of reprobation. After all, reprobation is just what we should want if we seek to bring home to people the shamefulness of crime.

A first reason why republican theory favours reliance on the socializing institution is that it promises to provide superior protection against crime than that provided by the coercive institution. Societies are bound to derive greater protection from crime when citizens view crime as shameful and unthinkable than when they calculate that in general crime is more likely to be unprofitable than profitable. Thus, the societies in which crime is lowest are likely to be those where criminals are most effectively exposed to reprobation (Braithwaite 1989).

A second reason why republican theory favours reliance on the socializing rather than the coercive institution is that it naturally requires that citizens should understand why the criminal justice system does what it does. When a citizen is coerced into not doing something by the imposition of a legal penalty on the activity, he may or may not understand why coercion is imposed. If he does not understand, then the subjective component is his dominion must be threatened, for he will see himself as subject to a randomly imposed coercive power. When on the other hand a citizen is brought to see that the activity is a matter for shame and why it is a matter of shame, the subjective component in his dominion is not jeopardized in the same way.

The consequence is that a republican theory of criminal justice makes for a presumption that the system ought to be orientated towards the reprobation of offenders, not just the imposition of coercive penalties. The reprobation required will be pursued in the design of sentences; we shall come to that matter later. But it will also be pursued at other levels of the criminal justice system. If the system is guided by republican theory, then we may expect the police officer, the prosecutor, the judge, and indeed ordinary citizens to be recruited to the project of reprobation. The paradigm form of reprobation will involve moral reasoning with offenders, since this is the most direct way of inducing an understanding of the wrongness of the act and eliciting a sense of shame about it. But reprobation is also communicated in other ways. It is administered by the health and safety inspector who threatens publicity if a firm does not put things right before his next visit; by the police officer who agrees not to press a charge but only after undertakings of good behaviour over a certain period; and by the judge who, publicly denouncing someone for an offence for which he has been convicted, still suspends sentence on humanitarian grounds.

The liberal may object that if punishment and coercion are threats that may not on balance protect dominion, why is this not also true of reprobation? But the objection misfires. Whereas dominion requires protection from the invasion of our persons, property, or province involved in either punishment or crime, it does not require protection from the moral reasoning and disapproval of others.

Nevertheless, the liberal might say that empirically a republic of citizens actively involved in disapproving the wrongdoing of their neighbours might produce a community that is oppressively stultifying of diversity. This question has been addressed at length in Braithwaite (1989). Shaming can be a medium for the tyranny of the majority. But a society that lacks a capacity to mobilize social disapproval will never guarantee freedom to deviate, will never offer the minority protection from the tyranny of the majority. This is because a society without the capacity to mobilize disapproval cannot exercise social control against those who trample on the freedom to be different. The good society, in the republican sense, will be strong on reprobation of those who violate the criminal law and strong on reprobation of those who trample on the freedom to deviate in those areas beyond the constraints of the law. A society that cannot organize reprobation to protect freedom will lose its freedom.

Reintegration

Our fourth presumption is that the criminal justice system should pursue reintegration in the community, in particular the restoration of dominion, for those citizens who have had their dominion invaded by crime or punishment. If we are focused as republicans on the promotion of dominion, then such reintegration must naturally assume importance. It is only too obvious that the after-effects of being the victim of a crime, or of being someone convicted of and punished for an offence, can militate against dominion. Hence the restoration of victims and ex-offenders to the enjoyment of full dominion must be a priority.

The more important target for reintegration is the victim of crime. The victim has been devalued as a person. She has been given the message by another human being that she is unworthy of enjoying rights to non-interference (Murphy and Hampton 1989: chaps. 2 and 4). Even with property crimes such as burglaries perpetrated by an unknown offender, victims regularly report emotional stress from a sense of having been violated. This sense of having been violated is enough to damage seriously the dominion of the victim.

The victim's dominion can be restored in a number of ways but the most effective is likely to be when the relevant community acts symbolically and tangibly to assure the victim that she is not devalued as a person, that her dominion is worthy of respect. Symbolically, this is done by condemning the crime and the criminal—reprobation. Tangibly it is done by restitution or compensation for the victim.

Consider the victim of sexual harassment or sexual assault in the workplace. She will feel violated and devalued because another human being thought her person and her province unworthy of respect. Respect is best restored symbolically by the community reprobation, in this case the workplace reprobation, of the non-respecting person, particularly by the offender being brought to express remorse and apology. But such symbolic restoration requires the tangible backing of compensation; otherwise it may come too cheap. Compensation will most powerfully assure the victim that she and her dominion are valued if it is paid by the very person who denied respect for her dominion—the offender. But if the offender cannot be made to pay compensation, still the community should compensate the victim to assure her that it recognizes her value and the value of the dominion that has been invaded.

A secondary justification for reintegration by victim compensation is that it must protect people's subjective sense of dominion if they know that should they suffer the misfortune of crime, the community will act to help repair the suffering. Perhaps one of the reasons citizens tend to fear natural disasters less than crime is that they know that when natural disasters occur communities work together to help the victims. The discrepancy between the communitarianism of our response to victims of natural disasters and the neglect of community response to crime victims is a sad fact of modern life, a fact that reinforces the fear of crime.

But the reintegration of ex-offenders is also bound to be of importance to us as republicans. Unless efforts are made at their reintegration, ex-offenders can easily slip into the status of second-class citizens, lacking the full enjoyment of dominion. And, a factor of perhaps equal importance, unless such efforts are made, ex-offenders can easily be drawn into offending again. When law-abiding communities confer a criminal status on offenders, they encourage these citizens to maintain a criminal identity, to align themselves with criminal subcultures and to persist in a life of crime. A case for reintegration has been made on the basis of the criminological literature in Braithwaite (1989). The important thing to note if that case is sound is that reprobation and reintegration are mutually reinforcing.

So much then for the four presumptions in favour of parsimony, the checking of power, reprobation, and reintegration. These presumptions will serve as supplementary interpretive principles when we try to work out the significance of the republican stance for the design of the criminal justice system. We turn now to consider the answer to each of the ten questions raised by that system.

1. What Kinds of Behaviours Should be Criminalized by the System?

The classical liberal position on this question is that no activity ought to be criminalized unless it causes harm to others. The best-known statement of that position is found in John Stuart Mill:

> The only purpose for which power can be rightfully exercised over any member of a civilized community against his will, is to prevent harm to others. His own good, either physical or moral, is not a sufficient warrant. He cannot rightfully be compelled to do or forbear because it would be better for him to do so, because it will make him happier, because, in the opinion of others, to do so would be wise or even right. (Mill 1910 edn.: 72–3)

The two major attacks on the liberal position come from legal moralism and legal paternalism respectively. Legal moralism would allow that an activity may be criminalized just because it is immoral or is at least regarded as immoral in the community at large. Legal paternalism would allow that an activity may be criminalized because it is likely to cause harm to the agent herself. The legal moralist questions the harm restriction in the harm-to-others constraint; the legal paternalist questions the restriction to others.

Where would the republican stance place us in relation to the liberal, legal moralist, and legal paternalist positions? It would replace the liberal concern with harm by a concern with activities that diminish dominion. And it would reject the legal moralist claim that the mere fact that an activity is immoral or is thought to be immoral constitutes a distinct reason why it should be criminalized. But it can, at least in principle, accept the legal paternalist claim that activities which undermine a person's own dominion are matters of concern as well as activities which diminish the dominion of others.

This bold statement may cause anxiety on two fronts. First, our theory may appear ominous, in so far as it broadens the target of concern from harm to the diminution of dominion. And second, it may seem ominous in allowing the criminal justice system to be directed against activities which damage only the agent's own dominion. But neither worry, we believe, ought to be taken very seriously. The reason is that the presumption in favour of parsimony ought to act as a severe constraint on what acts are criminalized. Thus, while dominion might be threatened by someone spreading false rumours about imprisonment without trial, parsimony suggests that the danger ought to be met by a public information campaign, or by a civil remedy under defamation law, not by criminalizing such an act. Again, while someone might be likely to undermine her dominion through taking a certain drug, parsimony suggests that the best way of coping with that problem might be to criminalize sale of the drug without a prescription rather than criminalizing its use.

We tend to believe, for the record, that on a republican theory only those activities would tend to be criminalized which threaten the persons, property, or province of other citizens. In other words, we think that the republican commitments would direct the criminal justice system towards the minimal type of institution which the liberal applauds. Still, this is not very radical, since most of our present criminal laws would remain. We would still want to criminalize offences against the person such as homicide, assault, and intentional or reckless endangering of life through lack of occupational safety; offences against property like robbery, burglary, theft, and fraud; and offences against people's province such as kidnapping, slavery, arbitrary arrest, and detention without trial. Equally, we would continue to countenance what Feinberg (1986: 19–22) calls derivative crimes. These are crimes which are not threats to dominion as such but which endanger the system whereby dominion is protected. Examples are carrying an unregistered hand-gun, escape from prison, tax evasion, practising medicine without a licence, and contempt of court.

But while such derivative criminal laws will often pass the republican test, it is important to note that they require careful definition. Thus the law of contempt of court is important in protecting the right to a fair trial and in ensuring a dimension of dominion. If people disrupt trials, improperly influence a jury, or subject the defendant to adverse publicity during the trial, then the right to a fair trial is put in jeopardy. It is proper that the law of contempt of court should criminalize such activities. As things stand, however, the law of contempt is often invoked, not just against such activities, but against protests by the defendant, as when she makes voluble remarks at the trial or calls the judge a fool. This use of the law is not designed to protect the right to a free trial, but to protect the sensibilities of those who inflict punishment and to maintain order in the courtroom. Neither of these goals justifies the application of the criminal law. On the important matter of securing order in the courtroom, we believe that this can be achieved by other, less invasive means than criminalization; a perfectly adequate remedy would seem to be restraint or removal from the courtroom until the defendant is willing to undertake not to interrupt.

Our commitment to criminalizing certain offences may be questioned on the following lines. It may be said that as consequentialists we should want to codify no offences at all, simply giving the state unbounded discretion to prosecute, try, and punish agents for acts of suitably serious intentional harm. But we hope it is clear that on our theory, not only should appropriate crimes be codified in law, they should also be defined as precisely as possible. If the criminal justice authorities are not bound by precise criminal laws, then their power is relatively unchecked and there is a threat to the subjective component of dominion. It is well known, for example, how the arbitrary use of the charge of unseemly language to victimize Australian Aborigines has generated insecurity within Aboriginal communities in their dealings with the police (Wilson 1978). Furthermore, if criminal laws are not precisely defined, then the pursuit of reprobation will be ill-served. To the extent that laws are vague, citizens will not pick up a clear understanding of just what it is that warrants reprobation.

We turn now to some difficult issues. We will look at three areas where criminalization is controversial: crimes of offence, consensual crimes, and strict liability crimes. We do this, not in order to defend a detailed set of proposals, but in order to give a sense of the impact which a republican theory is liable to have on some of the controversial matters that come up under this first question.

Crimes of Offence

Making unseemly or offensive language criminal is a clear threat to freedom of speech, providing a weapon for those who wish to use the power of the state to trample upon the dominion of others. Similarly, criminalizing blasphemy is an unjustifiable threat to religious freedom, criminalizing 'sedition' and offences against the flag a threat to political freedom. So too, criminalizing public drunkenness, vagrancy, or gambling might be conceived as an unreasonable threat to social freedom, and criminalizing obscenity or public indecency a threat to sexual freedom.

Issues of public indecency throw up what might seem a more difficult challenge. Suppose two young people engage in intimate sexual activities opposite a minister of religion on a bus; for argument's sake, imagine they are a homosexual couple. You might say that the dominion of the minister is assaulted by the behaviour, but this would be to adopt a much looser conception of dominion than we have advanced. The loss of dominion can only be that which forces the minister to close his eyes or move to another seat. But surely, you may counter, life would be unpleasant for most of us if this kind of behaviour were allowed to go in public and that we are entitled to protection from such an intrusion on our feelings. Not wanting to dismiss this concern out of hand, our response would be that there are better ways of dealing with the problem.

Being parsimonious and systemic in our thinking, we would prefer to move the solution to the policing part of the criminal justice system. The police have a role of maintaining public order and might be called in by the minister to ask the couple to desist from causing offence. Alternatively, the police might suggest that the minister move to another seat. In the unlikely event that both suggestions were ignored, the conflict would undoubtedly escalate. Ultimately, the police might have no option but to secure order by removing the offensive persons from the bus. The police have a concern with public order as well as with law enforcement and we would have no objection in principle to their being able to remove those giving offence from the bus in order to avoid an outbreak of public disorder. Maintaining public order and thereby preventing crimes from occurring can be an important means of promoting dominion.[1]

The irony is that the very offences against morality which seem to pose the most troubling challenge to decriminalization, such as the example above, are those least likely to require social control

[1] The public order function of the police is totally a dominion-protecting function, mainly justified by preventing crime before it occurs. The police officer pulls two drunks apart who are abusing each other not because a crime has occurred but to prevent violence; she keeps a crowd from milling too close to a head of state for the same reason. When public order policing loses sight of dominion, as when it arrests the man who heckles the head of state, it becomes dangerous.

by the criminal sanction. Intimate sexual activity on buses is not a widespread problem in our society, and this is so in the absence of effective criminal enforcement against the practice. The more offensive the behaviour is to large sections of the populace the more redundant the criminal justice system is. The minister in our example can easily spoil the couple's experience by audibly expressing objection. The more offensive the conduct, the greater the power of informal social control and the more susceptible is criminalization to rejection on grounds of parsimony. The less offensive the conduct, on the other hand, the more persuasive is the argument that criminalization is needed if the conduct is to be stopped; but in that case, of course, it ceases to be clear why the promotion of dominion requires that the conduct cease.

Consensual Crimes

A different kind of difficulty arises with behaviour that clearly does harm, but where the harm is freely accepted by the victim. The prostitute who provides a spanking requested by a masochist does harm, at least in one ordinary sense. But because the spanking is done with the consent of the victim and has no further effects on the victim's liberty-prospects, it does not reduce his dominion. Thus we certainly would not want to criminalize it.

The case of the drug dealer who supplies heroin requested by an addict raises different issues, however. In the long term, addiction will reduce the dominion of the consensual victim. Ultimately, it may give her no choice but to run every aspect of her life to service the habit; it may leave her with no resources to resist the manipulations of dealers who use her money, or pimps who use her body. This means that there is a case to consider in favour of criminalizing heroin use.

But our theory is very unlikely to support the criminalization of using heroin, given the presumption of parsimony. Criminalizing the use of that substance is an invasion of dominion and the alleged benefits are doubtful. Besides, criminalizing use of substances like heroin is likely to create an illicit market, an underground organization of racketeers, and the potential for great corruption.

We think that republican theory supports a policy of decriminalizing drug use but requiring that substances like heroin be available only on prescription, within the doctor–patient–pharmacist framework. We think that selling any potent pharmaceuticals without a prescription should be a criminal offence because there are so many thousands of them on the market, with such a diversity of side-effects unknown to the lay person, that the state cannot be assured that dominion is secure unless the transaction occurs within that framework. But while wanting to decriminalize drug use, we would be appropriately conservative about the methods and time-frame for implementing a decriminalization policy. The damage of criminalization having been done, the state must be very cautious in educating the community that decriminalization of drug use is not intended to indicate that it no longer views such activity as a serious problem. Decriminalization can only responsibly be undertaken after a community education campaign that reaches every group in the community, that communicates to families and schools and peer groups that it is their job to dissuade their members from drug abuse, not the job of the criminal law.

The open-system quality of the theory is clearly illustrated here. The theory requires us to ask whether the problem is better dealt with by informal social control outside the criminal justice system—via family socialization, doctor–patient interaction, and so on. But in recommending that the drugs problem be moved outside of the criminal justice system, the theory does not allow the system to ignore the problem completely; after all, selling without a prescription remains a crime. If the criminal law did not require a prescription, pharmacists and doctors would not have the authority to apply their professional skills in controlling drug use. This example should clarify how one of the challenges for an open systems approach is to co-ordinate interactions between the criminal justice system and other systems. Lawyers are familiar with this challenge with regard to harmonizing the criminal and civil law systems; but we can see that it is a problem of much wider import.

While we find it hard to think that criminalization would protect the dominion of drug users, legislators who pressed this line would be required to do a great deal of work under the strictures of republican theory. Systemic analysis demands attention not only to the dominion of drug users but also to the cost to dominion at the surveillance, investigation, and enforcement stages. The republican legislators would ask for an analysis of the dollar costs of criminalization in all these sub-systems; they would want to know how much could be achieved for the dominion of drug users by spending these sums on drug education programmes; they would want to know the cost-effectiveness of attempting to reintegrate drug offenders in prison versus outside programmes. They would want a report on whether criminalization has had the effect of expanding the black economy in a way that strengthens organized crime and encourages police and judicial corruption. They would want to know what proportion of murders are associated with the black economy in illicit drugs, what proportion of property crimes are associated with the need for addicts to fund their habits. In the absence of such knowledge, republican legislators should opt for the rest-position of minimal criminal justice intervention.

Strict Liability Crimes

A third area of difficulty in considering what to criminalize is strict liability crime. We naturally assume, given our theory, that only persons who are morally culpable for a prescribed encroachment upon the dominion of others should be convicted: those who engage in harmful acts should be protected from punishment which fails to take account of whether their behaviour was intentional, reckless, negligent, or just accidental. The criminal law is a decidedly unparsimonious way of dealing with harmful conduct that involves no fault, for if remaining blameless is insufficient to protect us from being punished, the subjective element of our dominion is under threat. Thus, the theory clearly forbids crimes of absolute liability where the offender is in no way blameworthy for the offence. However, the theory may permit what are often called crimes of strict liability, wherein the offender did not intend to commit the offence, but is nevertheless blameworthy at some lower standard of culpability.

Gross (1979: 342–740) provides an account of some forms of strict liability (offences of 'minimum culpability') which would be acceptable under the terms of his theory and ours. We can reasonably hold a manufacturer strictly liable for unintentionally selling contaminated food or drugs when two basic requirements are met. First, it must be possible as a practical matter for the risk of harm inherent in what was done to be appreciated by the person doing it. Persons involved in the drug industry know in advance that much higher than usual standards of care are required in their industry. Second, the person held criminally responsible must have been in a position to prevent the harm and it must have been part of her agreed responsibility to be watchful for this harm.

Thus, when the quality control manager is convicted for releasing an impure batch of drugs, it will not do for her to be able to plead successfully that she did not intend the people to die and that she exercised the usual degree of care to prevent a catastrophe. The usual degree of care is not good enough. She entered into her responsibilities knowing that society required her to take whatever measures were necessary to obtain the special degree of care essential for her industry. A condition of reaping the benefits of selling dangerous products is that the company must spend the extra time and money in deploying whatever extraordinary measures are required to protect the public. This is not to deny the quality control director an 'impossibility' defence (nothing could have been done) or a scapegoating defence (it was not truly she who was responsible and in a position to prevent the harm) (see also Sadurski 1985: 242–3). But it is to insist that dominion may be best promoted overall if releasing impure drugs is made a crime of strict liability.

We have seen in this section that republicanism conduces to the kind of minimalist policy on criminalization also favoured by liberals. Yet the strict liability case illustrates that where the threats to dominion are sufficiently profound the parsimony presumption can be overridden in a way that puts the republican on the side of criminalization. In practice, the republican legislator would have to embark on a programme of rather widespread decriminalization in most Western societies we know, and the only areas where there would very likely be a need for significant new criminalization would be where changing technology and changing economic institutions pose completely new threats to dominion.

2. What Sorts of Sentences Should be Permitted or Enjoined?

This question bears on two main matters: first, how far the discretion of the court should be limited in deciding on the nature of the response when someone has been convicted of a crime, in particular on the nature of any punishment prescribed; and second, how far that discretion ought to be limited when the court decides on the intensity of the response, in particular the severity of any punishment imposed. We mix consideration of these matters in the discussion that follows.

Our four presumptions serve us well in considering the proper answer to this question. A first lesson derives immediately from the presumption in favour of checking power. This is that there certainly ought to be a maximum sentence prescribed for every type of crime, a maximum which the courts are unable to breach. Unless there is such a maximum in place, no offender is proof against the caprice of the vindictive judge or prison official.

But is this really so? Will the dominion of the average citizen really be threatened by knowledge that there is no upper bound on the punishment that can be given, in the extreme case, to murderers? After all, the average citizen would never contemplate murder. The average citizen, however, is not our only concern. Members of oppressed racial minorities often believe, rightly or wrongly, that the police frame members of their racial group for serious crimes. Such people will feel threatened by the lack of upper penal bounds. And so will many others. We should not underestimate how common it may be for women subjected to domestic abuse to consider striking back at their husband with a weapon, or for sleepless parents of a screaming baby to be on the brink of hitting the infant against a wall. And it is not only people who have contemplated such a crime whose dominion would be affected by the prospect of unbounded punishment. A woman who reads a story of a teenage boy indefinitely imprisoned for intercourse with an underage girl will not directly fear that she might be so treated for this type of crime. But she might well tremble at the thought that she lives in the kind of society where any person can be subjected to such open-ended punishment. Historical experience, reflected in a whole genre of literature, makes clear that punishment of this kind allows selective victimization and small-scale terror.

Historical experience has a further relevant lesson to teach. Maxima are needed to assure equal prospects of liberty, for we know from historical precedents that open-ended maximum punishments result in selective victimization of the poor. Lifting maxima worsens the over-representation of oppressed racial minorities in prisons and execution chambers. Bias and selectivity in deciding who will suffer from open-ended punishment reduces dominion in reducing equal prospects of liberty.

A second general lesson on sentencing follows from the principle of parsimony, as distinct from the presumption in favour of checking power. This is that, while a maximum sentence ought to be identified for each type of crime, no corresponding minimum sentence ought to be imposed on the courts. Parsimony requires that no minimum sentence be set, because the court must be put in the position where, taking account of the particular circumstances of a crime and an offender, it may judge that dominion is best served overall if clemency is shown.

These first two lessons are of a relatively abstract kind. We enter more controversial territory when we begin to consider precisely what sorts of sentence ought to be available to the courts. The punishments imposed by courts can be neatly divided into three kinds, turning on our earlier distinction between an agent's person, his province, and his property. Punishments directed against the offender's property include fines, restitution, and seizure of assets. Punishments that encroach upon his province are imprisonment and, to a considerably lesser extent, community service. Finally, punishments which invade his person include capital punishment, corporal punishment, mutilation, and torture. The question then is whether the discretion of courts should be limited through the prohibition of any one of these penal categories.

We believe that it should, for we think that punishment directed against the agent's person should be proscribed. The presumption in favour of parsimony motivates this line, since intuitively such punishments would represent a greater invasion on someone's dominion than punishments of the other kinds and there is no evidence that punishments in this category are particularly effective as deterrents (Departmental Committee on

Corporal Punishment 1938; Kaiser 1986). But in any case the argument from parsimony against such punishments is buttressed by an argument from the presumptions in favour of reprobation and reintegration. The punishments in question are distinguished by the absence of any likely reprobative or reintegrative advantages. It might be thought that some sort of mutilation—perhaps a branding of some kind—would serve to reprove an offender effectively. The historical record, however, suggests that branding contributed to offenders becoming outcasts devoid of bonds and communication with respectable society (Braithwaite 1989).

Among the three types of punishments distinguished, our tendency is to favour putting a limitation on the courts which would restrict them in most cases to being able to impose only punishments against the offender's property. Parsimony suggests that such punishments are the most desirable, since we intuitively regard punishments directed against property as less invasive of dominion than those directed against province. Moreover, the offender's dominion loss is balanced by a dominion gain for taxpayers (with fines) or for victims (with restitution). The presumptions in favour of reprobation and reintegration suggest that ideally punishments directed against the offender's property ought to be of a kind which will maximize the reprobative and reintegrative effects. We think that they would be of this kind if they involved restitution to the victim or the victim's family. Fines are weaker on this criterion, even if they are earmarked for a general victim compensation fund.

Together, the presumptions in favour of reprobation and reintegration mean a first preference of voluntary victim restitution or compensation; a second preference for mandatory restitution or compensation; and if this is not possible a fine, with the money going to a state-administered victim compensation fund. This fund might be used in compensating the victims of proven but unsolved serious crimes, where there is no convicted offender to provide compensation. A parsimonious concern for the dominion of taxpayers requires us to limit such state compensation to serious crimes where the need for victim reintegration is strong; minor property crimes should not be eligible.

Notice that different responses may be called for with corporate offenders and corporate victims. We would not necessarily call for state-funded compensation for corporate victims, because here the case for victim reintegration is weak. And on the other side we do not think it is always going to be sufficiently reprobative just to impose a requirement of compensation or a fine on corporate offenders, especially where these costs are likely to be passed on to consumers. Consider a company that is found guilty of misleading advertising. Here an adverse publicity order or a corrective advertisement paid for by the offender fits best with our presumption in favour of reprobation (Fisse and Braithwaite 1983).

There are two sorts of circumstances, however, even with individual offenders, where punishments directed against property are not suitable. One is where the offender has committed a very serious crime and where the community has a justifiable concern to be protected from future acts of violence by the offender. In such a case it seems to us that imprisonment may be justified and should be available as a sentence to the courts. Because of the presumptions in favour of both parsimony and checking power, the legislature should give a clear statutory instruction to the judiciary that imprisonment should only be used as a last resort, as some recent Australian statutes have done (e.g., Sentences and Penalties Act 1985 (Victoria)). Further, the judge should be required to give reasons why there was no recourse other than to imprisonment in the particular case, and these reasons should be subject to appeal by the offender.

The other situation where punishments directed at property will not be suitable is when the offender is unable or unwilling to pay. Here we favour the community service order, as when the offender is required to do weekend work for a welfare agency. That sort of punishment, although it invades the offender's province, can be preferable in three ways to imprisonment. First, it is less invasive of dominion and so can be supported on grounds of parsimony. Second, it is more likely to have a reprobative effect, since it avoids isolating the offender in the company of those who have the least incentive to disapprove of what he has done. Third, when the community service is orientated to the needs of victims, it can have a reintegrative effect on the victim, and indeed also on the offender.

Before leaving this question, it is important to consider Graeme Newman's (1983) disturbing book which challenges one of the assumptions in our discussion above. This is the assumption that a punishment directed against an offender's person is always less parsimonious than one directed against his province, in particular less parsimonious than imprisonment. He makes the case for punishment by electric shock.

A flood of objections immediately spring to mind as we read Newman but it is surprising how many can be parried. Corporal punishment would return us to a society wherein order is secured by an ethos of terror. Yet this consideration may not be overwhelming, when young men in our prisons are routinely subjected to rape and brutal beatings by either inmates or guards; the terrors of prison only seem less because those of us who have not experienced prison are wilfully blind to what goes on within them. The same consideration applies should we seek to defend a preference for imprisonment on grounds that it better protects the value of human dignity from humiliation. We are inclined to object to the degrading relationship between the punishment technician and the offender—that it is wrong to put one human being in a relationship of such total control over another—but the prison officer is really in a quite similar relationship over a much longer period in a way that impinges on many more aspects of the offender's life. We may object that some people suffer from the pain and the terror of anticipating it more than others, so that corporal punishment can never be just. But Newman convincingly argues that this form of inequality is actually less profound with scientifically calibrated shock than it is with imprisonment that is terrifying for some, a time to rest and dry out for others, cause of permanent loss of employment and breakup of marriage for some, a period of retraining in illegitimate job skills such as drug distribution for others.

We think that Newman's book is a useful challenge to criminology, for we believe that the standard responses are less than overwhelming. Our own response involves three strands. First, we argue that any punishment which involves the person's body in the manner of electric shock is less parsimonious than one involving province or property. Second, we think it is important to avoid the threatening and brutalizing consequences of the state becoming a moral exemplar of the use of violence to solve problems. Third, we think that while both electric shock treatment and imprisonment fail to have a strong reprobative rationale, and fail on that account to be attractive responses, still imprisonment has one beneficial feature which shock treatment lacks. This is that imprisonment offers protection to the community from a dangerous offender. Better to have restrained Charles Manson by imprisonment than to have tortured him by electric shock. While we can reconcile imprisonment with the principle of parsimony in extreme cases, corporal punishment does not have the same feature.

3. How Should Resources be Allocated to the System, Among Different Parts Within the System, and Within a Single Part or Sub-System (e.g. the Police)?

Let us take the last of these three resource allocation issues first. Republican theory implies a radical departure from the way resource allocation has proceeded under past and present criminal justice administration. Consider a police department. Poorly run police departments deal with each complaint that comes in as best they can. The contemporary conception of a well-run police department has the department recognizing that it can only do an adequate investigative job on a fraction of the offences it might pursue, so it sets priorities according to the seriousness of the offence.

Our theory supports this as far as it goes, supplying the threat to dominion as the yardstick of seriousness. But the theory also implies, as our consideration of parsimony highlights, that the dominion gain from the crimes prioritized must be balanced against the dominion loss from police surveillance and investigation. This is a radical departure because the traditional police ethos has been to do whatever is necessary and lawful to bring the most serious offenders to book. A natural reaction is for readers to think it idealistic nonsense to believe that police can ever be expected to compromise their pursuit of maximum clear-up of serious crime with concern for civil liberties. But here the contemporary debate about police accountability to the community has useful lessons. The community has a fear of crime which is tempered by fear of the police. To the extent we succeed in making local police units accountable to their local communities through consultative committees and citizen management committees, the prospects for policing which is responsive to dominion overall, rather than simply to crime control and public order, are increased. Good police accountability mechanisms will seek out civil liberties groups as priority community organizations for nominating representatives on to consultative and management committees at both the local and agency-wide levels, representatives who can be expected to balance the police predisposition for law enforcement with a predisposition for resource allocation sensitive to other forms of dominion.

Civil libertarians are also needed as critics of the police to ensure, in accordance with the presumption in favour of checking power, that people's rights are taken seriously. Resource allocation difficulties should not be allowed to trump rights. For example, a right to protection from arbitrary searches of one's home should never be compromised because the division is so short-staffed that the paperwork to secure a search warrant is an excessive burden. Allocation decisions between criminal justice agencies must equally be constrained by rights. But we should not exaggerate the difficulty of meeting this constraint, because many rights are rights of *non*-interference that require the criminal justice system to use less resources: *not* to spy on innocent citizens, *not* to arrest arbitrarily, and *not* to harass homosexuals, prostitutes, drug addicts, and political activists so long as they are obeying the law. However, the right to a fair trial means that the courts must be supplied with whatever resources are necessary to guarantee this, and such a claim on resources should never be trumped by the police department arguing that it could prevent more crime by appropriating some of those minimum resource requirements of the courts. While the theory is clear that this is the principle involved, just what resources are in practice required to give all defendants a fair trial is a very difficult question indeed. Court administration research to clarify this matter is a high priority on the research programme commended by republican theory.

Within the constraint of ensuring that all criminal justice agencies have the minimum resources necessary to take rights seriously, scarce resources should be reallocated among criminal justice agencies in such ways as will be optimal for dominion overall. We would argue that lives would be saved and injuries prevented if some resources were diverted from relatively well-funded police forces to support the enforcement activities of struggling occupational health and safety, and consumer product safety agencies (Braithwaite and Grabosky 1985; Braithwaite *et al.* 1984). And, in line with the reintegration presumption, we would argue for taking more seriously the compensation of victims in the allocation of scarce criminal justice resources; victims are a weak constituency which has fared poorly in the struggle for resources.

But the ultimate allocative question is 'How many resources should the criminal justice system get compared with other government functions?' And when we ask this, we quickly reach the limits of our theory. One way of approaching the question is to say that taxpayers should certainly cease funding the criminal justice system when the point is reached where further funding will not enhance dominion but will have an effect which is either neutral or negative with respect to dominion. Further, we might think of saying that funding of the system should always be increased until this point is reached: that is, that we should keep spending on criminal justice until the declining marginal returns to dominion fall to the point where a further increase in funding will cause a loss of dominion to taxpayers equal to the dominion protected by that increment in criminal justice system activity.

Unfortunately, this second prescription is of little practical value since the budget process in all nations of which we have knowledge does not permit this kind of trade-off. More typically, the exigencies of fiscal policies first lead to the setting of a target budget deficit or surplus and then different spending programmes compete for the scarce resources available under the expenditure ceiling. That is, the choice in practical terms is not between taxpayers forgoing income and the criminal justice system getting it, but between the criminal justice system, or defence, or social security, or some other spending programme, getting more or less.

Our theory is a theory of criminal justice. It has nothing to say about whether defence or the arts should be higher expenditure priorities than criminal justice. We have argued that every theory should be pushed to the limits of its comprehensiveness and it is in the political process of framing a national budget that our theory clearly reaches its limits. Another theory—perhaps a more general republican theory of the state (Pettit 1989*a*)—is needed to determine how criminal justice claims against public expenditure should be weighed against those of national defence and the like.

4. What Kind and Intensity of Surveillance Should be Tolerated?

We have already partially answered the question of how decisions about the deployment of surveillance should be made in our response to the last question. The police, and any other enforcement agency, must balance the protection of dominion secured by a given surveillance option against the cost to dominion of those caught in the surveillance net. When we put a collection of suspects or a randomly selected physical location under surveillance we intrude into the privacy of many others besides the offender. Thus, parsimony suggests that we should be slow to adopt such measures.

In normal police work random surveillance is generally unproductive. As Reiss observed:

> Less than 1% of the time officers are on patrol is spent handling on-view matters. And, only 1% of the time on routine preventive patrol is spent in handling criminal and non-criminal incidents. Overall, 99% of the time in preventive patrol nets no criminal or non-criminal incidents, an indication that preventive patrol is markedly unproductive of police matters processed in the system of criminal justice. (Reiss 1971: 95)

In view of this, it is unsurprising that there is no persuasive evidence that police patrol strategies make much difference to crime rates. (For a review which puts a somewhat more optimistic view of this research see Rouse 1985.) It is possible that more aggressive and intrusive patrol strategies, combined perhaps with the use of decoys, might produce better results than the traditional methods. But until evidence of such effectiveness is produced, the presumption in favour of parsimony requires us to resist new techniques of surveillance. The new police surveillance, a growing concern for civil libertarians, includes expanded use of undercover agents and informers, public campaigns to encourage citizens to report drug users to the police (which have netted instances of children turning in their parents), phone tapping, electronic eavesdropping, hidden cameras, periscopic prisms, electronic bracelets for tracking persons under house arrest, lie-detector tests, 'spy dust', matching of information from computerized databanks, satellite surveillance, and more. Gary Marx (1977, 1980, 1981, 1982, 1985, 1988) has been the leading scholar in documenting what Foucault (1977: 220–1) called the modern state's 'subtle calculated technology of subjection'.

In the face of the dangers posed by the new surveillance techniques, one option suggested by the requirement to check power is to impose a form of civil liberties budget on the police akin to the regulatory budget idea of conservative business scholars. The idea is that business regulatory agencies should not be permitted to impose a compliance cost for its regulations in excess of a politically imposed ceiling, a ceiling which is believed to be the limit of what the business community should reasonably be called upon to bear. It is possible to imagine parallels in the area of police surveillance.

Conceivably, the range of new police powers being sought or new surveillance technologies being considered could be ranked crudely as high, medium, and low in terms of their incursion upon dominion. Existing police powers, surveillance activities, and techniques could be similarly ranked as involving high, medium, or low threats to dominion. Then, if the police wished to acquire a new power or technology of intervention into domains of privacy, they would have to give up an existing intervention of roughly equal cost to dominion (a high for a high threat to dominion, a medium for a medium).

The troubling expansion of the brave new world of surveillance by both public and private police (Shearing and Stenning 1987) also creates a need for countervailing power in the form of human rights commissions or similar bodies which have genuine authority in dealing with citizen complaints against both public and private agencies of social control.[2] One feature of dominion as the target of the criminal justice system is that it obliges us to consider

[2] How effective in crime control and how respecting of rights are private police compared with public police is an important item on a research agenda to inform republican judgements on the privatization of policing and its regulation. The republican must weigh the dominion of both crime victims and those intruded upon by the private security industry, as well as the savings to taxpayers from the privatization of policing, in forming such judgements.

such reforms. When our goal is simply crime prevention, in contrast, human rights commissions and civil liberties budgets could only be conceived as impediments to the police getting on with the criminal justice job.

In thinking about policing policies, we must not make the mistake of assuming that policing is mostly about making arrests. Police use a mixture of what Reiss (1984) calls 'compliance' and 'deterrence' models of social control. When the police officer encounters a street fight in which one protagonist threatens the other with a broken bottle, she may deal with the matter by taking the bottle from him and sending him home rather than by arrest—a 'compliance' solution rather than a 'deterrence' (or 'retributive') solution. Parsimony counsels in favour of such discretionary policing. Police departments driven only by punishment goals will serve dominion poorly. When the police officer arrives at an accident scene, the best thing she can do to protect dominion is to ensure that medical help is provided to victims and to clear the road; collecting evidence for a prosecution should be a lower priority, at least initially. Well-trained police perform an enormous service in comforting victims, mobilizing paramedical help, and in providing practical advice on matters such as insurance claims. When directing traffic, to take another sort of case, the police officer may do better by dominion to refrain from pulling over an unregistered vehicle when doing so would create a horrendous traffic jam. She may better protect the dominion of other motorists by towing away a car parked dangerously than by issuing a ticket.

Reiss (1984) points out that many police department policies are preoccupied with crime control by deterrence, when on the street many police are using their common sense by applying a 'compliance' model. This critique is less true of Japanese policing policy than of American (see Bayley 1976). Japanese policing is more focused on prevention than on deterrence, most particularly through attempts by the police to reason morally with alleged or potential offenders and to be catalysts of informal social control by families, employers, and local communities. It fits better with our presumption in favour of reprobation and indeed reintegration. The active participation of citizens in protecting their own dominion goes with the republican ideal of citizenship.

A concern with dominion therefore implies a shift from

surveillance for the purpose of collecting evidence for prosecution to surveillance for the purpose of solving problems in consultation with local communities—a key plank of the new (in the West) community policing philosophy. Instead of just issuing a lot of traffic tickets at a junction that has repeated accidents, the police would convene a meeting for local residents and road construction authorities to discuss the redesign of the junction. Instead of just lying in wait outside a club from which members regularly drive under the influence of alcohol, the police can work with the club to organize a 'server intervention program' (Jacobs 1989: 139–47) so that the club will take some responsibility for promoting responsible drinking from behind the bar. A school that has a particular drug abuse problem, say glue-sniffing, can be targeted for discussions with the students concerning an appropriate drug education programme. Republican policing fosters communitarian problem solving.

5. What Cases Should be Targeted for Criminal Investigation and How Should These Investigations be Conducted?

One approach to targeting suspects is a simple reactive one. The agency only acts on complaint, selecting for intensive investigation the complaints involving the most serious alleged invasions of dominion. The traditional reactive policing style does have a rationale which is well tuned to the dominion target. To the extent that the police respond to those crimes of sufficient concern to the citizenry to elicit a complaint, they are responding to an exercise of dominion by the victim, an expression that the crime was an intrusion upon her sphere of sufficient moment to elicit a plea for outside assistance or intervention. Reintegration requires investigation of victim complaints because a failure to investigate is a further communication to the victim that he and his dominion are unworthy of respect. Moreover, when police restrict themselves to responding to complaints, they implicitly render themselves more accountable to the community; the requirement of community complaint limits their discretion to target suspects on the basis of police prejudices about their politics, demeanour, race, or whatever.

On the other hand, proactive policing is necessary if some

types of crime are to be brought within the reach of effective enforcement. The domains which are most resistant to anything but proactive enforcement are corporate crimes, corruption and fraud. Occupational health and safety offenders, environmental offenders, insider traders, tax evaders, and corrupters of politicians will never be apprehended in numbers if enforcement personnel sit in their offices waiting for complaints to roll in. A proactive inspection or undercover programme is needed, focused on domains where intelligence suggests that offending is most common. Notice, however, that the checking of power presumption would require at least judicial approval of the 'probable cause' for more intrusive undercover operations.

We cannot offer detailed guidelines on the form which proactive policing ought to take. But a starting-point is the work of Moore *et al.* (1984), who advocated the targeting of police investigations on dangerous offenders. Their dangerous offenders are those who have offended at a high rate, and who have persisted in offending over a considerable period. In our terms, they are offenders who pose a major threat to dominion over our persons. Moore and his co-authors review the quite impressive evidence that a relatively small proportion of the offender population accounts for a high proportion of the most serious crimes Thus their work makes an important case for directing police surveillance to this category of potential offenders.

Two other aspects of that work are worth mentioning. One is that the authors warn against the over-zealous pursuit of the dangerous and, as a safeguard, argue for a very specific interpretation of their classification criteria. They suggest that dangerous offenders are those who have been convicted at least twice in a three-year period for violent street crimes and who satisfy one of two further conditions: they have been arrested twice for violent offences within that period or they have been twice convicted for property offences within that period. We find virtue in this approach in view of the presumption in favour of checking power.

The other aspect of the work of these authors is one that also attracts us. They explicitly recognize that a problem which has been traditionally associated with one part of the criminal justice system may be more effectively handled by another. Thus, they point out that changing sentencing practices to target dangerous offenders has proved to be a comparatively fruitless pursuit: dangerous offenders are already treated so harshly under existing sentencing practices that the scope for further crime prevention down this track is minimal. They argue that, in contrast, there is considerable scope for improved concentration on dangerous offenders in the area of police investigation. For a number of reasons the investigative process tends to be less effective against high-rate offenders.

In summary then, a republican policing strategy might give priority first to investigating serious complaints, and second to proactive investigation of serious white-collar crimes and crimes by targeted dangerous offenders. Such a strategy would be a radical departure from contemporary practice in many Western countries where considerable priority is given to drug investigations and to easy investigations that improve clear-up statistics.

One further comment, in connection with the first priority: the investigation of people's complaints. We think our theory supplies philosophical foundations for the shift to what has been called 'community policing'. The core idea of community policing is that police ought to be responsive to the fears and demands of local communities—maximum responsiveness replaces maximum deterrence or clear-up as the organizational goal. Police who are responsive to local communities are police who take dominion seriously. When local communities are empowered by criminal justice institutions, citizen rights against the police can be enforced through participatory politics. This gives rights a force under republican institutions that they lack under liberal institutions, particularly for the poor who lack the legal resources to enforce rights in the courts.

Cynics about community policing argue that it shifts emphasis from reducing crime to reducing fear of crime (and fear of the police) because these last are easier to achieve than crime reduction. True, there may be more evidence about the capacity of the police to reduce fear of crime (Kelling 1988) than evidence of their capacity to reduce crime. But the republican must view the reduction of fear as important in itself. Consider the fact that victim surveys consistently show women to be objectively less likely than men to be victims of crime, but subjectively more afraid of crime. If community policing enables the police to overcome the fear women have about walking around at times and in places when and where objectively they are quite safe, then it will have done something very important to secure their dominion.

6. What Cases Should be Selected for Prosecution?

For full retributivists, prosecutorial discretion is something to be hemmed in as much as possible. There should be rules requiring prosecutors to proceed to trial with cases where certain criteria of seriousness and quality of evidence are met. A much more ambivalent attitude to controlling prosecutorial discretion follows from republican theory. Even with the most serious cases, dominion overall is frequently best served by not prosecuting; the parsimony presumption means that non-prosecution is the rest-position.

In an earlier work, one of the authors discussed the dilemma of prosecutorial discretion in the thalidomide drug disaster (Braithwaite 1982*a*: 752). Nine executives of Chemie Grünenthal, the manufacturer of thalidomide, were indicted in Germany on charges of intent to commit bodily harm and involuntary manslaughter. After the complex legal proceedings had dragged on for five years, including over two years in court, the charges were dropped as part of a deal in which Grünenthal agreed to pay US $31 million in compensation to the German thalidomide children. The press cried 'justice for sale'. But the prosecutors had to consider the ongoing misery of the thalidomide families who up to that point had struggled for nine years, rearing their deformed and limbless children without any financial assistance. Would retribution against Grünenthal and its executives have justified perhaps another nine years of deprivation for the victims?

Andrew von Hirsch (1982: 1170), in a reply to this article, suggested that the idea that justice might be put up 'for sale' in this way was indeed offensive. But this is simply to state the clear difference between the retributivist and the consequentialist in such cases. To the full retributivist, the prosecution should proceed. To the consequentialist, whether it should or not depends on a detailed consideration of the relevant consequences of proceeding: on the one side, the public benefits in preventing future crimes (substantial benefits perhaps, with a case of such enormity and high public profile); on the other side, the costs of proceeding with prosecution to the dominion of the victims and their families. Under consequentialism, we can accept that the prosecutor is probably in the best position to exercise the discretion to balance these awesome considerations. Interestingly, very similar considerations confronted lawyers combating Union Carbide over the Bhopal disaster: a difficult balance had to be struck between getting money into the pockets of victims quickly and firing all litigation barrels at Union Carbide (Hager 1985: 6). Thalidomide and Bhopal are extreme manifestations of a dilemma that is not so uncommon. It is a dilemma to which the consequentialist but not the retributivist can respond pragmatically.

When one begins to consider the unusual but profoundly important consequences prosecutors must balance in cases such as these, the dangers of even the most seemingly uncontroversial limits on prosecutorial discretion become clear. A prosecutor who does not balance the dangers of a long trial to the health of a serious offender who is at high risk of a heart attack is not taking dominion seriously. Concerns of this kind are near-infinite in their variety, difficult to foresee, and unpredictable in the circumstances of their occurrence.

A parsimonious consequentialist might think of swinging from prosecution guidelines which mandate prosecution of the most serious crimes to the other extreme of having guidelines that prohibit the prosecution of minor offences. This would be a mistake; its effect would be to undermine the protection of dominion afforded by the criminal law. A guideline never to prosecute those who shoplift goods less than $10 in value would undermine the credibility of the law against shoplifting and risk an epidemic of this kind of offending; a prosecution guideline that all first offenders of a certain type will not be prosecuted would be an open invitation to all and sundry to chance their arm until they are caught for the first time, and only then begin to worry about the law.

Prosecutorial discretion may seem to go against our presumption in favour of checking power and we should stress the need for constraints of accountability. In this connection we might think of relying on publicly issued prosecution policies to achieve accountability (Davis 1969). But, following Baldwin and Hawkins (1984), we are not optimistic. Baldwin and Hawkins give a sense of why such policies are vague and in general justify the patterns of past prosecutorial practice. The policies will be used as a resource by prosecutors to justify their actions when they are subjected to public criticism, but will not create any serious obstacle when they point the prosecutor in an inconvenient direction.

There may be more hope for prosecutorial accountability through requiring prosecutors to give written reasons when they fail to prosecute, at least in cases above a certain threshold of seriousness and evidentiary adequacy. It is unnecessary for reasons to be given in cases where prosecutions are launched, because the court then provides the accountability check. The written reasons submitted by prosecutors for not proceeding in serious cases could be subject to occasional audit by an appropriately constituted community watchdog. The most appropriate bodies to have full access to the prosecutor's records would be perhaps those community management or consultative committees that perform the same role with police policies.

We have been discussing familiar reasons why non-prosecution can serve dominion—it can save taxpayers' money, save offenders from the pains of imprisonment, witnesses from the pains of recollection and degradation in the witness box, and the community from further victimization by a young man who comes out of prison more bitter and better trained for the illegal job market. These considerations suggest that if the parsimony presumption rules then prosecutorial discretion will certainly be wide. But it turns out that the presumption in favour of reprobation and reintegration also give us a reason to explore the possibilities of such discretion, in particular the possibility of a prosecutor referring an offence back to the community where it took place.

Handing an offender back to his community gives the community wherein the offence occurred—be it the offender's class at school, his workplace, his family, or his football club—control over finding the best way to help the offender to solve the problem he has created. A world in which the criminal justice system took over all the ugly conflicts of local communities would be a world in which communities would be enfeebled in their power to reprove offenders and also to reintegrate both offenders and victims. While the criminal justice system is uniquely concerned with the protection of dominion, it does not have a monopoly on this mission. In fact, most protection of dominion is secured by informal social control in the community, a type of social control the criminal justice system should seek to foster rather than supplant (see Braithwaite 1989). In our example from Chapter 1, when Braithwaite cracks Pettit over the head with a bottle, if a police officer called by a neighbour bursts in and puts Braithwaite under arrest, the criminal justice system has deprived Pettit and his friends of the responsibility for reproving Braithwaite and has put at risk the reintegration of both parties. It has affirmed for all observers of the incident that it is the job of police and courts to sort these things out, not the responsibility of the citizens involved. As Sandel (1984: 11) more abstractly expresses the problem: 'Western democracies have managed to represent interests but not to cultivate citizenship; they protect civil liberties but have not secured freedom in the sense of a shared public life.'

Our way of thinking about prosecution runs directly counter to the intuitions of retributivists. They tend to be critical of prosecutorial discretion not to proceed against offenders: 'No society which purported to be just would allow knowingly any of its members to break the laws with impunity. To allow the offender to get away with impunity would undermine the point of having rules in the first place' (Galligan 1981: 157).

But the oft-repeated retributivist plea that it is pointless to have rules without punishment is nonsense. If I play golf with a friend whom I perceive to cheat, and I choose to say nothing and refrain from punishing him in any way, this does not mean there is no point in the rules of golf. Oxford researchers found that while 30 per cent of effluents sampled by a British pollution authority were technically criminal, not one prosecution had been launched for eight years (Richardson *et al.* 1982: 124). While pollution regulation might be more effective with some prosecutions, it does not follow from these data that the law is pointless. Indeed, the Oxford researchers suggest that non-prosecutorial British environmental enforcement has been modestly effective in reducing pollution (Hawkins 1984; see also Vogel 1986).

The question of when to prosecute thus highlights a sharp distinction between republican consequentialism and retributivism. In accordance with the principle of parsimony, republican theory says: do not prosecute unless you believe that dominion will be increased overall as a result of the prosecution. Full retributivism says: always prosecute the guilty offender, and place the burden on anyone who would compromise this principle to show why the prosecution should not proceed. The republican onus of proof is on the agent who favours prosecution, the retributivist onus is on the advocate of mercy.

7. How Should Pre-Trial Decisions be Made—Decisions About Charge and Plea Bargaining, Full and Partial Immunities, Bail or Pre-Trial Detention?

For the full retributivist on matters of pre-trial decision, charge and plea bargaining are wrong, as is granting immunity from prosecution in exchange for the offender's acting as a prosecution witness. At best they allow justice to be trumped by the public good; at worst they are a sell-out to the administrative convenience of prosecutors. For the republican, on the other hand, these practices are right so long as they promise to increase dominion overall.

The republican theorist will often be critical of some of the actual practices we find in operation. Thus, we would argue in view of the work of Moore *et al.* (1984) that prosecutors should be more reluctant than they currently are in the United States to plea bargain with dangerous offenders. The point to stress is that the republican theory is open at least to the idea of charge and plea bargaining, and the granting of full or partial immunity. The presumption in favour of checking power would lead us, however, to recommend that pre-trial decision-making of this kind should be constrained in a way that guards against caprice or corruption. Bargains and immunities might be negotiated under the supervision of a magistrate, for example.

The position of the retributivist on bail or pre-trial detention is not clear, since the only justification of such measures would seem to be in terms of consequences rather than deserts. Our republican view, driven by consequentialist considerations, is that a defendant who satisfies the definition of a dangerous offender should generally be detained but that otherwise there should be a presumption, on grounds of parsimony, in favour of release. This policy, we believe, would further dominion overall. The problem of course is that it is liable to violate the right of the innocent not to be punished, since dangerous suspects whom we would lock up may indeed be innocent. In order to mitigate this evil we would argue for house-arrest or secure hotel-style accommodation during pre-trial detention and for the payment of compensation to defendants subsequently acquitted. This line would also give criminal justice agents an incentive to be parsimonious in seeking pre-trial detention and an incentive to give priority for speedy trials to defendants who are actually detained. Parsimony might therefore mitigate the considerable costs of taking the rights of the innocent seriously at the pre-trial stage.

8. What Adjudication Procedures Should be Used to Determine Guilt?

The presumption in favour of checking power uncontroversially implies that defendants ought to have a right to a fair trial under the republican theory; we assume, but shall not argue here, that this means a right to trial by jury,[3] and a right to appeal. Such rights should apply even to minor criminal defendants like alleged petty thieves. True, the adjudication of most property offences, even moderately serious ones like car theft, will cost the community more in the salaries of judges, prosecutors, police, and others than the original offence cost the victim. However, the theory does not allow us to balance the benefits of a fair trial against these costs; as argued in Chapter 3, to respect dominion we must tie our hands against deliberating over whether or not a defendant should get a fair trial. The theory directs our attention to the damage which must be done to people's dominion if it is not a matter of common knowledge that every alleged offender can expect a fair hearing. If the cost of trials is too great, then the only solution the theory allows is to have fewer prosecutions, fewer trials.

[3] At least within Anglo-Saxon cultural traditions, the institution of the jury is an important guarantee of the subjective dominion of defendants facing the awesome phalanx of the court. The injection of independent ordinary citizens at the ultimate determinative point of the process builds assurance against a conspiracy of 'the legal system' against the common person.

But if every defendant has a right to a fair trial, can we seriously contend that the assembly-line justice of lower courts grant it in even the wealthiest countries of the world? And can we seriously suggest that any state can afford to abandon the mass production of findings of guilt based on perfunctory hearings in lower courts?

One of the advantages of our consequentialist theory is that it opens up a more satisfactory approach to this problem than is available to retributive theorists who can say little more than that fiscal realities make justice an unrealized ideal. The consequentialist analysis of the problem begins with Feeley's (1979) finding that 'the process is the punishment'. For most offenders processed through the lower courts, the most serious tangible consequences are not the penalties imposed by the court but the consequences which flow from the process. On average, offenders processed in these courts spend longer periods under detention while awaiting trial than they do as a result of the imposition of sentence; and they lose more money through the cost of lawyers, bail, and workdays lost than they do to fines imposed by the court.

It follows that when the offender confronts the prospect of a fairly light sentence for a minor crime, it can be more in his interests to be subjected to an adjudication procedure which is quick, cheap, and rather informal. While the defendant has a right to a fair trial, rights generate no lesser dominion when they can be freely waived by those who hold them, and so we would provide for the defendant to opt for the assembly-line justice of trial before a single magistrate. The state should not be able to deny a jury trial, but the defendant should be able to decline it.

In agreeing that the process is the punishment, and that therefore the defendant can be better off with quick and cheap justice, we are by no means apologists for the status quo of lower courts. Our theory gives us independent reasons to advocate that rigorous jury trial be a right for any criminal case, and certainly for any case that risks the offender's liberty or person as a sentence, but that the right should be waivable. It just happens that if the theory were applied in practice the offender would often have an incentive to waive the right. Indeed he would have more incentive to do so than at present: in a world where punishment was used parsimoniously and where imprisonment really was a last resort, it would become even more true that the criminal process would be the greater part of the 'punishment'.

Moreover, in a parsimonious criminal justice system there would be fewer trials of any kind, so rigorous jury trials for all defendants who wanted them would become fiscally feasible. Indeed, an advantage of taking the right to a fair trial seriously would be that it would encourage the parsimony in prosecution which the pursuit of dominion requires. Not so for the full retributivist. By insisting on just deserts for all who are guilty, the retributivist advocates a criminal justice system in which it is a fiscal certainty that all but a few will be denied justice in the form of a fair trial.

The presumption of parsimony means fewer trials and the presumption of checking power means fair trials that protect the rights of the innocent. But we should notice, thirdly, that the presumptions in favour of reprobation and reintegration mean that we should not evaluate trials simply in terms of whether they reach an accurate verdict. Trials are at their best when the process is the punishment in the sense that the moral reasoning of the court and the testimony of the victim bring the offender to a posture of remorse, so that both reprobation and reintegration are secured. And even when trials fail to engender the self-inflicted punishment of remorse, the court must still be required to respect the right of the defendant to a reasoned explanation as to why she is worthy of reprobation (Duff 1986; Nozick 1981).

In recognizing the importance of reprobation and reintegration in criminal trials, we should not lose sight of the fact that these goals can be achieved outside the courtroom. They can be achieved by police, as in the Japanese policing tradition; they can be achieved by prosecutors; and even during the period of the trial a little imagination would enable these goals to be substantially advanced. After conviction but before sentence, the judge might ask a social worker to ensure that the defendant understands why what he has done is a crime, to give him a chance voluntarily to apologize and offer recompense to the victim.

But though reprobation and reintegration can be furthered outside the courtroom, they can also be promoted within, and promoted without any compromise of the defendant's rights. The judge has a moral authority far greater than that of the police officer or social worker, and the criminal trial is a solemn ceremony of unique symbolism. Thus, we would want the judge, in announcing her verdict, to explain why the crime was an affront to the rights of the victim, not just to announce the sentence as a morally neutral penalty or tax on rule-breaking. We would want her to exploit her unique opportunity for facilitating the reprobation and reintegration of the offender, as well as the reintegration of the victim. What the rules of evidence are, what defences are permitted, and other such questions should be primarily decided on the basis of what will maximize fairness and minimize conviction of the innocent. But once a fair hearing has been given and the finding of guilt made, we see no reason why reprobation and reintegration should not assume great importance in trial procedures.

Needless to say, we have done little more here than put the questions of the fairest rules of evidence and the best venues for reprobation and reintegration on the research agenda of republican criminology. However, the theory suggests some important advice on how to approach research on rules of evidence and adjudication procedures generally. A concern for dominion implies, because of dominion's subjective element, a concern for how citizens perceive the fairness of adjudication. When trials are not perceived as fair, even though they may be objectively fair, citizens will not enjoy dominion. It is not good enough for jurisprudents to persist in the tradition of resolving these matters by abstract argument. A research priority, therefore, is the relatively new social psychological work on procedural justice (Lind and Tyler 1988). This directly investigates whether the subjective element of dominion is better protected under adversarial or inquisitorial procedure, what procedural safeguards are viewed by citizens as important to the fairness of adjudication, and the like. Already this work is turning up surprising and important empirical findings—for example, that 'consistency' is relatively unimportant compared with other procedural justice criteria in explaining citizen perceptions of the fairness of their encounters with the legal system (Tyler 1988; Lind and Tyler 1988).

It should be clear that it is only through research on the social psychology of procedural justice that we can form an understanding of the procedures which secure reprobation and reintegration. But, more importantly, it is this kind of research on citizen perceptions of fairness which is needed to instruct us on how to protect the subjective element of dominion within the criminal process.

9. Within the Discretionary Limits Set, What Sentences Should Courts Impose on Those Found Guilty?

We have already argued that the legislature should set parsimonious maximum penalties for each type of offence in proportion to the harm and culpability generally associated with it, but that there should never be minimum punishments. The question now is what judges should do under the ceiling placed upon their discretion. Traditional or preventionist sentencing admits of four principal functions of the sentencing decision—rehabilitation, incapacitation, deterrence, and moral education. We will consider each of these in turn.

One of the great contributions of the new retributivists has been in exposing the dangers to dominion of punishment guided by the pursuit of rehabilitation. As the Soviets have shown most vividly, there is nothing quite so totalitarian as rehabilitation combined with punishment (Cohen 1985). Earlier, in discussing capital and corporal punishment, we suggested that citizens ought to have a right to non-interference with their persons by the state; punishment ought to be restricted to interference with property and province. Coerced attempts to rearrange a psyche are an interference with the rights citizens should have over their persons. Republicans should therefore disapprove of such efforts. But, of course, this is not to argue against making rehabilitative services readily accessible to offenders who need them and ask for them; indeed we would encourage the use of such services by offenders. This position also does not preclude coerced rehabilitation of a corporate criminal. A management restructuring order should be a permissible sentence upon an organization that has broken the law. Rehabilitation is a more viable doctrine with corporate offenders than with individuals, because coerced reorganization of a management structure is less oppressive than coerced reorganization of a psyche (Braithwaite and Geis 1982).

Corporate offenders aside, the prescription that follows from a right to non-interference with dominion over one's person is that a heavier sentence should never be imposed for the reason of securing greater rehabilitation of the offender. Obversely, parsimony implies the permissibility of giving a lesser sentence on grounds of superior prospects of rehabilitation. The latter is a common situation, of course, given that prison is the worst possible place to facilitate freely chosen rehabilitation. Quite apart from the impossibility of keeping offenders away from 'bad influences' in prison, if rehabilitation depends on maintaining legitimate work as an alternative to illegitimate work, then keeping an offender in a job may be the most rehabilitative contribution the criminal justice system can make.

The second traditional rationale for sentencing is incapacitation. Surprisingly, some retributivists, while rejecting selective incapacitation as a general policy, suggest that in cases of 'vivid danger' offenders ought to be incarcerated for a longer period than would be proportionate to the offence (Ashworth 1986: 17; von Hirsch 1985). Under our theory, an offender who has served the maximum sentence allowed by the legislature has a right to release that cannot be trumped by any such consideration.

Selective incapacitation seems to us a dangerous policy if it is allowed to trump the right to non-interference beyond the maximum sentence legislated in advance of the offence. It can reopen the floodgates of indeterminacy that we can thank the new retributivists for closing. This aside, however, to deny incapacitation as a consideration in sentences of imprisonment is to deny the one thing that imprisonment can do better than any other sanction. For Zimring and Hawkins, to be in favour of prisons but against any form of selective incapacitation is politically to support the institution but to deny the legitimacy of its unique function: 'It is as if someone were to acknowledge the refrigerator as the most important of kitchen appliances while denying the necessity to keep food cold' (Zimring and Hawkins 1987: 5).

Selective incapacitation is difficult in practice, however. Prediction of dangerousness is difficult and, even more important, some of the variables that enable us to improve prediction are morally suspect. Most pointedly, in the United States, knowing the race of an offender improves our capacity to predict reoffending. A narrow definition of dangerousness akin to that of Moore *et al.* (1984) is required, which takes into account only the record of past offending. But even the fact that someone is dangerous in this sense should not be allowed to override his right not to be punished beyond the maximum sentence, and we should be parsimonious and morally uncomfortable in allowing it to increase deprivations of liberty within the permitted limits.

After rehabilitation and incapacitation, deterrence is the third function traditionally associated with penal sentences. Positive criminology has, at least to date, proved incapable of showing the levels of punishment necessary to achieve different levels of deterrence. As will be argued in the next chapter, there are reasons for believing that crime would increase if there were no punishment whatsoever. But there is little support for the view that increasing levels of punishment increases the deterrent effect. Even if criminology could tell the judge that six-month sentences achieve on average 15 per cent more deterrence than three-month sentences, this is of little use in individual cases. We know that prison is likely to be more painful to a sick old man than to a healthy younger man, to a mother separated from her baby (cf. Daly 1987), to an effeminate male teenager likely to be raped. And so on.

As a general principle, then, there is no point in judges weighing the speculative deterrent effects of different punishments. But none the less judges will secure for the community the benefit of having some deterrence if they occasionally impose punishments for other reasons: say, reasons of incapacitation. People will at least pick up the message that if they offend they are liable to some level of punishment.

Durkheim is the pre-eminent theorist of the fourth traditional rationale for punishment—moral education:

> Since punishment is reproaching, the best punishment is that which puts the blame—which is the essence of punishment—in the most expressive but least expensive way possible . . . It is not a matter of making him suffer . . . Rather it is a matter of reaffirming the obligation at the moment when it is violated, in order to strengthen the sense of duty, both for the guilty party and for those witnessing the offence —those whom the offence tends to demoralize. (1961: 181–2)

Not surprisingly, in view of the presumption in favour of reprobation, we argue that moral education should be the primary purpose considered in sentencing decisions. Elsewhere one of the authors has argued that community habits of law observance arise partly because the moral educative effects of the criminal process renders crime unthinkable for most of us most of the time (Braithwaite 1989). We refrain from crime not so much because we fear or even know the punishment we are likely to get, but because it simply seems wrong to us; and one reason it seems wrong to us is that people are punished and shamed for it.

The reprobation and reintegration presumptions lead us to favour restitution as a form of punishment; it symbolizes the harm, connoting through its content the wrong that was done. A major advantage of adverse publicity orders as sanctions against corporations is equally their expressive communication of the harm done (Fisse and Braithwaite 1983). What better way to communicate the wrongdoing of a pharmaceutical company that has made a false claim about its product in a medical journal advertisement than to require it to place remedial advertisements confessing to the falsity of their earlier claim to the very audience that was misled? Community service orders can also be very expressive sanctions—the man with a job who falsely claimed welfare benefits being required to work for a welfare agency, the coal-mining company that exposed its miners to unsafe roof conditions being required to undertake research and development on new roof-bolting technology. Sanctions which expose offenders to the community have more moral educative and reintegrative potential than sanctions which secrete them away in prisons.

Service to the moral educative purposes of the criminal sanction implies a degree of judicial creativity in sentencing. This causes objections from retributivists who wish to see sentences ordered along a proportionality metric on which equal wrongs can be given equal sentences. But we do not have to labour the silliness of an assumption, say, that twelve months of imprisonment for one person is remotely likely to be twelve times as painful as one month's imprisonment for a different kind of person. Proportionality metrics will always be rough and we should not be seduced by the fact that some things have numbers attached to them and others not. There is scope for ordering different types of alternatives to incarceration along a punitiveness gradient (Freiberg and Fox 1986; Wasik and von Hirsch 1988) but that is all.

This last possibility is important, because the criminal law should give moral guidance to the community, signifying the relative seriousness of different crimes with sanctions of differing severity (more on this in Chapter 8). Imagine a new crime is created—dumping a new kind of nuclear waste—that the legislature views as of enormous seriousness, even though the community has not yet come to grasp the reasons for this seriousness. The state can effect the desired moral education by providing for high maximum penalties and by judges imposing heavy penalties to signify the seriousness of the crime. At the other extreme, when the state does not provide for severe penalties or when judges never apply severe penalties, the community is apt to get the message that this type of crime is not regarded very seriously. We are not suggesting here that every offence of a serious type needs to be punished severely to give the community the message that the crime is of a serious sort; the community is quite intelligent enough to get this message from a few cases aggressively brought to its attention. There is more moral educative impact from a press release on the conviction of one restaurant for selling contaminated food than from ten being denounced only to the motley assembly in a courtroom.

Whenever judges decide a sentence then, not only our checking of power presumption, but also our reprobation presumption suggests that they must make clear why they do so. The criminal justice process should always seek to be a communicative process that engages the defendant in moral discourse. At its best it would argue with her as a rational agent who is shown respect through reasoning over the responsible exercise of her dominion (Duff 1986). That promises to be the most reprobative as well as a parsimonious response to criminal activity. Punishment should supply citizens with moral reasons for choosing not to engage in crime; and it requires respect for the capacity of citizens to make morally responsible choices (Hampton 1984).

Of the functions traditionally associated with penal sentences, our conclusion is that in exercising whatever discretion is left to them, judges should primarily have an eye to moral education and, though only in exceptional circumstances, to incapacitation. The notion of forced rehabilitation is obnoxious, and there is little point in judges trying to measure the different deterrent effects of the different sentences that they might impose. The considerations judges should take into account are the education of the offender, and of the community at large, the protection of the community by the incapacitation of the offender, and the reintegration of both offender and victim.

Judges who are moved by these considerations will generally sentence with a presumption against punishment. They will frequently record a conviction without penalty, or impose a probation order in place of prison or a fine. In any case they will try to elicit from the offender an indication that she understands that she has done wrong, that she stands denounced, yet has been granted mercy by the court. They will also do what they can to return the problem to the dominion of the relevant community of concern. If the offence was an assault which occurred in the changing-room of the football club, club members and officials could be asked to meet an officer of the court to give guarantees that they will keep the protagonists under control in future; if the assault occurred in the family, family members could be called in.

When punishment is required, we argued earlier that deprivation of property rather than liberty should be the presumptive punishment. For a large proportion of crimes, restitution or compensation, with 'interest' for the inconvenience or anguish of the victim, is the appropriate response.[4] With major property offenders, and wealthy organized criminals for whom voluntary compensation would be a farce, large-scale seizure of assets will be justified, perhaps to the point of seizing every asset owned by a corporation or wealthy individual. For a host of minor crimes where concerns about victim compensation do not arise (e.g. contempt of court), fines are certainly the appropriate sanction.[5]

Even when an incapacitative option is required, the parsimonious judge should consider liberty-depriving options short

[4] If all the prosecutor seeks is mandatory restitution, then there will be circumstances where the least costly (most parsimonious) way to achieve this will be by proceeding civilly rather than criminally. Harmonizing of civil and criminal law here is not a major challenge. Where a criminal restitution order is followed by a civil proceeding, obviously any civil order allows for the pay-out already made.

[5] Of course, flat fines punish the poor more than the rich, but 'day fines' calculated as so many days of the offender's income can be used instead. Moreover, the poor constitute most of the fodder for our prisons at present, and imprisonment implies a total loss of income more economically damaging than even very heavy fines, so policies to replace prison with fines will structurally advantage the poor, even if they are flat. Another possibility with the poor offender is for the probation officer, with the offender's permission, to negotiate with his employer for overtime, the extra income being directed to pay the fine. The employer could be given the extra hours of labour at a below-market rate as an incentive for her to co-operate in keeping her employee out of prison.

of full imprisonment. The violent football hooligan could report to the local police station every Saturday afternoon during the next three football seasons to wash out the cells or the police cars. The malpractising doctor or lawyer could be struck off, at least for a period. The corporate crook could be disqualified from ever serving again as a company director. The possibilities for non-incarcerative incapacitation are an important research project for republican criminology.

In urging judges to be creative in finding alternatives to prison, there is the risk that the alternatives will prove so attractive as to widen the net of social control, to bring people under the control of the criminal justice system who otherwise would have been left free. Such a risk is a challenge to our presumption in favour of parsimony. Concern over net-widening is one reason, along with cost and victim compensation, why property sanctions rather than community corrections should supply the sentence of choice for most offences.

10. How Should the Sentence be Administered by Prison, Probation, and Parole Authorities?

We have already said that coerced rehabilitation should be prohibited, and freely chosen rehabilitative services readily available, in our prisons. There is no need to make prisons horrible, unpleasant places when incapacitation rather than deterrence is the reason offenders are sent there. In any case, there is no evidence that crime prevention through deterrence will be advanced by making the experience even more painful than it is. Of course, it is theoretically possible to make the food so good, the accommodation so luxurious and the recreational activities so much fun that some people commit crime to get in. People with experience of prisons know, however, that this will never be a problem of widespread practical significance.

Prison administrators should use their limited resources to maximize dominion. That means that trade-offs must be made between serving the dominion of the outside community through expenditure on security and spending on things which enhance the dominion of prisoners. Such trade-offs inevitably occur anyhow and so in this sense republican theory can give its blessing to existing practice. In contrast, it is difficult to see how preventionist theory could ever justify spending resources on better food for prisoners in preference to installing extra razor-wire on the wall.

As against preventionists, though not retributivists, republicans will say that prisoners should only be deprived of those rights explicitly incorporated into their sentence. With imprisonment, that right is essentially freedom of movement. Why should the offender also lose other democratic rights such as the right to vote or read newspapers? The republican has a clear answer. The offender should be explicitly sentenced only to that deprivation of liberty needed to protect the dominion of others. Both parsimony and the checking of the power of prison administrators mean that any additional deprivation of liberty is wrong. Part of the insatiability problem with preventionist theories is that their advocates can approve of the prison administrator who capriciously deprives prisoners of their right to read newspapers in order to make their prison experience more deterring.

Existing practice is notoriously flawed when tested against the presumption in favour of checking power. Prison administration is rarely constrained to be rights-respecting and, in closed institutions, public accountability for the exercise of discretion is difficult. Authoritative outsiders, who can demand access to secret places at unexpected times, such as Ombudsmen, are needed to protect the rights of prisoners, take their complaints seriously, and call prison administrators to account.

If incapacitation is the only reason for resort to the unparsimonious sanction of imprisonment, then parole is needed for cases where there is a change in the circumstances the judge gave as written reasons for imprisonment. The man is sent to prison because he vows to attempt again to kill his wife, and his wife dies. The manic-depressive murderer, locked away because of his periodic outbursts of violence, is cured with the help of the prison psychiatrist. For the full retributivist, parole boards should be abolished, because they arbitrarily vary deserved sentences and undermine justice. For the parsimonious consequentialist, it is wrong to brutalize a human being in a prison for no better reason than retribution. Hence, justice means letting as many out as is possible, consistently with protecting the dominion of members of the outside community.

Work release, study release, and compassionate leave should

be encouraged whenever prisoners can be trusted under supervised periodic release, though not trusted to unconditional release. Further, these means of graduating reintegration back into the community can be used to test the prisoner's readiness for parole. Here too our republican line is probably going to be very different from the retributivist one. Remission of sentence for good behaviour in prison is also difficult for retributivists to justify because it is a variation of the deserved sentence. For the republican consequentialist, however, the rioting and chaos which would otherwise prevail in our prisons, with all the suffering that entails for those who have to live in them as prisoners or prison officers, justifies the retention of remission for good behaviour.

Our presumption in favour of reintegration, specifically reintegration of the offender, means that we believe prison administration and prison research should give priority to the question of how to prepare prisoners for return to society, and how to facilitate that return. There is an instrumental reason and an intrinsic reason for that priority. Reintegration might help to prevent ex-offenders going back to crime and threatening the dominion of others. And of course it would help to restore ex-offenders to the status of full dominion themselves. It would save them from becoming stigmatized, second-class citizens.

In conclusion, we would observe that the fundamental problem of prison policy in most systems is overcrowding. This problem requires a response at many different levels in the system. It is a classic case of a problem which cannot be solved within the sub-system where it falls, but only via a systemic, open-systems analysis (Welsh *et al.* 1988). Hall (1985) has outlined the sort of approach for which it calls:

> many jurisdictions have succeeded in curbing jail population growth and avoiding the need for larger facilities without compromising community safety or the integrity of the justice system. These measures have been based on: (1) a realization that the factors determining jail population go well beyond the local crime rate; (2) a recognition of joint responsibility for jail population levels among agencies involved in criminal case handling; (3) an understanding of the overlapping functions and interdependence of all criminal justice system components; and (4) careful planning involving all components of the local criminal justice system. (Hall 1985: 4)

Conclusion

In this chapter we have tried to draw some of the lessons of a republican theory for the shaping of the criminal justice system. In this conclusion we will look quickly over the points made, highlighting some differences between our theory and alternative theories like retributivism and preventionism; differences between what our theory would recommend and existing practice; and the significance of the theory for reorientating the research agenda of criminology.

We have seen that if the criminal justice system is orientated to the promotion of dominion, then four presumptions ought to rule: parsimony, the checking of power, reprobation, and the reintegration of victim and offender. The chapter went on to consider in turn the ten key questions raised by the criminal justice system and, invoking the presumptions mentioned, an indication was given of the answer that might turn out to be appropriate for each. Our discussion of how to handle the ten key questions was in each case unsatisfactorily brief, but we hope it was sufficient to show that the theory is capable of generating comprehensive answers which have some chance of satisfying reflective equilibrium. Notwithstanding its sketchiness, this is quite an achievement, and certainly one retributivism cannot boast.

All versions of retributivism fail to provide practical guidance on what to criminalize, how to allocate resources within the system, what kind of surveillance to permit, which suspects to target for investigation, which to prosecute, and how to conduct trials and pre-trial negotiations. There are seemingly insurmountable difficulties in ever adapting retributivism to such tasks. If retributivism only allows us to treat as means people who are guilty of crime, then any kind of preventive or investigative work that seriously interferes in the lives of non-offenders, treating them as means, requires a justification. It is difficult to see how such justification can be other than consequentialist.

The advance of retributivism over preventionism and utilitarianism is that it corrects the neglect of the right of the innocent to be protected from punishment and the right of the guilty to be protected from open-ended punishment and enforced therapy. But this is a short list of rights. Retributivism is better, but not much better, than preventionism in taking rights seriously, for other crucial rights cannot be derived within the doctrine. In what circumstances should a defendant have a right to release on bail? When should he have a right to a jury trial? While our own treatment of such matters has been cursory, we hope it has been sufficient to show that rights can be derived from republican theory to check power at all crucial points in the criminal justice process, points where retributivism is silent on rights. Preventionism and utilitarianism are theories that are suspect on taking any rights seriously; retributivism is a theory that takes a very short list of rights seriously; republican theory can at the very least take seriously all uncontroversial rights in the area of criminal justice.

It is not only on the question of rights that republican theory contrasts with preventionism and utilitarianism. We saw that republicanism can make sense of shifts from 'deterrence' to 'compliance' policing, from sentencing practices that give deterrence priority to sentencing practices that give priority to moral education. We saw how republicanism rejects any attempt to enforce rehabilitation through the criminal justice system, while making access to rehabilitative services a right, and how the pursuit of incapacitation must be constrained by unbreachable maximum punishments.

So much for the comparison between our theory and others. We also saw that the theory, grounded though it is on uncontroversial premisses, suggests some controversial departures from existing criminal justice practice. It suggests a system in which there are fewer criminal trials, but where no one should ever be incarcerated without the right to a full jury trial. The principle of parsimony would mean a substantial emptying of our prisons. The presumption in favour of checking power would mean credible community accountability mechanisms for police, prosecutors, and prison administrators. Under the status quo these are among the most powerful and least accountable actors in modern societies. The presumption in favour of reprobation would mean that Western criminal justice would become more like Eastern criminal justice with respect to moral education. And the presumption in favour of reintegration would imply a massive redistribution of resources from deterrence or retribution to such activities as the helping of victims.

Finally, we hope to have indicated that republican criminology suggests a recasting of the research priorities within criminology. It would mean a new pre-eminence for psychological research in criminology: not the sort of psychology that we saw in the heyday of the Gluecks, when psychologists also dominated criminological research, but the sort we see in the procedural justice tradition (Lind and Tyler 1988). If we are serious about being consequentialists, we must be empirically rigorous about assessing consequences. Take the issue of whether the inquisitorial procedure we see in Continental criminal law is superior to the adversarial procedure of Anglo-American criminal law. Already there is a growing body of research on how fair each of the adjudication procedures is perceived to be by those who experience it, a central issue given the importance of the subjective element of dominion in our theory. Do the advantages of the two methods vary according to whether it is a simple crime like murder or a complex economic crime? Under which procedure are offenders more likely to understand exactly why the law says they have done wrong, to report feeling ashamed, to express remorse, and voluntarily to offer victim restitution? These questions can be investigated within the research tradition of the psychology of procedural justice.

Of course preventionism has always directed us to the empirical study of the effects of deterrence, rehabilitation, and incapacitation. But our republican theory suggests a much wider vision of the consequences that should be researched. Matters that have traditionally been settled by clashes of opinion between lawyers should be targeted for systematic empirical research. Thus, debated rules of evidence should be tested by interviewing jurors to see how they understand the import of the evidence under different rules. A slowly growing band of psychologists is becoming interested in this kind of research, although it is a scholarly enterprise that does not enjoy high status in psychology or law or criminology. Republican theory would elevate this research tradition to a position of central importance.

Another relatively neglected sort of research to which our approach would give priority is work on interactions among sub-systems. Criminology has too many experts on criminal law, on police, on courts, on sentencing, on prisons, and not enough experts on the way these sub-systems affect each other. In some parts of the world there are inter-agency criminal justice authorities, policy research institutes, and commissions that are beginning to build system-wide perspectives on problems. We applaud that development.

If the policy inferences in this chapter are insufficiently detailed, one reason is that for any given question the consequentialist is required to gather a great deal of empirical evidence, and should reserve final judgement until this hard work is done. A second reason is that the consequentialist requires an implementation strategy for this theory before he can begin to detail his recommendations. We turn to the question of implementation strategy in the next chapter.

7

Implementing the Republican Theory

Real world policy choices usually involve incremental changes from the status quo; revolutionary changes wherein utopian visions of the best possible system can be implemented are rarely or never possible. Whether incrementalism is or is not the best way of making policy is hotly disputed, but that it is the way that most policy is in fact made is rarely contested. Common law systems, for example, are in a sense structurally incremental.

A theory that cannot be applied to the real world of incremental change is of limited use and in this chapter we will suggest how our theory can be applied to the practical politics of incremental change. This is a more important task than pushing on further with the work of the last chapter by designing in detail the criminal justice utopia prescribed by republican theory.

Though we require a theory to be capable of incremental implementation, we should stress that we are not incautious enthusiasts about incrementalism. Thus we recognize that an incremental strategy unguided by a theory of the good is vulnerable to internal contradiction and to capture by those with the greatest power to put their stamp on the strategy (Goodin 1982). Atheoretical incrementalism inevitably strengthens entrenched interests: in the criminal justice world, the police, the legal profession, and law-and-order scaremongers who build political reputations by appealing to retributive emotions. We require a theoretically guided incrementalism which connects a long-term vision with immediate political practice.

A feature of our theory that makes incremental implementation rather easier than is normally the case is the presumption in favour of non-intervention rather than intervention by the criminal justice system. This is the principle of parsimony which we have already discussed. Whenever the criminal justice system criminalizes, investigates, or punishes, there is a certain loss of dominion to those imprisoned, those who have their privacy intruded upon by the police, and those compelled to testify in the trial. There is also of course a cost to the dominion of those compelled to pay through their taxes for laws, police, prosecutors, judges, and prison space. As against these certain costs, however, the gain in dominion for any increase of state control is uncertain. This then implies a presumption against any increase: a presumption which should only be overridden given solid evidence that crime control progress can be made and dominion enhanced by greater intervention.

Obversely, it implies a presumption that opportunities should be seized that narrow the net incrementally, that have the criminal justice system do less. This is because doing less will produce a certain benefit in protecting the dominion of suspects, witnesses, and taxpayers, while it will not certainly do harm to the victims of crime. But of course any deficit in dominion of crime victims is of great concern, and our central question is how to satisfy that concern.

In the discussion that follows, we speak of incremental cuts —decrements—in line with the presumption of parsimony, as if there were no question about the sort of intervention to which the cut would lead. One point that needs to be added, and something that we shall take for granted in discussion, is that where possible the cut should always further the reprobative and reintegrative effects that we wish the criminal justice system to have. If we are cutting a financial punishment, we should also try to see that a purpose like restitution is served by the penalty that remains. If we are reducing a punishment that curtails a person's province, better that it involves a more useful form for purposes of reprobation and reintegration: say, community service. Our preferred line will be obvious from the analysis in the last Chapter. We should monitor every change made to try to ensure that they serve the purposes of reprobation and reintegration. Similarly, of course, we should monitor for any effects on the checking of power. But this exercise is not going to be overly demanding, because decrementalism means that there will be less power to be checked, not more.

Some may find our theory rather impractical, believing that it must fail to take account of the retributive beliefs and emotions of ordinary people. But that view would be mistaken. Our theory requires sensitivity to and monitoring of the retributive-reprobative beliefs that are widespread facts of all societies. It is a theory that seeks to ride the tiger, to harness the retributive dispositions of citizens to the pursuit of reprobation. The theory tries to build those dispositions into a powerful and desirable cultural force, preventing 'anger and resentment from flooding destructively down the well-worn canyons of revenge' (Blanshard 1968: 80). As Chan (1986: 43) concludes (drawing on Lukacs), normative criminological theory can borrow from revolutionary praxis; we can harness the positive power of reprobation while charting a stormy course buffeted by the winds of revenge. Alert to how the wind is blowing, the yachtsman does not let this determine his course; he defies and exploits it to pursue the course required.

An Empirical Presumption About the Causes of Crime

The literature on the relationship between criminal justice expenditure—on levels of policing, of punishment, of imprisonment—and crime is voluminous. We will not try to summarize that literature here but will boldly put a position on the state of the evidence; most criminologists, we believe, will agree with this position.

Between different countries, and different jurisdictions within the same country, there are enormous variations in the size and intrusiveness of the criminal justice system. Some jurisdictions, for example, have imprisonment rates more than ten times as high as others. Despite substantial research efforts, persuasive evidence that variations in criminal justice expenditure and interventionism cause substantial variations in crime rates has not been produced. There is certainly no evidence that small incremental changes to the status quo make a difference to levels of crime. Neither the theories which suggest that widening the net makes things worse, nor the theories which predict crime reduction from a more powerful criminal justice system, can claim vindication by the data on policy outcomes.

While there is a criminological consensus that changes at the margin of criminal justice intervention make no detectable difference to the crime rate—up or down—there is also a consensus that if the criminal justice system were abolished—if there were no police, no courts, no prisons—there would be more crime. We accept both these propositions. The implication of the two considered jointly is this. We can reduce expenditure on criminal justice—decrease the size of the police force, prosecute less, punish less—without producing an adverse effect on crime sufficient to be detectable after controlling for other influences on the crime rate. This holds, we believe, even in the comparatively non-punitive jurisdiction in which both authors live (which has an imprisonment rate of 32 per 100,000). However, we cannot persist indefinitely with decrements (minor contractions) to the criminal justice system without reaching the point where adverse consequences for crime will become evident. We confidently presume that some level of monitoring and punishment of crime is better than no monitoring and punishment, that there is an irreducible minimum of state intervention which must be sustained for the law to have credibility as a constraint. But we have little idea of the exact point where further cuts to the criminal justice system would damage the dominion of crime victims more than it would benefit the dominion of taxpayers, witnesses, and suspects.

The Decremental Strategy

It follows that it is safe to begin incremental cuts to the criminal justice system confident that this is right according to the theory. It is right because we are effecting a certain increase in the protection afforded to the dominion of those intruded upon by the criminal justice system without any evidence that this will diminish the dominion of persons who will be victims of crimes that would not otherwise have occurred. But because we also assume that progressive decrements will ultimately lead us to the point where crime is increased by the cuts to the system, we must monitor the accumulating effects of the decrements on the crime rate.

The difficulties of doing this are considerable. Crime rates fluctuate in response to many structural factors which are more powerful in their effects than those of the criminal justice system.

If after a decade of decrements the crime rate is higher, it may be difficult to tell whether this has been produced by the decrements or by a change in the age structure, for example, with adolescents becoming a larger proportion of the population. Multivariate statistical techniques to control for variables such as age structure can be applied to the problem, however, and should be so applied.

More importantly, what is required is a decrementalist strategy designed to secure the most useful feedback on the effects of changes. Thus, instead of cutting police expenditure by 1 per cent in every region of the state at one point in time, the government might cut only half the regions in the first year. Assume crime rates increase overall that year (because of other factors). We then have greater analytical leverage with the feedback because we can see if the crime rate went up more in the regions which experienced cuts in expenditure compared with those whose budgets remained untouched.

The kind of data one would monitor in the first instance would be in the form of Figure 1, which plots the relationship between decrements/increments to the speed limit and road accident fatalities in Denmark. One would then move to multivariate

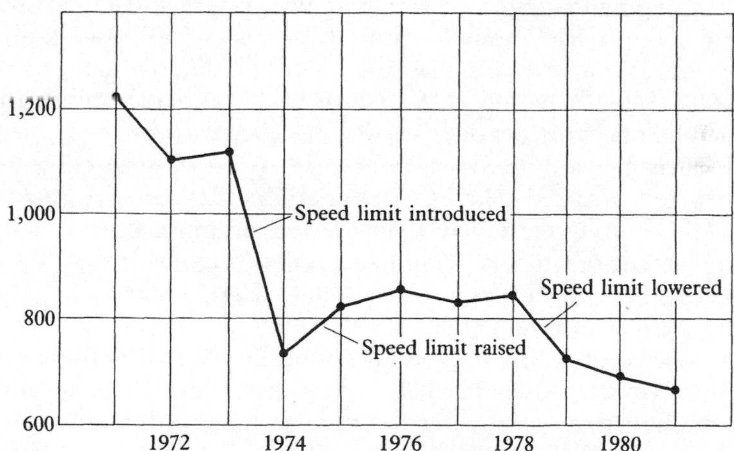

Fig. 1 Motor Vehicle Crash Fatalities in Denmark Before and After Speed Limit Law Changes, 1970–1982
(Insurance Institute for Highway Safety, 1987)

modelling of fatality rates and comparisons with control jurisdictions or locations unaffected by the speed limit changes.

We believe that there are good theoretical and empirical reasons for predicting that cuts to the level of punishment in the society would have to be very substantial indeed before persuasive evidence of crime increases would be produced. Elsewhere one of the authors has argued at length the basis for this belief (Braithwaite 1989). Mostly we do not refrain from crime because we calculate that the certainty and severity of punishment exceed the benefits of crime; rather we refrain because to kill, to rape, to steal a handbag is simply unthinkable to us. We are deterred from crime mainly by our own consciences and by the shaming of others whose respect we value, not mainly by rational calculation of the costs imposed by courts of law. This is the theoretical basis for our prediction (which may be found to be wrong) that any apparent increases in crime associated with early cuts to the criminal justice system would be shown by sound multivariate analysis to be increases that cannot reasonably, let alone certainly, be associated with the criminal justice cuts.

When the first evidence is produced which justifies the belief that the accumulation of criminal justice cuts has lifted crime rates, further cutting should be stopped. There should not be a rush into reinflating the criminal justice system, but a freezing at that point to allow time for more rigorous empirical work to be done and public debate to occur. Then, guided by that research and public discussion, a decision should be made on whether increments or further decrements are called for.

Once it has been established that an increase in crime has occurred, we need to know what degree of increase, in what kind of crime. Of course, it may well be that a community concerned to implement our theory would make the judgement that the increases are insufficiently major in nature and quantity to justify the sacrifice of dominion involved in widening once again the net of state control. The judgement might be made that the loss of dominion from crime has been significantly less than the gain in dominion from narrowing the net, so that further cuts to the criminal justice apparatus are justified. If the latter judgement were made, an extremely cautious strategy for implementing further cuts would be required. Caution would require a long period of evaluation and public debate between the first new decrement and the next one. Randomized experimental evaluations of the impacts of further cuts on crime and on the dominion of citizens other than crime victims would be desirable.

To be frank, we see this latter part of the implementation strategy as one that would never be invoked. We believe this because the entrenched interests in maintaining wide nets of state control are so strong that a struggle for decremental reform would never succeed in cutting the system to anywhere near the point where the dominion loss of victims from crime was sufficiently strong to outweigh the certain loss of dominion to citizens constrained in various ways by the net of state control. At least we believe this to be true in the English-speaking countries we know, where the police are a powerful lobby, and law-and-order constituencies are influential in politics and vocal in the media.

System and Sub-System Decrementalism

Thus far we have discussed decrementalism pitched at the level of the whole criminal justice system. The theory leads us to begin a process of decrement and feedback towards a smaller criminal justice system. Within the macro-pruning, however, choices must be made as to which areas will be pruned most and which least. Political reality dictates that these choices will be made on the basis of opportunism; chances to cut most sub-systems will be infrequent given the vested interests in bureaucratic growth. Nevertheless, the theory should provide guidance as to which opportunities are the highest priorities to seize.

The first element of guidance is that cuts should not be made in an area that jeopardizes a citizen's rights. Thus, the courts should not be deprived of the resources necessary to offer defendants a fair trial and the police should be prevented from paying for their cuts by collecting evidence cheaply through currently illegal invasions of citizens' province. The theory recommends monitored decrements in the variety of behaviour that is criminalized, in the maximum punishments provided by the legislature and the average punishments imposed by the courts, in the intensity of surveillance, in the number of cases targeted for criminal investigation, in the number of cases taken to trial, and in the portion of their sentence convicted offenders are required to serve under confinement.

A priority in reform should be to repeal criminal laws that do not in fact protect dominion. This is a priority because a cut at this fundamental level will have consequential positive effects at every subsequent stage. If we eliminate an environmental law that imposes enormous compliance costs, yet which forbids a kind of effluent found by new research to be harmless, decriminalization not only liberates the dominion of agents within a sector of the economy, it also liberates taxpayers from the costs of enforcing the silly law, citizens from being spied upon by investigators collecting evidence of non-compliance, witnesses and jurors being required to participate in litigation regarding it, and other citizens from being punished for non-compliance.

As for other areas where there is no evidence for an association between an increase in crime and introduction of a decrement, we should explore most vigorously those where the decrement will best serve to recover dominion previously eroded by the criminal justice system. Since capital punishment and imprisonment are the most comprehensive assaults on dominion inflicted by the criminal justice system, those reforms which will reduce the number of citizens who suffer these fates should become the highest priority. This view is also reinforced by the staggering costs to taxpayers of appeal processes associated with sentencing a citizen to death and the high costs of imprisonment. Sentencing reform is therefore of special importance. We will devote more attention to it later in this Chapter.

Cuts to the police are not as high a priority as sentencing reforms, partly because a substantial proportion of police activity does not involve trampling on the dominion of citizens; rather it involves responses to simple calls for help as well as peacekeeping activities. The police officer threatens a drunk with arrest unless he goes home to bed and desists from harassing women passing by; he pulls apart two youths brawling in an alley; even though he can do little to catch a burglar five hours after the crime occurs, he consoles the householder, explains how to claim insurance and increase security, and records the offence for statistical purposes. The police actually spend only a small proportion of their time slapping handcuffs on people and using intrusive surveillance techniques which invade the privacy of citizens. It follows from the theory, however, that such cuts as are made to the police budget should be concentrated on activities that are maximally intrusive while minimally adding to the protection of citizens. Significant slices of police time and resources are devoted to intrusive activities such as posing as clients to trap prostitutes, petty drug dealers, unlicensed bookmakers, and the like. These are areas where resource cuts could be targeted. Negotiating cuts in the 'civil liberties budget' of police departments, as discussed in Chapter 6, is one strategy for targeting reductions in police resources so that they reduce activities that maximally intrude on the dominion of citizens.

Some enforcement agencies spend even smaller proportions of their resources on dominion-invasive activities than the average police department. A British environmental inspector would seem to do very little to trample upon the dominion of citizens (see Hawkins 1984), and certainly comparatively less than the British police officer. So the theory provides stronger grounds for experimenting with cuts to the police budget than the environmental protection budget.

Sub-Systems Where Increases Can be Justified

A consideration of environmental enforcement leads us to wonder whether there are not in fact some areas where the theory implies an increment in enforcement rather than a decrement. There are such areas, and they are disproportionately located in the domain of law enforcement directed against business. The realities of political power discussed earlier, wherein entrenched interests resist cuts to police enforcement directed at common crime, are reversed with corporate crime. Here it is the law breakers, rather than the law enforcers, who enjoy the greater political power and the stronger ties with political leaders.

One of our empirical presumptions was that, in order to secure compliance, some enforcement of a law is better than no enforcement. Many business regulatory laws are never, or almost never, the subject of criminal enforcement. Grabosky and Braithwaite (1986) found that a third of 96 Australian business regulatory agencies had not secured a criminal conviction (or civil penalty) during the three years of their study.

With most areas of business regulation in most countries, the criminal law has not been used to the minimal level of our presumption; there has not been a demonstration to the community that in these domains the law is capable of keeping its promises. So we do accept that in most business regulatory domains there is a need for increased criminal enforcement, at least to the point of that modicum of enforcement which sets the lower limit on incrementalist experimentation. Beyond that point neither the political realities of power nor the principled pursuit of incremental improvements in crime control would allow punishment to be increased very greatly. The theory could never justify widespread use of criminal punishment to secure social control in this area for two main reasons. First, excessive use of punishment can generate an organized business culture of resistance to the law (Bardach and Kagan 1982). Second, non-punitive techniques of moralizing and persuasion are routinely more effective than law enforcement for securing compliance. The dominion of victims of most types of business offenders will be best secured by regulatory persuasion. Persuasion works best, however, when the government negotiates against the background of a demonstrated capacity for tough criminal enforcement against companies that resist good faith negotiation or that perpetrate unusually evil crimes (Scholz 1984; Braithwaite 1985).

The occasional resort to prosecution necessary to optimize business compliance with the law does involve increases in criminal justice invasions of dominion. But these are very minor ones which go to levels of enforcement far below those that apply, or are ever likely to apply, to blue-collar crimes. A case can also be made within the terms of the theory (though we will not devote the space to doing so here) that it would serve well the protection of dominion to increase the resources available to many business regulatory agencies. Business regulatory agencies, we have said, are and should be mostly about educating, persuading, reproaching businesses on their responsibilities to comply with the law. In practice, and according to the theory, they do not and should not massively restrain the dominion of the regulated with widespread criminal enforcement. Further, a business regulatory inspectorate employing a strategic mix of punishment and persuasion can demonstrate better protection of dominion in the community from modest increases in its resources. The level of serious coal-mine accidents, for example, would seem to be reduced by increased funding of mine-safety inspectorates (Braithwaite 1985; Lewis-Beck and Alford 1980). Very substantial decreases in the levels of some—though only some—environmental pollutants have been achieved in most developed countries since the expansion of environmental protection agencies in the late 1960s and early 1970s. Limited regulatory intrusions into the motor vehicle industry since the late 1960s seem to have achieved massive saving of life (Department of Transport 1982). While there is some empirical controversy surrounding the short-term effects of such regulation, not many would dispute the long-term importance of regulation in reducing the horrific nineteenth-century death-toll from fires in poorly designed buildings, railway accidents, and workplace catastrophes.

There are, of course, business regulatory enforcement domains which would not qualify for expansion under the tests of our theory. Moreover, under the scrutiny demanded by the theory there would be particular laws under every regulatory regime which would be candidates for repeal. Within a general cut in the criminal justice budget, however, overall resources for business crime enforcement should probably be somewhat increased. There are enough large domains of business regulation devoid of criminal enforcement for such an increase to be required for minimal protection of dominion from white-collar predation. This at least is what we suspect the theory will imply when this topic is treated more rigorously by future research.

Beyond corporate crime enforcement, we find it difficult to think of pockets of common crime where enforcement increments above the status quo would be shown to increase community protection. Perhaps domestic violence is one, driving under the influence of alcohol another (Homel 1988). But, again, there is a need for more research here. While there may be areas for which the theory would prescribe modest increases in criminal justice intervention, however, we can think of none where massive enforcement increases would improve the protection of dominion overall.

Of course, we can only find out what would happen by putting our theoretically guided incrementalism-decrementalism into practice. But from what we know from empirical criminology, implementation would be likely to result in massive reductions of punitive and intrusive social control across a broad front and very modest increases in punitiveness across a number of business regulatory areas: these areas currently constitute a tiny fraction of the criminal enforcement action.

What is the Right Punishment?

Let us now illustrate in just a little more detail how a decremental implementation of republican theory can solve problems previously viewed as insoluble. The question which, more than any other, has eluded a satisfactory answer in the literature is how severe should punishments be for particular crimes?

The new retributivists have persuasively demolished the leading utilitarian and preventionist works on optimal penalties. There is neither evidence that rehabilitation can work in prison nor even in community-based programmes, let alone data to guide how long offenders should be locked up to provide for their rehabilitation. While extreme cases of violent or vindictive offenders who obviously require incapacitation do arise, as a general principle we cannot begin to allocate the severity of punishments on the basis of predictions of dangerousness. Similarly, the new retributivists have shown that it is beyond existing or foreseeable technical competence to use the data on the deterrent effects of different levels of punishment to specify in advance an optimal deterrent penalty. Moreover, there remain good grounds for wondering whether different levels of formal state punishment affect offending much at all.

Old-fashioned retributivists once had an answer to the question of what is the right punishment—an eye for an eye, a tooth for a tooth, a life for a life. But the new retributivists have rightly torpedoed the *lex talionis* as well; it can never provide guidance with offenders who cannot be punished in the same manner as their offending—rapists, bribe-payers, environmental offenders. Unfortunately, the new retributivists have not come up with a theoretical substitute. They tell us only that punishments for different crimes ought to be ranked according to the harm done and the degree of culpability of the offender for that harm (Nozick 1974, 1981).

Harm done and culpability involved may enable us to rank-order crimes, and may even enable us to rank intervals between crimes, so that we can say that the interval between that shoplifting and this burglary is smaller than the interval between that assault and this murder. But quite a lot more than this is required to generate a set of correct retributive punishments. Let us list systematically what is required:

1. A suitable scale of the harm or seriousness of all crimes: for example, a scale which would tell us that stealing $100 is twice as serious as stealing $10; stealing $1,000 ten times as serious as stealing $100.[1]
2. A scale of culpability or responsibility which would enable us to say, for example, that Jack had a 50 per cent level of responsibility for the crime, Jim 100 per cent.
3. A strategy for combining seriousness and culpability into a single desert metric, such as Nozick's (1981) suggestion of multiplying harm by responsibility.
4. A scale for punishments which would tell us, for example, that five years' imprisonment is five times the burden of one year's imprisonment; one year is three times the burden of one month.
5. A strategy for matching the scale of crimes and the punishment scale.

We will not comment on the first four requirements, which can be resolved to varying degrees of satisfactoriness, because the fundamental stumbling-block is the utter intractability of the fifth (matching) requirement. Suppose we identify the least serious crime. With which punishment should we match it? What is it that the stealing of $10 deserves? Von Hirsch (1985) concedes that this 'anchoring-point' problem is intractable within the terms of retributivist theory. He solves the problem by conceding that consequentialist concerns like deterrence and the capacity of the prisons system should be used to settle on anchoring-points for penalty scaling. But we have already agreed that von Hirsch was

[1] In this example, and in others, we suggest that the retributivist may need a ratio scale. In fact an interval scale might suffice: a scale which was sensitive only to the order of the intervals, without enabling us to say that an item at one point was so many times higher on the scale than an item at another.

right in concluding that the deterrence literature cannot guide us in setting optimally deterrent punishments. We cannot set a torch to preventionism, build a new theory on its ashes, and then scrape together the ashes to construct such a fundamental prop to the new structure. Besides, prison capacity is an arbitrary basis for deciding when it is right to deprive citizens of their liberty. We should be troubled if, within a federal structure, punishments in State *X* are twice as severe as in state *Y*, simply because state *X* has a lot of spare cells.

Kleinig (1973) has explored the possibility of a non-arbitrary basis for levels of punishments (see similarly Davis 1983). Kleinig's analysis, however, depends on the (arbitrary) assumptions that the worst crime possible deserves the heaviest morally acceptable punishment, and that the least serious crime possible (whatever that is) deserves the lightest punishment possible. For us, the lightest punishment possible would be a judicial reprimand; for others the heaviest morally acceptable punishment would be death. Neither are useful extremes for scaling deserved days in prison. But let us be as helpful as we can to Kleinig by positing one day in prison as the lightest punishment possible and life imprisonment as the heaviest morally acceptable punishment. In abstract, we might see no moral objection to life imprisonment. None the less, our arbitrary view might be that no crime committed in the past has ever deserved life imprisonment. Obversely, we might see one day in jail as too lenient or too severe for the least serious crime possible. The anchors are in fact adrift. The simple fact is that retributivism cannot supply a unique non-arbitrary way of translating a scaling of crimes into recommendations for levels of sentences.

Our consequentialist theory does instruct us in how to find the right scaling of sentences. First, it forbids the enshrining of a minimum penalty for any offence because the principle of parsimony counsels mercy and reconciliation unless there are good grounds for believing that dominion will be better protected overall by punishment. Second, it requires the enshrining of a maximum penalty, with that maximum being gradually decreased until the iterated process of decrement and monitoring reveals the first solid evidence of an adverse effect on levels of crime. The sentencing level is frozen at that new point for a considerable period of more thorough empirical study and public debate; then either a decision is made that dominion can be further protected by another cut in the maximum sentence, or the process incrementally backtracks to higher levels of punishment. The right maximum penalty is as low as experience shows we can achieve without failing to protect dominion overall.

The critics will raise questions about how revealing this experience is likely to be. It could happen that reducing the maxima would have no effect on the average penalties imposed; that judges would dig in their heels, refusing to change their sentencing practices. Our systemic methodology, which requires us to monitor effects in the judicial sub-system of changes in the legislative sub-system, would then give us solid data on the consequences of the change: there would be no consequences at all. We would have to choose in that case between judging this kind of reform a waste of time and persisting in the reduction of maximum penalties below the penalty levels actually being imposed by judges.

Assume, in contrast, that the judiciary responds to the signals from the legislature by lowering average sentences. Would we really find out if crime increased as a result? The data will often not be very revealing in such cases. But such empirical difficulties confronting the criminal justice policy-maker are not so very different for those who must make judgements on rough short-term data about the multiple systemic effects of tightening fiscal or monetary policy one extra notch. And they are not necessarily more difficult than those confronting the business policy-maker who evaluates whether a cut in the advertising budget was good or bad for profits. If sales went down, how much of the drop was in orders placed before the advertising cuts came into effect, how much was due to an economy-wide recession, how much to the fact that a competitor increased its advertising budget? Criminology should be able to cope with these policy-monitoring challenges in the same admittedly rough ways that policy-makers cope in those other arenas. We have the luxury in criminal justice policy (compared with economic policy) of being able to move slowly without a decision-point for the next change being forced upon us before we have had time to analyse the consequences of the last change. And we can do all of the things that are done in those other policy-evaluation arenas to clarify the effects of what we do. For example, we can reduce the maxima for burglary but not for car theft and observe whether the ratio of burglaries to car thefts increases.

While there are things we can do to improve the sophistication and informativeness of our monitoring, there can be no denying that it may fail to detect crime increases or decreases caused by the reform. Yet confronted with these inevitable difficulties, the criminal justice policy-maker following our theory is in a much better position than the utilitarian economic policy-maker or the profit-maximizing business executive. This is because the theory gives her clear advice on what to do when confronted with conflicting or equivocal data on the effects of a decrement in punishment—add another decrement. The theory instructs her that it is wrong to tolerate the certain evil of a more intrusive criminal justice system for a crime control benefit that cannot be demonstrated.

Consider in contrast the difficulties of a retributive reformer. She cannot enjoy the benefit of our simplifying principle. Retributive theory, because it includes no principles to weigh in deciding the right absolute level of punishment, cannot tell the reformer whether to struggle overall for changes up or down. An incrementalism advocating increases in punishment is just as defensible, in the terms of retributive theory, as an incrementalism arguing for reductions in punishment. And even when retributivists do agree on incremental reduction, there are no grounds for hoping for or aspiring to convergence on where this reduction should stop. In a world of perfect information, in contrast, different republicans will converge on support for the same level of punishment. While such a world is impossible, the point is that as we approach closer to it, republicans will move closer to agreement. No amount of information, in contrast, can help resolve the arbitrariness of retributive presumptions.

Decrementalism and Being Systemic

It may seem unlikely, but still it is conceivable that judges, angered by a lowering of maximum sentences for serious crimes, strike back by actually increasing the average sentences they impose under the new maxima. The criminal justice system is full of political actors with views to promote and interests to protect, so that counter-intuitive outcomes such as this are always a possibility. Therein lies the danger of implementing a neat sub-system theory without monitoring the way changes in that sub-system elicit responses from actors in other sub-systems.

A decrease in average sentences may not produce an increase in crime, but under the sway of law-and-order rhetoric the community may become convinced that it has dramatically increased crime. An epidemic of fear of crime in the community might grow to be a serious threat to the dominion of citizens who are suddenly afraid to walk in their neighbourhood at night. Vigilantism might arise. Such consequences cannot be predicted in advance; but neither can they be ignored. A decrementalist strategy with constant monitoring of system outputs will move slowly, watching for any such community reactions and attempting to cope with them.

We believe, therefore, that our theory avoids what Feeley (1983: 194) calls 'the fallacy of formalism'. Our theory is not bound to formal descriptions of what criminal justice actors do. It seeks to render reform responsive to the logic and incentives manifest in concrete historical settings among those whose practices we wish to change.

Beautiful Theories and Ugly Practices

Normative social theories tend to construct a package of measures that together are supposed to herald the good society. They have a beautiful coherence and a vision of the ideal world which sounds attractive. But the whole package is never implemented. In addition to our beautiful theory with elements *A*,*B*,*C*, and *D*, there is a competing beautiful theory with elements *W*,*X*,*Y*, and *Z*. One powerful constituency lines up behind the first theory because it will benefit from elements *A* and *B* of that theory; another lobby lines up behind the second theory because it will benefit from *Y* and *Z*. A likely result then becomes a compromise policy package, *A*,*B*,*Y*, and *Z*. Now this might be the worst of both worlds, a package that defeats the goals targeted by the coherent policy packages of both theories. In criminal justice, this political dynamic often accounts for Sellin's dictum that 'beautiful theories have a way of turning into ugly practices' (Cullen and Gilbert 1982: 151).

A strength of our theory is that it does not set down a definitive package of interdependent reforms. It is a theory which sets the reformer on a certain course, giving instructions on how to evaluate her progress, and how to use this feedback in deciding whether to change course. It is not a beautiful theory ripe to be turned into ugly practice: its accountability against a yardstick of 'beauty', its systemic focus, and its monitored incrementalism combine to arm it against such practices.

Reformers armed with no more than beautiful theories are no match for boots-and-all opponents. It is hard for caring souls who balance a concern for the dominion of crime victims with a concern for the dominion of those caught in the net of state control to win battles against blood-and-guts campaigners who peddle a glib retributive or deterrent message. Simplistic attacks on evil have the upper hand in emotive debates.

To resist such campaigners, reformers must take their chances as they come: to call for the abolition of mandatory minimum terms of imprisonment for a particular offence by playing up a poignant case of an offender who warranted mercy; to call for the abolition of capital punishment after it is found that the executed suspect was innocent; to call for the demolition of an oppressive prison following a riot. A blueprint, a utopian vision for an ideal system, is not enough. A theory is needed that can guide the *Realpolitik* of exploiting opportunities for incremental reform. We hope we have provided such a theory. It is a theory which can say to the pragmatic reformer: take your chances for decremental changes to criminal justice policy as they arise, then argue for thorough evaluation of the system-wide effects of the reform when secured. Given what we know about the minimal impacts of criminal justice reforms on crime rates, the probability is that there will be no evidence of adverse effects on crime and the reformer can then wait for her next opportunity to cut back the system, using the data on the absence of ill effects from the earlier decrement. Of course, if the point is reached where evidence does emerge that dominion has been set back by the reform, then the reform agent has the much easier task of joining forces with the law-and-order lobby.

But this will rarely happen, because the law-and-order lobby will stave off most changes advanced by dominion-respecting, rights-respecting reformers. In English-speaking countries, one-sided support for retribution and deterrence has been so strong that the difficulties of what should be done when the scales approach balance between protecting the dominion of crime victims and protecting the dominion of those caught in the net of social control are judgements which will not be confronted by this generation.

Incrementalism is a barren practice unless informed by a comprehensive normative theory. Without theoretical guidance, incrementalism can never be more than the practice of political pragmatism which allows this year's change to contradict last year's change, unencumbered by any analysis of the right direction to take the system in the long haul. But a normative philosophy which cannot inform the real world of incremental change is equally a barren theory. Neither atheoretical pragmatism nor unpragmatic utopianism will advance the protection of dominion. Our theory, we hope, escapes these dangers. It is designed to satisfy both the philosophers and the politicians, drawing on a nuanced view of the good and the right and pointing the way to a sophisticated intervention in the real world of pressure politics.

8

Retributivism: An Inferior Theory

We hope that by now we have persuaded readers that a comprehensive theory of criminal justice is preferable to a sub-system theory, and that our republican theory is comprehensive; that a consequentialist theory is preferable, and that our theory is consequentialist; that a target is required that is uncontroversial, stabilizing, and satiable, and that dominion passed these tests; and finally that the theory is one that can be applied to the political realities of incremental struggle. The present chapter is aimed at readers who, while they may have accepted some of the above, still feel compelled by retributive intuitions.

Retributivists, as we have already seen, support all or at least some of the four constraints distinguished in Chapter 3. Full retributivists support all four, arguing that the guilty and only the guilty should be punished, and that they should be punished at the level proportionate to their crime and culpability: no higher and no lower. Negative retributivists agree that only the guilty should be punished and that they should not be punished at any level higher than the proportionate one: they allow that sometimes the guilty need not be punished or that they may be punished at a lower than strictly appropriate level.

Whatever batch of constraints they defend, the feature that distinguishes retributivists proper is that they regard the constraints as fundamental criteria of right and wrong, not, for example, as guidelines derived from consideration of how best to promote some more fundamental goal. They take it as a matter of the most basic, underived fact that there should be punishment for crime; that the guilty or at least only the guilty should be punished; and that punishment should be at, or at least not above, a certain proportionate level.

Retributivist discourse is not confined, however, to rehearsing such constraints. It mainly consists in justifying and elaborating the constraints. Three questions dominate discussion: first, why we should punish; second, who we should punish; and third, how much we should punish. In this chapter we turn to consider what retributivists have to say on such questions. We know the sorts of answers that republican theory would support: that we should punish, if at all, only when it will promote dominion; that we should punish only those found guilty, since otherwise dominion at large is jeopardized by the system; and that we should be parsimonious in punishment, not going beyond the lowest level which will certainly promote dominion. We shall argue that though republican theory does not focus exclusively on punishment in the way that retributivism does, the answers provided by retributivists are manifestly less satisfactory than the republican responses. Republican theory defeats retributivism even on the home ground of retributivism.

Why Punish?

Different answers to this question are defended by different adherents of retributivism. In the pages that follow we try to show that the answers supplied by the major supporters of retributivism are unsatisfactory.

The first kind of answer is supplied by what Honderich (1984: 212) calls intrinsic retributivists. This is that we should punish because there is intrinsic good in the guilty suffering. Defenders of this variant of retributivism simply say there is no good argument against the view that having the guilty suffer is intrinsically good, and that there is a widespread acceptance of this view in the community. Both assertions are questionable. Against the first, we can put the intuitive claim that it is generally bad to cause people to suffer intentionally. Against the second, we can argue that there is no empirical evidence to suggest that the intuitions of most citizens support the intrinsic good of the guilty suffering. Most citizens, we suspect, support retribution up to a point, and will give reasons for that support. They will not rest with the blunt claim that it is good the guilty suffer. Indeed, most retributivist philosophers are unhappy to rest with this claim and that is support enough for our suspicion.

The second and more dominant line of retributivist argument on why to punish invokes notions of balancing benefits and burdens which are discussed in Chapter 4. Ashworth (1983) talks of the general justifying aim of punishment as being

> to restore the balance which the offence disturbed. It is unfair that the offender should be allowed to 'get away with' that advantage, and it is therefore right that he should be subjected to a disadvantage so as to cancel out (at least symbolically) his ill-gotten gain. (pp. 16–18)

Similarly, Sadurski (1985: 225) follows Kant in suggesting that the why of punishment is 'restoring an overall balance of benefits and burdens' (see also Morris 1968; Murphy 1979; Finnis 1980). Von Hirsch also, in his pioneering 1976 work, was a devotee of this answer to the 'why punish' question, although by his 1985 book he had abandoned it. And most recently Sher (1987) has provided an eloquent defence of this doctrine, albeit from a target-retributivist perspective.

A first objection to this justification for punishment is that law-abiding conduct is not always burdensome and crime is not always advantageous. The rapist might contract syphilis or the burglar break a leg. The conspiracy or the attempted murder might fail. Is the crime to be punished even though no benefits accrued?

The benefits and burdens theorist has a reply to this. He can say that it is self-restraint which is the burden, and unrestricted liberty the benefit that criminals gain by eschewing self-restraint. But is the self-restraint of not committing murder really a burden to our law-abiding readers? Indeed is it so great a burden that failure to bear it warrants a greater balancing punishment than for any other crime? Or is it that murder brings such greater benefits than other crimes as to warrant more punishment than, say, insider trading? Even under conditions of unrestricted liberty most of us have no interest in or attraction to committing murder, and so the burden is no actual inconvenience. On the contrary, one influential view is that educating ourselves to adopt a moral character which abhors evil makes us 'better off' (Falls 1987).

Herbert Morris, who had been a leading advocate of the benefits and burdens approach (Morris 1968), now advances 'A Paternalistic Theory of Punishment' (Morris 1981). In this account, far from punishment being a burden, it has become a benefit: punishment helps the offender to comprehend the evil involved in crime both for others and for herself. The offender is morally better off when she is brought to feel contrition via punishment. That someone like Morris can shift view so dramatically gives substance to our suggestion that it is less than clear what constitutes a burden in this area, and what a benefit.

Sadurski (1985: 226) is unpersuaded, because the burden of self-restraint still does limit options, he says, and to have choice is better than not having it: this, notwithstanding Dworkin's (1982) argument that sometimes having fewer choices is preferable to having more. Is it a burden in this sense that you are unable to fly to Mars tomorrow? The point we would stress is that some burdens have practical significance for people and some do not. It seems a weak basis for locking people up that they renounced burdens which are not felt to be burdens by most law-abiding citizens. The same point applies to Sher (1987). He argues that because murder entails violation of an unusually strong moral restraint, the murderer assumes an unusually large freedom. But if it is a freedom that most people in no sense view as a benefit, then what is it that calls for a balancing to occur?

In any society with gross inequalities of wealth and power, restoring the balance of benefits and burdens is a troubling notion. How can we talk of a pauper's punishment restoring the equilibrium of benefits and burdens in the same way as does a millionaire's? The equilibrium was never there to restore. Even more fundamentally, the reciprocal obligations of self-restraint are rarely reciprocal. Anatole France is repeatedly cited on this: 'The law in its majestic equality forbids the rich as well as the poor to sleep under bridges, to beg in the street and to steal bread.' Obversely, corporations and their executives have other burdens of self-restraint which paupers do not—to refrain from rigging prices, making unsafe products, polluting the environment. And even if we achieved a socialist or libertarian utopia, there would still be a lack of reciprocity. Refraining from rape will always remain a greater burden for men than for women.

A third, closely related retributivist account of why we should punish invokes the Hegelian notion that punishment annuls the wrong done, re-establishing the status quo (Hegel 1942). Jean Hampton discusses a rationale of this kind, although in the spirit of target-retributivism, when she talks of punishment defeating the offender. Punishment, she admits, cannot annul the act itself. 'But it can annul the false evidence seemingly provided by the wrongdoing of the relative worth of the victim and the wrongdoer' (Murphy and Hampton 1989: 130). She sees crime as an act of mastery; punishment, she thinks, is 'a second act of mastery that denies the lordship asserted in the first act of mastery' (p. 127).

This conception might make limited sense with some violent crimes. But how much sense does it make of more common crimes like employee pilfering or embezzling from an employer? Can we account for this as the employee achieving mastery over the company, and the punishment as necessary to deny this mastery? Is a tax offence 'evidence of superiority' of the tax offender over the state? When an offender sees himself as a junkie, will it be sensible to conceive of punishment annulling his 'prideful and inflated sense of his own importance' (p. 144)? Hampton suggests that punishment 'can annul the message, sent by the crime, that they [victim and offender] are not equal in value' (p. 130). It should be clear that this equality account suffers the same problem as assuming that there is an equilibrium of benefits and burdens to be preserved when in fact the starting-position is a disequilibrium.

Increasingly, to turn to a fourth major variety of argument, modern retributivists have jettisoned notions of balancing and annulment, in favour of reprobation or denunciation as the justification for punishment. Lord Denning (1984) has been a prominent advocate of the view that 'the ultimate justification of any punishment is not that it is a deterrent but that it is the emphatic denunciation by the community of a crime'. Some defend denunciation on a variety of consequentialist grounds: denunciation strengthens inhibitions against crime in the community (e.g. Braithwaite 1989); it 'contributes to a society's identity as a self-respecting community' (Oldenquist 1986: 75; Oldenquist 1988); to fail to denounce would 'depreciate the importance of the rights that had been infringed' (von Hirsch 1985: 53). But a number of retributivists, notably von Hirsch (1985) and on one interpretation Nozick (1981: 363–97), are at pains to argue that reprobation of criminal conduct is a good in itself independently of any good consequences that follow from it.

This intrinsic reprobationism is not so troubling a philosophy as intrinsic retributivism. We are compelled to give reasons for an intuition that it is right intentionally to inflict suffering on the criminal because it must be reconciled with another intuition that it is generally wrong intentionally to inflict suffering on another human being. In contrast, the intuition that it is right to denounce criminals is not troubled by any contrary intuitions about the wrongness of criticizing others.

The trouble with reprobationism, however, from the retributivist's perspective, is that it is not clear that it will support the sorts of punishment favoured by retributivists. The point ought to be obvious from our discussion in Chapter 6. We argued there for a presumption in favour of the pursuit of reprobation, but this presumption directed us away from the measures supported by retributivists, not towards them. We were prepared to allow imprisonment as a punishment of last resort but that was because of the need to protect society from dangerous offenders, not for reprobative purposes.

It is doubtful if a system of proportionality of punishment is the best way of assuring proportionality of reprobation. Denunciation, we believe, is determined less by the length of sentence than by whether the trial is reported in the media, whether it is held in open court in the presence of significant others, how many of the offender's acquaintances come to know of the conviction throughout the rest of his life. The shame directed at a respectable businessman who spends two months in jail may be no less than it would have been, had he been sentenced to six months. Compared with the denunciation associated with arrest and indictment, the actual sentence might be associated with a withering away of denunciation. As an American judge has argued:

> Pronouncing of the sentence is not as injurious to the person, his relationship to the community, to his family, as the return of the indictment. A loss of credit, a loss of bank credit, a loss of friends, social status, occasionally loss of wife, members of family, children around the father. They react to this more when they hear that an indictment has been returned and he has been charged than they do after they have gotten used to the idea and he is sentenced for it. (Mann 1985: 224)

Moreover, the actual locking away of the offender can be associated with a further erosion of reprobation, a point Dr Johnson made about Georgian prisons: 'The misery of jails is not half their evil . . . In a prison the awe of public eye is lost, and the power of the law is spent; there are few fears, there are no blushes. The lewd inflame the lewd, the audacious harden the audacious' (Johnson 1759: 38).

Consider in this connection, not just what happens in prisons, but what happens in the sentencing process itself. About 85 per cent of those who face felony court charges in California are convicted of some offence, but only about 10 per cent are tried before a judge and jury (Rossett and Cressey 1976: 33–4). Most criminals are not confronted with the community's disdain for what they have done in the solemn ceremony of the criminal trial. Their fate is sorted out technocratically, quietly, often in deals done between prosecutors and defence lawyers. Rossett and Cressey argue that when defendants do appear in court, their appearances are almost always short, and from the defendant's point of view, full of legal talk the import of which is not comprehended. The offenders are on an assembly line populated by lawyers who are anything but moralizing about what the offender has done; the lawyers are matter-of-fact, worldly-wise, keen just to do their job, and move on to the next case. Given the case-load pressures on modern courts one wonders if things can ever be greatly different from an assembly line which is the antithesis of reprobation.

There is a strong tradition in criminology which says that formal punishment is not the way to maximize the possibilities for denunciation. Denunciation is something that occurs in the community; so it is silly to assume that taking legal conflicts out of the community and putting them into courts is the way to nurture reprobation. Christie (1981: 93), for example, talks of crime victims as having their conflicts stolen by the state. To the extent that we formalize and professionalize criminal justice, the community is deprived of pedagogical possibilities for clarifying norms. It is a commonplace in debates on business regulatory strategy to observe that formally punitive regulatory strategies undermine cultural commitments to the law as well as informal reprobation for non-compliance. Persuasion and education about legal obligations are strategies which minimize the risks of subcultures of business resistance arising in response to excessive litigiousness (Bardach and Kagan 1982). When the community genuinely comes to believe that criminal justice is something best left to the experts—either the technocrats of preventionism who administer the optimum deterrent, or the technocrats of retributivism who calibrate the just punishment—there is a risk that they will neglect the denunciatory obligations which are in their hands as citizens.

In another work one of the authors has argued at length that a way to reduce crime is to exploit better the power of reprobation by shifting away from punitive social control and towards moralizing social control (Braithwaite 1989). If the analysis in that book is right, reprobation would be well served by a widespread policy of giving offenders less than most retributivists would regard as the deserved punishment. It implies that reprobationism, even of a strictly retributivist sort, requires a shift away from punishment by moving many cases out of the criminal justice system into informal arenas of denunciatory social control. So reprobationism hardly supplies a satisfactory answer to the 'why punish?' question. Frequently punishment will heighten reprobation; but in other cases a concern about reprobation will cause us to want to shift existing practices away from punishment.

Consider Nozick, who justifies punishment as 'reconnecting' the offender with correct values from which her offence has disconnected her. Nozick is obscure on what being 'reconnected' means, except that it is clear that it need not mean remorse or repentance or any sort of internalization of these correct values. Rather, we punish the offender because we want these correct values to have 'some significant effect in his life' (Nozick 1981: 375). A significant effect seems to mean that the offender is brought to understand the correct values without necessarily accepting them (Nozick 1981: 380). We can therefore only agree with Ten that this seems to provide less a justification for punishment than a justification for institutions concerned with communication and moral reasoning:

> But if the recipient of retributive punishment can be connected with correct values merely by his understanding that he is being punished because others regard what he is doing as wrong, and without his accepting their values, then punishment has not been justified. For we can surely ensure that the offender understands even when the message is conveyed to him verbally in appropriately strong terms. (Ten 1987: 45)

The reprobative retributivist has quite a research agenda on hand if he hopes to show that imposing formal punishments commensurate to the wrongdoing of offenders is the way to advance reprobation or to issue reprobation commensurate to the wrongdoing. For the reasons we have discussed, our prediction on this empirical question is that the correlation between length of prison term and reprobation, however defined, will be low. Most variance in reprobation will be explained by such variables as whether or not there is an arrest, a conviction, media coverage of the crime, and whether the trial convinces friends and relatives of the offender that he is blameworthy. If length of prison term explains very little variance in reprobation, then attempting to guarantee proportionate reprobation by calibrating months in prison is crudely misplaced quantification.

What have we established in this section? We have shown that intrinsic retributivism is unattractive. Because punishment must be reconciled with the intuition that it is generally wrong to inflict suffering intentionally, reasons must be given for punishment; it is not enough to claim merely that it is good that the guilty suffer. We also argued against the views that punishment is warranted to restore the balance of benefits and burdens disturbed by the offence and that punishment is warranted to annul the crime. We spent considerable time, finally, dealing with the retributivist theory that the point of punishment is to denounce crime: to provide due reprobation. Denunciation of crime is an unexceptionable good and the pursuit of just reprobation is a fundamentally important way of preventing crime and protecting dominion. We argue, however, that punishing people commensurately to their deserts is not even a remotely satisfactory way of maximizing reprobation or of exemplifying a reprobative stance.

Apart from specific criticisms of specific proposals, there is a general point that we would like to make against all the retributivist rationales for punishment. This is a point we noted in Chapter 4. Giving a rationale for a retributivist constraint can easily slip into identifying a goal whose promotion generally justifies, in consequentialist fashion, the honouring of that constraint. Yet putting the goal in our sights in this way can easily mean the betrayal of the proper retributivist attitude, according to which the relevant constraints are fundamental moral factors, on a par with the natural rights invoked by some political theorists (cf. Hampton 1984: 215–16; Ten 1987: 60). Indeed,

Sher and Hampton are explicit on the point that the rationales they respectively favour—the balancing of benefits and burdens and the annulment of wrongdoing—should be seen in a consequentialist light; they are target-retributivists to this extent, not retributivists proper.

Our own attitude is this. We think that retributivists face a difficult choice. They can refuse to give a rationale for the desert-constraints they invoke, as many natural rights theorists refuse to give a rationale for rights. In that case they certainly cannot be accused of covert consequentialism but their attachment to the constraints in question looks arbitrary; fundamental natural rights are difficult enough to stomach, fundamental natural deserts look wholly unpalatable. Alternatively, retributivists can offer a rationale for their favoured constraints, in the fashion of the theorists reviewed in this section. In that case they may succeed in making the constraints look more attractive but their retributivism begins to look questionable; they begin to look like consequentialists who want to promote the factor quoted in the rationale and who defend the constraints as means for generally promoting it.

In conclusion, it may be useful to add a further general point against certain retributivist rationales. This is that so far as retributivists represent punishment as good in itself, a way of producing a certain equilibrium or annulment, or a form of moral education, they raise a question about whether punishment is the sort of thing with which the state should concern itself (Gross 1979: 378–9). A leading retributivist thinker, Jeffrie Murphy, has posed the question nicely (Murphy 1985: 6):

> legal punishment must be justified in terms of compelling *state* interest, and it is hard to see that there is any state interest at all in bringing about this (perhaps ultimately desirable) state of affairs [just deserts]. There are many states of affairs that we might regard as desirable but for the achievement of which we would not form a state or government. If we lived in the absence of law and government, we might agree that it is in our rational interest to form a government for protection against external and internal violence (the basis for utilitarian deterrence theory). But is it likely that rational contractors would form a government and accept all the resulting limitations on freedom simply to bring about a proper apportionment (whatever that means) of evil and suffering? The very suggestion seems preposterous.

Murphy concludes that perhaps the only explanation of why we punish that is compatible with liberal attitudes is the preventionist one: 'deterrence (or some form of crime prevention) will always be the dominant general justifying aim of punishment' (Murphy 1985: 7). We can accept this further challenge to retributivist accounts of why to punish, confident that the challenge does not touch our own republican theory. It is hardly any more controversial to allocate to the state, through the criminal justice system, the role of promoting dominion than it is to give it the task, in Murphy's words, of protection against external and internal violence. Dominion is negative liberty, albeit liberty construed in a republican fashion, and few will reject the idea that the promotion of such liberty is a proper task for the state, at least in its criminal justice role. One of the authors has argued that the promotion of dominion is a proper task for the state in other roles too (Pettit 1989*a*). We do not have to go that far, however, in order to show how republican theory, unlike retributivism, is proof against Murphy's challenge. Even a libertarian about the state in its other aspects could reasonably endorse a republican view of the criminal justice system.

Who to Punish?

Retributivists who think that their explanation of why to punish holds up under our criticism will also hold that it provides guidance on who to punish. Full retributivists will say that we ought to punish only and all those who are guilty, negative retributivists that we ought to punish only those who are guilty but not necessarily all of them. But even retributivists who agree that they have no explanation of why to punish, even indeed retributivists who admit that the institution of punishment is best explained by consequentialist considerations—say, preventionist goals—hold that at least they have something to say on who to punish. Such retributivists follow Hart in distinguishing the general justifying aim of punishment from the aims to be followed in distributing punishment and argue that retributivism, full or negative, gives the proper answer to at least the distributional question.

Before turning to consider the answers provided by retributivists to the question of who to punish, we would like to comment on the position of retributivists who take this latter line, being, say, preventionist about why to punish but retributivist about who to punish (e.g. von Hirsch 1985). There is a tension, even an incoherence, in the position which, we believe, is often overlooked. The tension appears once we recognize that there will often be cases where the overall goal of the institution of punishment—say, crime prevention—is frustrated rather than furthered by the distribution of punishment according to retributivist standards of desert. How can something like the prevention of crime or the maximizing of utility be the overall goal of the institution, if punishment is distributed by standards that are not attuned to the promotion of the goal? If we give the deserved punishment in cases where doing so has bad consequences, the distribution of punishment defeats the general justification of engaging in the distribution.

To this charge it may seem that the retributivists in question can provide an answer derived from Rawls (1955) and indeed developed by us for our own purposes in Chapters 5 and 6. It may seem they can say that the retributivist standards should be such that the goal is furthered if the standards govern the distribution of punishment. But there are a variety of points to make. Whatever of a utilitarian goal, a preventionist goal can hardly be served by distributing punishment according to negative standards; refraining from punishing the innocent and refraining from punishing the guilty beyond the deserved level can hardly be construed as rules that prevent crime. And no matter which is held to be the goal of the system, it should be transparent that positive standards, standards which require us to punish all the guilty at the desired level, will make for a pattern of punishment which poorly promotes that goal. The possibilities of bargaining, persuasion, mercy, and voluntary compensation made possible by relaxing those standards would help the promotion of the goal, not hinder it.

Mixed retributivists of the sort under discussion argue rightly that punishment is sometimes necessary to achieve a good consequence like preventing crime or protecting the community: hence their resort to a consequentialist justification of the institution. But it is irrational to conclude that because punishment is *sometimes* necessary to protect the community, we should then set out to punish *consistently* or presumptively in accordance with full retributivist standards. Punishment that is driven by such standards will not always protect the community and may even weaken community protection. Full retributivists on matters of distribution must insist that desert be dispensed even when this has such a weakening effect. Their position is scarcely coherent, if they try to argue at the same time that the point of having a system of distributing punishment is to promote community protection.

We make these points here, because we think that the sort of retributivism which combines utilitarian or preventionist goals for the institution of punishment with a retributivist system of distribution has a false charm, a charm that may beguile anxious retributivists who are worried about our criticisms of the standard responses to the 'why punish?' question. But now we must return to consider in their own right the answers given by retributivists to the question of 'who to punish?' Here the salient distinction is between those who uphold just negative desert constraints and those full retributivists who also uphold positive constraints.

We take issue with both full and negative retributivists, so far as they invoke constraints that are meant to be fundamental and underived. The only constraints we would countenance are ones that can be derived from the republican goal of increasing dominion. But we have a much greater quarrel with full retributivists on the question of who to punish than with negative ones. Most of this section then will be devoted to a discussion of full retributivism. Before getting on to that discussion, however, it may be useful to comment fully on our attitude to the negative doctrine.

We agree with negative retributivists, for republican reasons, that indeed only the guilty ought to be punished, and we agree with them further that mercy is often desirable. For us, mercy is simply refraining, for good reasons, from imposing legally legitimate punishment. We will not comment on retributive arguments in support of mercy (e.g. Smart 1968; Card 1972; Sadurski 1985; Raphael 1955; McCloskey 1965; Armstrong 1961; Gross 1979; Garcia 1986; Murphy and Hampton 1989). But we have some remarks to make on the case retributivists often put for why it is legitimate to punish those found guilty of crime. We are not impressed by this case. We think it is conspicuously unpersuasive beside our own argument that we may punish the guilty when, and of course only when, it is certainly necessary for promoting dominion.

The retributivist case for why it is legitimate to punish the guilty is that the offender forfeits her claim to freedom from suffering. Enjoying rights normally entails duties to honour the same rights of others and the argument is that when we neglect these duties, our rights cease to exist. But Burgh (1982: 198) points out that a judge who violates a defendant's right to a fair trial does not forfeit her own right to a fair trial. If *X* violates a contract or the right of *Y* to free speech, *X* does not forfeit her right to enter contracts or to free speech. Violation of the rights of others is not sufficient to justify loss of one's own rights; intentional infliction of suffering on others does not, necessarily, justify the loss of one's own right not to suffer. To believe otherwise is to accept the reasoning of the *lex talionis*—because I violate a right by taking an eye, the state can violate my right by taking my eye.

Hart and others attempt to justify the required reciprocity of rights by defining the law as a choosing system 'in which individuals can find out, in general terms at least, the costs they have to pay if they act in certain ways' (Hart 1968: 44–7). 'The price is justly extracted . . . within this framework the individual is given a fair opportunity to choose between keeping the law required for society's protection or paying the penalty by being punished' (Hart 1968: 44, 22). Burgh compares this scenario, however, with the terrorist putting captives on notice that should they choose to attempt escape, they will be beaten. Does the fact that there was due notice of the rules, a fair opportunity to avoid punishment, a free choice to break the rules, make punishment just? The conclusion from his terrorist example is that 'if we begin with the presumption that punishment is prima facie wrong, in virtue of its involving the deliberate infliction of suffering, we do not make it right by distributing it on terms that are fair' (Burgh 1982: 200).

There is an obvious objection to this conclusion but it is easily resisted. The victim of the terrorist beating may have freely chosen to be liable for the beating, it will be said, but she did not choose the rules which made her liable. The laws of a democracy, in contrast, are freely chosen by its citizens. But this is nonsense: the rapist can justly claim that he had no influence whatsoever in writing rape laws enacted before his birth; and similarly for most other criminal offenders.

So much for our differences with negative retributivists on their approach to the question of who to punish. We turn now to full retributivism, and in particular to the positive retributivist claim that all those found guilty should be punished. For full retributivists, as John Rawls describes their position, 'the state of affairs where a wrongdoer suffers punishment is morally better than the state of affairs where he does not' (Rawls 1955: 4). Giving the guilty less than the deserved punishment is immoral (Morris 1968; Hestevold 1983). According to Kant, the guilty person must be punished and if we remit the penalty we are guilty ourselves: 'and woe to him who creeps through the serpent-windings of utilitarianism to discover some advantage that may discharge him from the justice of punishment, or even from the due measure of it' (Kant 1887: 195). Or to quote Kant's most famous illustration of the categorical obligation to punish:

> Even if a Civil Society resolved to dissolve itself with the consent of all its members—as might be supposed in the case of a People inhabiting an island resolving to separate and scatter themselves through the whole world—the last Murderer lying in the prison ought to be executed before the resolution was carried out. This ought to be done in order that every one may realise the desert of his deeds, and the bloodguiltiness may not remain upon the people; for otherwise they might all be regarded as participators in the murder as a public violation of justice. (Kant 1887: 198)

There is a major divergence here between full retributivism and our republican theory, or indeed almost any consequentialist doctrine. Instances where withholding desert is in the interests of crime control are not 'crazy cases'. Any schoolteacher or parent knows that it is often in the interests of building commitment to future compliance with the rules to give the child a second chance, a warning that she has been let off this time. It is a sociological fact that any system of social control which attempts consistently to punish every detected infraction of the society's norms will collapse under its own totalitarian weight. Perhaps the most effective systems of social control carry pretty big sticks, but they use them with reluctance.

Earlier we spoke of the literature on business regulation which suggests that compliance is more likely to be maximized by policies which confront most detected offences with warnings and persuasive overtures on the need to comply in future, saving punishment for recalcitrant offenders (Braithwaite 1985; Scholz 1984). The fact is that moralizing social control in general works better than punitive control (Braithwaite 1989). If this empirical claim is right, then preventionism and our republican theory require widespread resort to mercy and forgiveness, while full retributivism 'bars disproportionate leniency as well as disproportionate severity' (von Hirsch 1976: 73).

However, full retributivism should be abandoned not only because mercy has good consequences, but because in any possible world, criminal justice policy and practice cannot be faithful to the adage that 'justice requires the conviction of the guilty' (Morris 1968: 478). The infeasibility of denying prosecutors the discretion to be selective in deciding who to prosecute is beyond doubt, and retributivists do not generally denounce such discretion (but see Murphy and Hampton 1989: 173). However, a policy of prohibiting non-punitive judgements, even only at the sentencing stage, is also of doubtful feasibility. Could the criminal justice system cope with all judges insisting that offenders convicted be given a punishment commensurate with the seriousness of their crime? Prison systems would be overwhelmed if the common practices of letting offenders off with a warning, bond, suspended sentence, or probation were ended.

If we think comprehensively about the problem, going beyond the ordinary limits of retributivist concern, it is clear that equally one cannot operate a police force, an environmental inspectorate, or a prosecutor's office which adheres to the principle that it is obligatory to convict all who are guilty. It just cannot be done. Most crimes will continue to have surveillance and investigation costs which will render conviction impossible for the majority of suspected offences. Police and prosecutors have no choice but to breach positive retributive constraints on a daily basis.

The retributivist may say that retributivism was only ever intended to be a theory of sentencing and that these observations about police and prosecutors are irrelevant. But we saw in Chapter 2 that sentencing is a process embedded in a wider network of interacting processes, and that if judges suddenly ceased extending mercy to minor offenders, prosecutors and police officers may take it upon themselves to extend that mercy by declining to bring minor cases before judges. Besides, if it is wrong for the judge not to punish the guilty man, why is it not also wrong for the prosecutor or the police officer to let the guilty man go free? We decide not to criminalize most of the things in this world that are very wrong (lying, infidelity, unkindness) because criminalizing them would not secure good consequences. On the same grounds why should we not decide against uselessly punishing something already criminalized?

To mandate punishment of the guilty is to propagate a legalist imperialism. The legalist leaves no space for other values to play a part in the interpretation and resolution of social problems. Legalism in this way is anathema to the republican sense of a shared, participatory public life. Christie (1981: 57) captured the problem eloquently when he talked about training in law as training in simplification, of the danger of 'a trained incapacity to look at all values in a situation'. Insistence on the retributivist constraint that the guilty must be punished means that all known crimes must be legally processed; to deal with them extra-legally, under the auspices of soft values like mercy, forgiveness, education, tolerance, shaming, recompense, repentance, turning the other cheek, is wrong. Societies that do not rein in legalism (which full retributivism manifests) beget levels of litigiousness which leave less space for the dominion of citizens.

Retributivists have provided a sound analysis of certain problems such as the way agents of the system arbitrarily abuse the power they derive from unbridled discretion under indeterminate sentencing. Yet the cure prescribed is sometimes worse than the problem diagnosed. 'A system is created where the whims of the administrators are exchanged for an enormously powerful, simple and centralized system of state control' (Christie 1981: 52). Rather than try to confine discretion in a state-imposed straitjacket we should be searching for ways of making the exercise of discretion more directly accountable to those citizens most likely to suffer from its abuse—searching for a republican rather than a formally legal model of accountability.

We have made two criticisms of the full retributivist policy that all those found guilty should be punished: first, that it is likely to worsen crime problems needlessly; and second, that it is neither affordable nor feasible.

Finally, we would like to comment on the line which full and indeed also negative retributivists sometimes run that in considering who to punish they think of offenders as persons in their own right, ends-in-themselves, whereas consequentialists treat offenders as means or fail in some other way to respect them as persons (Morris 1968). We agree that enforced therapy of the kind that some preventionists have supported is inherently disrespectful and, as indicated in Chapter 6, we join with retributivists in rejecting it. But we would argue that the responses we favour towards offenders, and the grounds on which we think that the responses should be decided, do not involve us in treating offenders less as persons than retributivists.

Retributivists argue that punishment is superior to enforced therapy because it treats individuals as persons. They may be right. But on the criterion of treating individuals as persons, persuasion and reprobation—the responses favoured in republican theory—are surely the responses to be preferred. People tend to resent punishment as an affront to their sense of responsibility; they view themselves as capable of seeing reason about any wrongdoing they may have perpetrated without being coerced into remorse by a spanking. Persuasion and reprobation treat people as responsible moral agents who choose what to do on the basis of reasoning that is sensitive to moral considerations. The punishment model of social control, in contrast, projects an image of human agents as amoral calculators, weighing the benefits of crime against the costs of punishment.

Retributivists also argue that they treat individuals as persons, so far as the question of whether to punish someone is decided by the inherent desert of that person, not by whether punishing him will mean that some distinct end like overall dominion is promoted thereby. As against this line, however, we would urge that republican theory is no less fair than retributivism, so far as it allows only the guilty to be punished—say, to be imprisoned—and that while it may justify punishment for consequentialist reasons, this generates far more humane and respecting attitudes.

Under republican theory, we make the guilty suffer only to prevent the greater evil of more suffering elsewhere. It follows then that we should feel morally uncomfortable about what we are doing, just as we should feel morally uncomfortable rather than morally upright about killing the soldiers of an evil dictator, locking up a mental patient, or putting in quarantine the carrier of a contagious disease. The retributivist will certainly feel morally uncomfortable about the quarantine of an innocent, but when it comes to intentionally inflicting suffering on the criminal, her approach allows her to feel morally upright: after all, the suffering is deserved. But this feeling is misplaced in our view; it is a dangerous practice to foster the belief that the criminal has forfeited his claim on our concern about making him suffer.

A virtue of the republican theory is that it compels us to confront the unpalatable fact that we cannot run the criminal justice system without treating people as means by imposing upon their dominion. It accepts the inevitability of arresting and trying the innocent, of imposing upon witnesses and taxpayers as means to secure the protection of others. At times, if we are unwilling to arrest and interrogate a number of (mostly innocent) suspects, we will increase the risks of conviction of the innocent. Unless we are willing to treat these suspects, subpoenaed witnesses, and taxpayers as means, the ends of justice cannot possibly be served. Republicanism accepts that as we treat such people as means so we punish guilty criminals as means to secure the protection of dominion for others. This treatment of people other than as ends-in-themselves invites a posture of moral reluctance rather than moral smugness, and that is surely a strength.

How to Punish?

There are really two questions here: what should be the severity of the punishment where punishment is imposed, and what should be the nature of the punishment?

We can dispense very quickly with the deficiencies of retributivism in recommending the nature (as opposed to the quantum) of punishment. While our republican theory can give clear guidance on the nature of punishment (see Chapter 6), retributivism supplies no means for evaluating which form of punishment is better than another. If five lashes (*A*) are as painful as two months in prison (*B*) or as restitution of $10,000 (*C*), then in the terms of neo-retributivist theory, there is no way of choosing among them. Von Hirsch (1988: 557) readily concedes that 'a desert rationale addresses only the severity of penalties, not their particular form'. This was not true of the old retributivism of an eye for an eye, a tooth for a tooth. Having torpedoed such views from the old retributivist tradition, the new retributivists have left themselves with nothing to say about the form of punishment, at least nothing that is derived from their theory.

It is on the question of severity in the allocation of punishment that retributivism is generally believed to be on its strongest ground. The retributivist critique has shown that it is impossible to go to the criminological journals to ascertain the level of deterrence, incapacitation, or rehabilitation required to bring the level of any kind of crime down to a preventionist target. We will first consider the likely retributive critique of this aspect of our republican theory, and then we will look at the positive credentials of retributivist theory: here we cover ground already traversed in Chapter 7.

Retributivism has generated quite a detailed working through of how to decide which crimes deserve greater punishment and which less, led by the creative scholarship of Andrew von Hirsch. Retributivists will be critical of the incrementalism outlined in Chapter 7 because it threatens the well-ordered gradation of penalties that has been the major policy contribution of their tradition. It might well happen, they will say, that punishments for murder can be drastically cut without adversely affecting the murder rate, while any cut in sentences for burglars will accelerate an ever-increasing burglary rate. In the end, we might be sending burglars away for longer average terms of imprisonment than murderers, and this would be palpably unjust.

Our first response to this is that we are against pointless suffering, even of murderers. The reason murder is not very susceptible to deterrence is that so many of these offences are one-off crimes of passion. For the woman who murders her husband in a moment of provoked anger, who understands the enormity of what she has done, who is already punishing herself terribly with guilt and remorse, who is never likely to reoffend, it may be better to leave her in the hands of the informal social control of her family; some of those wounds will have a better chance to heal if she is with her family rather than in prison. This is not such a radical proposition. In 27 per cent of murder cases in

Japan, sentences of imprisonment are suspended; many of these are cases where the criminal justice system decides that the family or community of the offender can do a better job of dealing with the problem than it can.

Yet to be against pointless suffering is perhaps not a totally satisfactory stance. Even within a republican theoretical framework, we must be concerned if the community becomes so exercised about serious offenders getting lighter sentences than minor offenders that it loses confidence in the criminal justice system. Voluntary compliance can break down and even vigilantism can arise when community respect for the law and its institutions is sufficiently eroded. This surely is one of the most important consequences to monitor should we ever achieve marked success in winding back punishment. Indeed, we would not have to set out to monitor it; the political realities are that even the slightest rumblings of this kind of concern are magnified by the law-and-order lobby. It is a near certainty that a stop would be put to any movement towards a system where serious street offenders systematically were being punished less than minor offenders. At least this is true in the punitive cultures of contemporary Western societies. Note that this political certainty relates to street offenders. There is no certainty about halting the situation where serious white-collar criminals are punished less than minor criminals.

But it is interesting to note that even in Japan the non-incarceration of murderers is achieved by suspended sentences of imprisonment, not by declining to impose a prison term. Retributivists find this hypocrisy deplorable. As consequentialists, however, we can tolerate the hypocrisy of maximum penalties being set reasonably high without being used, of sentences being imposed only to be suspended, because this may achieve the symbolic reprobative functions of the criminal law while toning down the excesses of its repression of dominion.

This is the bark-and-bite theory of criminal justice. If we take denunciation seriously as a way of controlling crime, then the criminal justice system should bark a lot. We cannot afford a system that bites every time it barks. So long as it bites often enough to make the bark credible, that is all we need. Even the watch-dog who never bites demonstrates that bluff is not without power in social control.

A common ground we share with von Hirsch (1985), Nozick (1981), and Hampton (1984) is that denunciation is a central justification for the criminal justice system, though we are moved by different reasons. Under our theory, denunciation can contribute towards crime control (Braithwaite, 1989), while showing maximum respect for individual persons: that is, while minimally encroaching upon dominion. The maximum penalties set down in law, we believe, do give an important reprobative message to the community. It is the job of the legislature to deal with the symbolic end of the problem, to declare solemnly in its enactment of laws that this is more evil than that. So we would be troubled by a legislature that reduced the penalties provided for murder to the point where the community was given the message that our political leaders no longer believe that taking the life of another human being is the ultimate evil. Those of us who believe in denunciation and reprobation must take symbolic politics seriously. That does not mean, however, that the *Realpolitik* of implementation must be brought into line with symbolic politics. Is this an undemocratic duping of the people? We think not; we think the people are sophisticated enough to understand that action thoroughly consistent with our symbolic politics would not be in our interests. They like a government which denounces foreign repressive regimes that are considered deserving of reprobation; but that does not mean that they think the state should be so imprudent as to bite as often as it barks.

So while we think it important for the legislature to reduce maximum penalties and to abolish all minima in order to manifest and implement its commitment to a dominion-respecting criminal justice system, and while we would want penalty reductions to be pursued most aggressively with crimes where there will clearly be no adverse consequences on the crime rate from doing so, we would want to constrain this process by a need to preserve the crude but nevertheless important message the legislature gives, namely that some crimes are more evil than others. The latter constraint is one which leaves wide scope for the pursuit of good consequences because it would be foolish to assume that there is much precision in the nexus between the level of statutory maxima and the reprobative message on the hierarchy of criminal evils. The constraint does not inhibit general reductions in maxima that maintain a rough ordering, or lower average sentences under the maxima. So long as the statutory maximum for murder is significantly higher than that for burglary, it probably is of no great consequence for this reprobative purpose whether it is 20 per cent higher or twice as high or ten times as high. Yet whether the achievement of reprobative purposes is sensitive to the ordinal but not the interval scaling of maximum penalties is an empirical question, a question which can and should be put to the test under a decremental policy. We reiterate that the constraint of maintaining a rough ordering of maxima in proportion to the seriousness of the crime is so politically impregnable that the possibility of its breach is not a major practical concern.

But it is misleading to suggest that republicans are on the defensive on the question of how to punish. We have already argued in Chapter 7 that retributivists should not be smug about the superior justice of their commitment to neatly calibrated penalties. For all the rhetoric of just deserts, no retributivist can answer any question about what is the deserved punishment for any given act. As Pepinsky and Jesilow (1984: 122) quip, they cannot tell us 'how many years of a person's liberty equals the value of a lost television set.' Retributivism cannot tell us what is the right punishment for murder, whether it should be 20 per cent higher or twice as high as that for burglary. The eighteenth-century judge who sentences the burglar to torture followed by death, the judge from Alabama who sentences him to ten years, and the judge from Amsterdam who sentences him to victim compensation all pronounce that they are giving the offender what he deserves. There is no retributivist answer as to which judge is right. On the retributivist's view, so long as they are all handing down sentences for burglary that are proportionately more than those for less-serious crimes and proportionately less than those for more-serious crimes, they could all be right.

There is quite an impressive consensus within and even between modern societies on which types of crimes deserve most punishment and which least (Rossi *et al.* 1974; Newman 1976; Thomas *et al.* 1976; Wright and Cox 1967*a*, *b*; Sellin and Wolfgang 1964; Wilson and Brown 1973; New South Wales Bureau of Crime Statistics and Research 1974; Chilton and DeAmicis 1975; Figlio 1975; Hamilton and Rytina 1980; Riedel 1975; Rose and Prell 1955; Wellford and Wiatrowski 1975; Pontell *et al.* 1983; Kwasniewski

1984; Rossi *et al.* 1985; but note the caveats of Miethe 1982, 1984, and Cullen *et al.* 1985). But there is enormous disagreement on how severely we should punish in general (Wolfgang *et al.* 1985; Durham 1988). The new retributivism gives us detailed guidance on the easy question but none on the hard one. In Chapter 7 we could not accept Kleinig's (1973) valiant attempt to make headway on the matching of punishment to crime. But even if we did assume that it was reasonable to allocate the lightest possible sentence to the most minor possible crime and to limit the scaling of penalties to days in prison, the decision of what the lightest possible sentence will be has such dramatic implications as to render the whole exercise arbitrary. In jurisdiction *A*, the lowest allowable sentence of imprisonment is one month; in jurisdiction *B* it is one day or three eight-hour periods of weekend detention. Suppose that armed robbery with violence is scaled as 300 times as serious as the most minor crime conceivable. In jurisdiction *B*, this means armed robbery with violence will attract 300 days; in jurisdiction *A*, 25 years.

The spuriousness of retributivist precision in calibrating commensurate deserts should be unmasked in other ways as well. One of the advantages of preventionism is that its mistakes are frequently visible—under policies of selective incapacitation or rehabilitation, a convicted rapist is shown to commit another rape as soon as he is released. The vagueness of desert, in contrast, masks mistakes. To define systematically the factors that are major determinants of desert is a tall order. When people are misclassified into the wrong category of desert, this cannot be at all obvious in a world where each crime is unique and will never occur in the same circumstances again. Mistakes are covered up by the jumbled nature of facts about blameworthiness and the limited time available for anyone bar those intimately involved to comprehend them. Lawyers' reifications of blame and harm elevate the cover-up of misclassification to a high level of technocratic rationality under retributivist sentencing grids. But, as Zimring (1976: 331) queries, 'Can we rigorously patrol the border between forcible rape without additional bodily harm and that with further harm—when that distinction can mean the difference between six months and six years in the penitentiary?' If the rape victim is so brutalized that she can never enjoy sex again, is this bodily harm? If we do so count it, does it rate the same score on the sentencing grid as a black eye? Events which fall between the conceptual cracks of the sentencing grid get forced into a category of desert.

Is the caprice of forcing human beings into state-imposed categories which have little to do with the subtle realities of their predicament, and which allow the more quantifiable to drive out the more important, better or worse than the caprice of the therapist making judgements about the future of human beings? We don't know. We only know that the mistakes of the former are less visible. The only accountability is to other legalists who, in appeals, apply the same reifications even further removed from the raw data of complex human interactions. Of course, simplification of complex and subtle social processes is inevitable in criminal justice systems. We bear no easy solutions. But we do warn against false promises of fairness from quantification of the human condition, from an assumption that non-discretionary quantification of evil is a good reason to sacrifice other values.

A crucial distinction between consequentialists and retributivists lies in the commitment of consequentialists to seek to understand all of the values in a situation, at least all of those relevant to the preferred goal: in our case, the protection of dominion. Christie (1981) talks of the 'hidden curriculum' of retributivism in these terms. We are familiar with the idea of the dangers of the 'hidden curriculum' of the education system—that there is a correct solution to problems, and only one solution, and this is to be found by reference to the authority of the teacher or textbook, and so on. For Christie, the hidden curriculum of retributivism is that the unproblematic notion of something being defined as a criminal act is all that matters in deciding what to do about a social problem; the criminal category is the decisive fact, not the wishes of the victim, the family circumstances of the offender, non-retributive value claims such as the demands of compassion, nor the possibility of a community solving its own problems rather than handing them over to professionals.

Conclusion

In this Chapter we have tried to tackle retributivism on its own ground. Abstracting from the retributivist failure to provide a comprehensive theory, we have attempted to show that retributivism provides inferior answers to the 'how', 'who', and 'why' questions of punishment, in particular answers inferior to those supplied by republican theory. While retributivism is already deficient in focusing more-or-less exclusively on such issues, it is doubly deficient in providing inferior answers to them.

9

Retributivism: An Inferior Practice

What we will show in this Chapter is that retributivism is incapable of dealing with the complexities of modern society, in particular complexities associated with white-collar crime. We shall argue that the just deserts model is neither desirable nor feasible as a response to such crime and that its implementation would have the practical effect of increasing rather than decreasing certain unjust inequalities.

Just Deserts and Injustice

The critique which follows applies to positive or full retributivism. It does not apply to negative retributivism, which outlaws only punishment of the innocent and punishment beyond that which is deserved. The problem arises with those who want to constrain the criminal justice system to punish the guilty, and to punish them in proportion to their desert.

There are a number of facts about the way the world works, mostly facts about the distribution of power, which prevent punishment from being imposed on those most deserving of it. A policy of attempting punishment of all those who deserve it (and who can be caught) has the effect of increasing injustice, worsening tendencies to punish most where desert is least. This is because of a tendency for the law to be 'the most powerful where the least needed, a sprinkler system that turns off when the fire gets too hot' (Geertz 1983: 217).

To begin to document this claim, consider first that there are a number of bureaucratic realities about criminal justice systems which conduce to the theorem that *where desert is greatest, punishment will be least*. One is the problem of system capacity (Pontell 1978; Nagin 1978). System capacity theory suggests that those locations in space and time where crime is greatest, and those types of crime where offending is most widespread and serious, are precisely where the criminal justice system resorts to leniency in order to keep cases moving and avert system overload. This can happen in many ways. The prosecutor in a high crime district who is presented with evidence of ten possible charges against an offender prosecutes only on the easiest to prove, so that she can move on to the next case; the prosecutor in the low crime district is under less pressure, so finds the time to develop a case with respect to all ten. The prosecutor overwhelmed with serious cases might cave in to a cosy plea bargain on a serious case more readily, while the prosecutor with only a couple of serious cases in his case-load would take all of them to trial. Plea bargaining is perhaps so much more endemic in the United States than in other developed countries because, with its rampant crime rates, there are more criminals deserving of severe punishment in that country.

The bureaucratic realities of criminal justice administration inevitably result in systemic pressures towards lenient treatment of sophisticated criminals and tough treatment of unsophisticated ones. Organized crime is costly to investigate; why bother when disorganized crime supplies plenty of easy marks to make the department's prosecution, clear-up, or conviction statistics look good? When organized crime is investigated, it is soon found to be easier to get evidence against fungible operatives than against the bosses and criminal strategists. Again, punishment becomes toughest where desert is least. For all types of crime, the offence perpetrated by a serious professional repeat offender is less likely to be punished than one perpetrated by an amateur or first offender (Moore *et al*. 1984). Kids are more likely to be caught than hardened adult offenders.

But these bureaucratic pressures towards a negative correlation between desert and punishment are not the most fundamental ones. The most deep-seated pressures have to do with power. What we will now set out to show is that in the terms of retributivist theory, there are more white-collar criminals deserving severe punishment in any society than blue-collar criminals deserving severe punishment. Attempts to give all who are guilty what they deserve, however, will successfully impose desert on blue-collar offenders and will be unsuccessful with white-collar crime. It is a sociological inevitability that most of those in our prisons will have blue collars or black faces, while just deserts implies that most of our prisoners should be white-collar criminals. But let us now go back to the first point in this allegation and try to defend the contention that white-collar criminals make up the majority of those deserving severe punishment.

The Volume of White-Collar Crime

Even on the basis of limited data sets for limited time periods, the work of Sutherland (1949) and Clinard *et al.* (1979) leads to the conclusion that most major corporations are recidivist law-breakers. It is difficult to find any large American corporations which have not been responsible for a serious corporate crime in recent decades.

If we exclude from consideration victimless crimes (for example, drug-use or consensual sexual offences) and traffic violations, the volume of offences is almost certainly greater for white-collar crime than for blue-collar crime. This can be sustained by showing that certain offences which constitute only a minor part of the white-collar crime problem are so common as almost to equal in number *all* the traditional offences dealt with by the police.

For example, a study of milometer fraud in Queensland found that over a third of vehicles randomly selected from used car sale-rooms had had their mileage readings turned back (Braithwaite 1978). The sample in this study is not sufficient to permit us to assert with confidence that this kind of fraud occurs for a third of the used cars sold in Queensland. Nevertheless, using a third as the best estimate available, there would be about 70,000 milometer frauds in Queensland each year. This is almost equal to the total of 80,181 offences of all types (including victimless crimes, but excluding public-order offences such as drunkenness and vagrancy) reported to the Queensland police in the year of the study. Moreover, in most milometer frauds there is a conspiracy involving more than one offender (Braithwaite 1978: 108–9). There were no prosecutions whatsoever for this offence in the year of the study, nor in the year previous or subsequent. Moving to a more respectable profession, Quinney found that 25 per cent of pharmacists in Albany, New York had been found by government investigators to have violated prescription laws. Government surveys in two Australian jurisdictions have found 15 and 32 per cent of petrol pumps respectively to be giving short-measure petrol to motorists (*Sunday Telegraph*, 3 Feb. 1980; *Canberra Times*, 13 Jan. 1981). When one considers the number of times each car has its tank filled, the number of offences annually is in the millions in each of these jurisdictions, though in one of them there had not been a prosecution for this kind of offence for twelve years.

What then of serious crimes by large corporations, as opposed to the widespread dollars and cents frauds of petrol station proprietors, used car dealers, and pharmacists? Few crimes could be more serious than bribing government health officials to entice them to allow a drug on the market which is banned in many other parts of the world. Yet in many countries this is common practice by transnational pharmaceutical companies (Braithwaite 1984). Nineteen of the twenty largest American pharmaceutical companies have disclosed foreign bribes to the Securities and Exchange Commission (Braithwaite 1984). Every significant coal-mine in the United States receives at least a few fines each year for violations of mine safety laws. Each year the Mine Safety and Health Administration fines over 100,000 offences (Braithwaite 1985). Kesner *et al.* (1986) estimated violation rates of antitrust laws and the Federal Trade Commission Act between 1980 and 1984 and concluded that Fortune 500 companies averaged nearly one violation apiece. With these kinds of offences, the number of individual offenders is often large. Wheeler *et al.* (1988: 339) found that twice as many white-collar crimes as non-violent common crimes involved six or more persons. All in all, the volume of corporate offences, combined with the high probability of multiple offenders for each offence in a complex organization, is sufficient to invert conventional assessments of the class distribution of crime.

Of course the data we have on the volume of white-collar crime is rather inadequate. It is much easier to determine how many bank robberies there have been in the United States during a year than it is to count the violations of the Occupational Safety and Health Act. Victim surveys are possible with common crimes but not for white-collar crimes, which mostly have diffuse, unidentifiable victims or victims who do not know they are victims.

Antitrust offences provide the classic illustration. Consider the tetracycline class actions allegations that as a result of an illegal price-fixing conspiracy a large proportion of the population of the United States and the whole world suffered artificially high prices during the 1950s and 1960s whenever they consumed broad-spectrum antibiotics (Braithwaite 1984). The many people in the Third World who died because they could not afford the new wonder drugs would never have conceived of themselves as having been victims of a violation of US antitrust laws.

Thus, there can never be a systematic comparison of the volume of white-collar crime with that of common crime. All we can do is demonstrate what we know to be the minimum volume of certain offences which constitute a minor part of the white-collar crime problem. It is then up to readers to judge whether this enormous volume is sufficient, when put against our knowledge of common crime from reports to the police and victim surveys, to make it plausible that there is more white-collar than common crime. If we exclude victimless crimes and traffic violations, we think that the inference, even in the absence of systematic data, is not only plausible, but overwhelming.

The Seriousness of White-Collar Crime

White-collar crime may be common, but is it serious, and therefore deserving of severe punishment? Until recently it was usual for criminologists to account for the non-punitive nature of the response to white-collar crime by presuming community tolerance towards this kind of offending. Now that a great deal of evidence from public opinion surveys on this question has been gathered from many countries, we know this is not so (Grabosky *et al.* 1987). The community views most kinds of white-collar crime as very serious (tax offences and false advertising being notable exceptions); when asked what sort of punishments different white-collar crimes deserve most people recommend horrendous prison terms well beyond those imposed even in extreme cases of the type.

Community perceptions of the deserved punishment is, of course, only one way of operationalizing desert. Mercifully it is not the way favoured by most retributivists. Retributivists generally favour implementation of desert by sentencing commissions of jurisprudential experts. These gurus are allegedly more sophisticated in their judgements of how many years' prison a lost television set is worth.

One principle for determining desert is endorsed on all sides. This is that offences which do more objective harm deserve more punishment. The lesson of this principle is obvious, for Sutherland (1949), and others since, have demonstrated that white-collar crime costs the community more than traditional crime:

> The financial cost of white-collar crime is probably several times as great as the financial cost of all the crimes which are customarily regarded as the 'crime problem'. An officer of a chain grocery store in one year embezzled $600,000, which was six times as much as the annual losses from five hundred burglaries and robberies of the stores in that chain. Public enemies numbered one to six secured $130,000 by burglary and robbery in 1938, while the sum stolen by Krueger is estimated at $250,000,000 or nearly two thousand times as much. The New York Times in 1931 reported four cases of embezzlement in the United States with a loss of more than a million dollars each and a combined loss of nine million dollars. Although a million-dollar burglar or robber is practically unheard of, these million-dollar embezzlers are small-fry among white-collar criminals. The estimated loss to investors in one investment trust from 1929 to 1935 was $580,000,000. (Sutherland 1949: 121–2)

In fact, at the end of the last century Barrett (1895) showed that banks lost more from fraud and embezzlement than from bank robberies. More recently, Johnson and Douglas (1978: 151) pointed out that the losses from the Equity Funding securities fraud alone were greater than the losses from all street crime in the United States for one year. Official inquiries consistently reach the conclusion that the cost to the community of white-collar crime exceeds that of other property crime (General Accounting Office 1978; Joint Economic Committee of the US Congress 1976; Saxon 1980: 8–13) with estimates of the cost differential ranging widely. At one extreme is the conclusion of the House Judiciary Subcommittee on Crime that white-collar crime cost the community fifty times as much (Conyers 1980), at the other the more guarded conclusion of the President's Commission on Law Enforcement and Administration of Justice:

There is no knowing how much embezzlement, fraud, loan sharking, and other forms of thievery from individuals or commercial institutions there is, or how much price-rigging, tax evasion, bribery, graft, and other forms of thievery from the public at large there is. The Commission's studies indicate that the economic losses those crimes cause are far greater than those caused by the three index crimes against property.

In addition to causing greater economic losses, white-collar crimes also pose the greater threat to relationships of trust which are vital to our political and economic systems. A spate of securities scams or bankruptcy frauds can threaten investor confidence, thereby capital formation, and thereby employment.

On the other hand, it can be argued that blue-collar crimes cause more fear in the community than white-collar crime. This may be so. But we should not underestimate the fear associated with many white-collar crimes. Anyone who has had to deal with panicked consumers fearing loss of life savings from the collapse of a bank, building society, or savings and loan association, knows the fear that a major fraud can cause. Anyone who has heard the screams of a nursing home resident as she resists the straps being tied around her arms and legs can understand the fear caused by facilities that flout laws regulating the use of restraints. These are not rare events: countless Americans have been affected by the recent savings and loans frauds; 38 per cent of American nursing home residents are physically restrained.[1]

Product-safety violations are perhaps responsible for more serious injuries than any other type of corporate offence. Magnuson and Carper (1968: 125) reported in the 1960s that in the United States each year, 150,000 people 'suffer excruciating pain and often lifelong scars from fires, resulting from a match or a lighted cigarette dropped on flammable clothing or upholstery', a problem that has been considerably reduced by consumer product-safety regulation since then. The National Commission on Product Safety estimated an annual rate of twenty million serious injuries associated with consumer products, with 110,000 resulting in permanent disability and 30,000 in death. The way large

[1] Data supplied by the Health Care Financing Administration from inspections of all American nursing homes.

numbers of people have been killed and injured by misrepresentation in the advertising of drugs has been well documented (Braithwaite 1984). One could go on to document the thousands of injuries and deaths caused annually by violations of automobile safety standards, foodstuffs legislation, pollution laws, and various other laws to protect the safety of consumers and workers. Single crimes on their own can cause massive injury. Consider the thousands of deaths and deformities to infants around the world caused by the fraud of a drug company in the thalidomide disaster (Knightley *et al.* 1979) or the thousands killed by the industrial-safety crimes at Chernobyl and Bhopal. Geis concluded, after referring to findings such as those of Ralph Nader on the building of potentially lethal cars and electrocution deaths caused by the failure to enforce legal safety requirements on electrical equipment, that 'support clearly seems to exist for the view that acts reasonably defined as white-collar crime result in more deaths and physical injuries than acts which have been traditionally defined as murder and manslaughter' (Geis 1973: 89; see also Monahan *et al.* 1979; Cullen *et al.* 1987).

But retributivists argue, correctly, that the seriousness of crime has two elements—the degree of harm and the culpability of the offender for that harm. Many white-collar offences (e.g. pollution offences) do not require proof of *mens rea* for a conviction. Nevertheless, the ethnographic evidence on regulatory inspection suggests that, at least in some important domains, inspectors do not recommend prosecutions unless they believe there to be intentional violation of the law (Hawkins 1984); accidental violations tend to be dealt with by warning and entreaty. It is naïve to assume that because a business offence is penalized under strict liability laws no intent was involved. Following more lengthy deliberation on this in an earlier work, one of the present authors concluded that:

> among that subset of crime which is intentional, white-collar crimes are greater in number and in harm (measured either objectively [in dollars or lives lost] or subjectively [by community ratings of seriousness or deserved punishment]). Therefore, it is reasonable to assert that just deserts, whether based on a subjective or objective calculus, implies that there should be more white-collar criminals sent to prison than common criminals. (Braithwaite 1982*a:* 750)

Why White-Collar Criminals Do Get Mercy

All too briefly, we have attempted in this Chapter to sketch how vast are the numbers of serious white-collar crimes in the community. To mobilize criminal enforcement against even the tiniest proportions of them would bankrupt the wealthiest of governments in the world. It is not just a matter of their number, but also their complexity. And it is the most serious white-collar crimes which tend to be the most complex. The complexity is partly inherent in the intricacy of the organizational structures within which they are embedded, in the complexity of the accounts, in technological complexity, and in jurisdictional complexity with offences which transcend national boundaries. But there is also contrived complexity arranged by sophisticated criminals who seek to make the paper-trail so difficult to follow, or the principles of organizational accountability so confused, that the investigator is led to drop the case in exasperation, and return to the less frustrating work of punishing small-fry. Needless to say, white-collar criminals are also generally well able to retain the legal talent who can exploit both the inherent and contrived complexity of the events to make proof beyond reasonable doubt a very onerous burden indeed.

An alternative to using their power to contrive complexity in order to deter investigation is for the powerful offender to buy off a junior scapegoat, or indeed to set him up as an easy victim without bothering to buy him off. Elsewhere, one of the authors has demonstrated, with many examples, that white-collar criminals use their power to pass blame downwards in the class structure (Braithwaite 1982*b*). So even within the white-collar crime category, the theorem holds that where desert is least punishment is greatest.

A further reason why white-collar offenders are more likely to escape punishment than blue-collar offenders is that while the latter are dealt with by the police, business offenders are mostly dealt with by specialized business regulatory agencies—environmental offenders by environmental protection agencies, food standards' offenders by food inspectorates, radiation offenders by nuclear regulatory inspectorates, and so on. Compared with the police, regulatory agencies are systematically less orientated to prosecution as the favoured means of securing compliance with the law. A study of 96 Australian regulatory agencies, for example, found that even though the smallest of them confronted thousands of offences each year, a third of the agencies had not launched a single prosecution during the three years of the study (Grabosky and Braithwaite 1986). In every country where empirical work on business regulatory enforcement has been done, a similar picture of more benign enforcement by the regulatory agencies than by the police has emerged. One of the authors has done research on dozens of business regulatory agencies on four continents without discovering one agency for which just deserts was a significant priority or even a subsidiary goal. The day the literature reports a business regulatory agency driven by desert, it will be akin to a zoologist announcing the discovery of a new species. While there are important differences of degree, there is almost a sociological inevitability that ruling-class constituencies will mobilize their political and economic power so that enforcement directed against them will be more muted than that which the police deliver against the working class.

That those white-collar criminals who deserve more punishment systematically get less than blue-collar criminals is not just a matter of power or regulatory capture. In the next section, we will see that regulatory officials find that it is in the public interest for them routinely to grant mercy to corporate criminals. It is generally both the easiest and best way for them to get their job done.

Why White-Collar Criminals Should Get Mercy

A literature is accumulating in the field of business regulatory enforcement which suggests that great sensitivity is required when punishment is used as a method of social control (Bardach and Kagan 1982; Braithwaite 1985; Scholz 1984; Cranston 1979; Hawkins 1984; Shover *et al.* 1983). Business regulatory agencies can sap the will of business to comply with the law by remorselessly punishing them whenever they slip up by breaching health and safety, consumer protection, pollution, antitrust, and other laws.

This is because, at its worst, an uncompromising punitive strategy can lead to what Bardach and Kagan call an 'organized culture of resistance'—a culture that facilitates the sharing of knowledge about the methods of legal resistance and counter-attack. As an example, Bardach and Kagan cite the advice of one legal expert: appeal all Occupational Health and Safety Administration (OSHA) citations, not just those to which companies object strongly, so that they can 'settle a case by giving up on some items in exchange for dismissal by OSHA of others. Those who leave certain things uncontested are needlessly giving up this possibility' (1982: 114).

Dissipating the motivation of business to strive for compliance with the law is a disastrous consequence because the punitive law enforcement alternative can never fill the gaps left by the failure of persuasion and education as compliance strategies. With all complex areas of business regulation one can never write rules to protect people against all the unsafe or exploitative practices that can occur. Since building consensus to write new rules is a difficult and time-consuming process, since rule writing does not keep up with rapidly changing technology, and since every business poses unique problems, government regulations never cover the field. The British, who have achieved the safest coal-mines in the world, make the point that if their inspectors enforced strict compliance with the Mines and Quarries Act 1954 and the regulations arising therefrom, they would enforce a far lower standard of safety practice than they in fact do (Braithwaite 1985). It is persuasion, heeded by responsible managers, which achieves the higher standards.

Achieving better than the minimum standards set down in law is imperative, but inspectors will not succeed if punishment has been used with so little finesse that they lose their capacity to persuade. Perhaps one reason why the United States has such a shocking coal-mine fatality-rate is that trust and respect between inspectors and managers has been lost by blunderbuss punishment policies. As the chief executive of the Bituminous Coal Operators' Association said when one of the authors interviewed him in 1982: 'Lives are lost because of inspectors with the paper syndrome and companies with the "How do we minimize the violations?" syndrome.'

Government inspectors achieve more by adopting a diagnostic and catalytic role than they can by focusing excessively on punishment. Bardach and Kagan underlined this point by quoting the safety director of a large corporation on what he thought OSHA inspectors should do:

> OSHA inspectors have the right to talk to employees. They'll go up to a machine operator and ask if everything is OK. What they really mean is, 'Is there a violation I can write up?' If the man points out a broken electrical cord or plug, the OSHA guy will just write it up and put it on the list of citations. What they should do is this: He should ask the employee 'How long has it been that way? Did you tell your foreman about it?' He should call over the foreman and ask why it was still that way. Maybe the foreman will say, 'I've told him three times . . . you're supposed to go to Supply and get a new cord.' Then why didn't he? Maybe his job is set up so he can't. Maybe the inspector will find out there's no procedure for checking cords, or that there is, but that the employees don't know it well. (1982: 148–9)

For white-collar crimes against the person—the very white-collar crimes about which the data show greatest community punitiveness—the case for selective enforcement is strongest. This is because the offence so often poses a continuing danger to the community. Just deserts must at times be sacrificed for protection of the public. Regulatory agencies often resist the urge to prosecute guilty parties when the co-operation of those parties is needed to safeguard the public health. If a drug company has criminally reckless quality control procedures which are putting the community at risk, an injunction to close down the plant followed by a criminal prosecution can set company lawyers to work on very effective delaying tactics (Braithwaite 1984). Justice delayed is profits retained. The public interest will often be better served by an approach to the company offering immunity from prosecution if it will co-operate in a package of measures which might include a voluntary recall of certain batches of impure drugs from the market, dismissal of certain irresponsible quality control staff, revision of standard operating procedures to improve product quality, and compensation to victims of the impure drugs. In a haphazard fashion, such negotiated settlements foster deterrence, often more so than the paltry fine which might be handed down by a court. But more importantly they do so while minimizing the risk to potential victims and maximizing help to existing victims. A voluntary recall of drugs already on the market is almost invariably more rapid and efficient (in the sense of maximizing the proportion of the batch which is located) than a court-ordered seizure (Hutt 1973). Only the company knows where all of its product has gone. A seizure that is resisted by the company faces considerable practical difficulties.

The same considerations apply with serious violations of food hygiene laws that result in widespread distribution of contaminated product. As a top executive of the Victorian Health Commission explained in an interview with Peter Grabosky and John Braithwaite:

> Prosecution then becomes rare for another reason. That is that our prime concern at that time is to lead to the discovery of the source and the termination of the outbreak. Now if you go in with a very punitive approach that we are trying to get evidence on somebody . . . then they do not want to incriminate themselves. Naturally, they are going to be difficult to get evidence from, they are not going to cooperate to the degree that we feel would be needed to speedily resolve an issue. So if we take that as our prime aim—the resolution of the problem—we very seldom automatically would take that to a prosecution.

In Chapter 6 we discussed how the thalidomide drug disaster prosecutions were halted in exchange for a quick compensation payout of $31 million to the long-suffering victims of the tragedy. The hard fact of life is that white-collar offenders often have some things of real value to offer the community in exchange for legal immunity. It is a sad reality of power that cannot be wished away by pious sloganeering about justice. The most regular occurrence of this sort occurs with financial institutions deserving of criminal prosecution, where regulators are reluctant to prosecute for fear of causing a run on the institution, ruining small investors who are slow to get their money out.

There are many reasons for not prosecuting even some violations which endanger human life. It is usually not good inspectorial practice to recommend a prosecution when the company comes forward and admits a violation. Thus, for example, airlines must be encouraged to report near disasters, however culpable they may be in relation to them: this way real disasters can be prevented, not only with the airline concerned, but with other airlines around the world. It would be the height of irresponsibility to allow policy in relation to such matters to be driven by considerations of retribution rather than protection of the community.

Although there are many more compelling reasons for not consistently prosecuting white-collar offenders, cost is undoubtedly the most influential reason in practice. Philip Schrag's (1971) gripping account of what happened when he took over the enforcement division of the New York City Department of Consumer Affairs underlines the inevitability of a retreat from commitment to consistent and equitable enforcement of the law when dealing with white-collar crime. When Schrag began in the job he adopted a prosecutorial stance. In response to a variety of frustrations, however, especially the use of delaying tactics by company lawyers, a 'direct action' model was eventually substituted for the 'judicial' model. Non-litigious methods of achieving restitution, deterrence, and incapacitation were increasingly used. These included threats and use of adverse publicity, revocation of licence, writing directly to consumers to warn them of company practices, and exerting pressure on reputable financial institutions and suppliers to withdraw support for the targeted company.

Whether we approve of the retreat from the justice model with white-collar crime, it must be conceded that, given the social system we have inherited, the public gets most of its protection from extra-legal muscle-flexing by regulators which persuades companies to change their ways. We might shudder at the cavalier disregard of due process by the inspector who says (or implies), 'fix that up or I'll be back once a month looking for things to nab you on'. But to the extent that white-collar crime is prevented by modern states, such muscle-flexing may be the most important way it happens. Moreover, we suspect that most companies would prefer to live with a little of such coercion every now and then than with the legal costs of a more litigious relationship with government agencies.

At the same time, many regulatory agencies are cognizant of the need for a degree of formal and public punishment to maintain the reprobative value of law, to foster deterrence, and indeed to protect dominion by showing ordinary citizens that the rich and powerful are not beyond the reach of the law. These ends can be achieved by highly selective white-collar crime enforcement policies in which only occasional offenders are made an example of. The offenders chosen are usually those for whom none of the foregoing arguments against prosecution apply. In practice, regulators choose them not because they are the most deserving of punishment, but because their case would be less costly than others, because their co-operation is not required to retrieve dangerous drugs from the market, and so on.

In summary, two things have been suggested. In this section we have argued that to allow retribution to take precedence in regulating businesses such as airlines, food and drug manufacture, coal-mining, and many others, is to make retributive justice a more important societal goal than protection of human life. No government would or should ever allow this to happen. Earlier we urged that the reality of enforcing the law against business violations which are vast in number, complex in nature, and formidably defended, is that there is no society, and never will be a society, that can allow the dispensation of deserved punishment to be the principle which guides efforts to secure business compliance with the law. A just deserts model of business regulatory enforcement is neither desirable nor feasible. But we now wish to develop a third point which relates closely to these two. This is that the just deserts model does not do as well as the republican even in the promotion of justice, specifically justice as equality.

Whither Equality?

One of the grounds for retributivist attacks on utilitarianism and preventionism, and one of the main retributivist boasts, has been that retributivism manifests the greater concern for justice as equality. We may define justice as equality in the criminal justice context by this principle: those who are equally culpable for equal wrongs (are equal in desert) should be equally punished. A special case of the principle is that more disadvantaged citizens should not be punished more severely than more advantaged citizens who have done equal wrongs. We shall argue that republican theory involves practices superior in their compliance with justice as equality than retributive theory. In Chapter 6 we saw how the presumption in favour of the checking of power motivates a variety of policies to guarantee equal treatment before the law, unless some publicly recognized reason for differential treatment is announced. Republicanism may not measure up perfectly against the yardstick of justice as equality but any injustice which it tolerates, it tolerates in the name of promoting dominion in an accountable manner; and, as we shall see, it will not have as much injustice to tolerate as the retributivist alternative.

Retributivists sometimes delude themselves with platitudes about the commitment of liberal democracies to equal enforcement of the law, blind to class differences, but these are empty slogans. Long ago Ehrlich (1936: 238) pointed out that 'the more the rich and the poor are dealt with according to the same legal propositions, the more the advantage of the rich is increased'. Or as Galanter (1975: 363) more colourfully put it, 'the sailor overboard and the shark are both swimmers, but only one is in the swimming business'.

There are two states of complete criminal justice equality. One is where every guilty person is equally punished. The other is where every guilty person is granted mercy. The sociological and fiscal realities of criminal justice mean that every society is always closer to the latter state of equality (zero enforcement) than it is to the former (100 per cent punishment). If we lived in a world where 90 per cent of the guilty were punished, then the way to make the system more equitable would be to pursue the 10 per cent who were getting off. But the reality of societies we know is the opposite. We are lucky to punish 10 per cent of the guilty, leaving 90 per cent of crimes unpunished. It follows that the more of the currently punished 10 per cent that can be extended mercy, the more equitable the criminal justice system will become.

In this most fundamental sense, the principle of parsimony is a principle for maximizing equality. Norval Morris, the most prominent advocate of the principle of parsimony, has been overly defensive of his position against the principle of equality (Morris 1983: 194–5). Let us illustrate the point with Morris's discussion of the sentencing of purse snatchers who had not used or threatened violence beyond the snatching of the purse. Morris found that about two-thirds of repeat offender purse snatchers were sentenced to probation or some other form of community-based supervision, and one-third to prison for about six months, with a handful getting longer or shorter prison terms.

The positive retributivist, as Morris points out, might pursue a version of equality by enforcing the same presumptive sentence for all repeat offender purse snatchers. Looking at the range of existing sentences between the majority who get probation and the substantial minority who get six months, he might be expected to set a presumptive sentence of two months in future for all convicted offenders of this type. This equality-driven solution to the problem is unpalatable to Morris. The amount of suffering inflicted by sentencing 99 offenders to two months is much greater than that from sentencing 33 to six months and granting mercy to 66. The prison threshold is consequential; the dominion difference between non-incarceration and two months' imprisonment may be far greater than that between two and six months. If so, we have substantially increased suffering in the name of equality.

It is this Morris finds unacceptable, and we agree with him. We, like Morris, find it morally repugnant to increase the suffering of one person for no better reason than to establish a greater equality of suffering with others who have done equal wrongs. If we have evidence against six tax offenders but only need punish one of them to get the required message to the community (that this kind of non-payment of tax is a crime), then we should select the most culpable or serious of the six for prosecution. The principle of parsimony counsels against punishment of the other five just so we can treat like cases alike.

Morris says that equality is simply a lesser value than doing what is necessary to protect the community, and doing it with a state which is as parsimonious as possible in its interventions. But there is no need for him to be so defensive, for there is more to be said. If we think systemically about criminal justice, the less we punish, the closer we approach a system in which those who have done equal wrongs are equally punished. So the retributivist who sentences all the purse snatchers to two months' imprisonment increases equality in the punishment of convicted purse snatchers, but does so at the cost of greater inequality in the more morally important category of all guilty purse snatchers (since most purse snatchings do not result in a conviction).

Retributivists can retort that while, in an ideal world, equal treatment of all who are guilty would be preferable, it is sensible and practical to lower our theoretical sights to a concern only about those who end up in court, to ensure only that those convicted of equal wrongs are given equal punishment. But what we have here is just another illustration of the folly of non-comprehensive thinking. One reason for emphasizing the wider category of all guilty criminals of a given type is that there are systematic reasons why the offences perpetrated by more professional and ruthless criminals will be less likely to get to court in the first place. By punishing unsophisticated criminals equally, we increase the inequality between unsophisticated and sophisticated crooks. Taking this point further, by presumptively punishing all the purse snatchers, we increase inequality of punishment among all kinds of property offenders who have done equal wrongs. We increase, for example, the tendency for those who steal by crude physical means to be punished more than those who steal by electronic means or by deception—fraud, embezzlement, insider trading, price-fixing. We increase class-based inequality in punishment.

Non-comprehensive theorists of sentencing play a remarkable game of self-delusion. They agonize over how to give sentences equitably to convicted tax offenders when they know full well that the real action is with the 90 plus per cent of tax offenders who the tax authorities do not send to court—the ones they strike a bargain with, process civilly, or just ignore because they only have the resources to run a small number of easy cases. The big inequality picture is between what happens to these people and what happens to those who are convicted, not inequality among the handful who are sentenced. This is not to deny that, other things being equal, there is real importance in reducing disparities among those who are convicted. But we have attempted to show that other things are not equal. With tax enforcement in Australia, and in most other countries we suspect, minnows are landed in court while the sharks break free of the legal net. Transnational corporations and their executives are never convicted for the widespread practice in Australia of illegal profit-shifting (transfer-pricing). Just as we saw in Chapter 2 that killing discretion in one sub-system can actually increase discretion in the whole system, here we see how increasing equality in one sub-system can worsen inequality in the whole system. Genuine concern about discretion or equality requires systemic analysis.

Some kinds of inequality among persons who are equal in culpability are more important than others. Inequality based on chance should be of less concern to public policy than inequality based on power or class. We are regularly victims of chance inequality. Some of us go through life without breaking a bone in our bodies, while others, without being deserving of more suffering, are forever falling down stairs. Public policy does not concern itself greatly with inequality based on chance alone because it is assumed that while misfortune will frown on us with suspect to some chance inequalities, good luck will smile on us with others. Not so with inequality based on power. The fact that a person suffers because of powerlessness increases the probability that she will suffer in countless other kinds of ways. Powerlessness begets victimization begets powerlessness begets more victimization. This is what is meant by 'self-perpetuating poverty' or 'cycles of disadvantage' (Rutter and Madge 1976). Public policy therefore rightly has a greater concern with rooting out structural inequality based on power in all its insidious forms than with removing inequality based on chance.

Implementation of our theory would reduce class-based inequality of punishment in two ways: in a major way, by showing mercy to more blue-collar criminals; and in a minor way by punishing some types of white-collar crime which currently enjoy virtual immunity from the criminal law. Although it is not designed to conquer the problem of class inequality, its application would reduce class-based inequality in punishment. Retributivism, which sets its sights on injustice, worsens class injustice before the law. It imposes desert with some success against the powerless, but it cannot do so with the powerful. While presumptive sentencing according to desert increases certain narrowly defined equalities in sentencing when compared to the parsimonious sentencing required by our theory, presumptive sentencing worsens overall inequality in the punishment of criminals who have committed crimes of equal seriousness. Our theory therefore implies a criminal justice system in which those who have done equal wrongs are more likely to get equal punishment than under retributivism.

Conclusion

Retributivism has been found to fail in three distinct and important respects. It is not a feasible theory of criminal justice, because its consistent application in the area of white-collar as well as blue-collar crime would require resources and commitments well beyond the reach of any society. It is not a desirable theory of criminal justice, because its application, particularly its application to white-collar crime, would probably increase such crime rather than reduce it. And finally retributivism is such that if it were applied in practice, then there would be less of that equal justice which it hails than we would expect to find under a republican dispensation.

10

Conclusion

In this chapter we will do no more than touch upon some salient conclusions. A summary of the book has been provided at the end of Chapter 1. First, we will highlight the key features of our theory; second, note major complaints against retributivism; and third, identify the common ground between the two theories, with a view to further dialogue.

Seven Key Features of the Republican Theory

The seven key features are that the theory is comprehensive; consequentialist; republican; rights-respecting; limits-respecting; supportive of presumptions in favour of parsimony, the checking of power, reprobation, and reintegration; and practical.

The first key feature is that it is a comprehensive normative theory of criminal justice; it supplies a basis for handling the main questions of criminal justice policy, from deciding what should be a crime to assessing how to run a prison. Second, it is a consequentialist theory, a theory which would evaluate the criminal justice system by the consequences it promotes, not by the constraints it satisfies. Third, it is a republican theory, a theory which sets up as the consequence of concern the republican target of maximizing dominion.

A feature of dominion as a target is that it requires a restrictive form of consequentialism: the good consequence of maximizing dominion can only be secured when agents restrict their deliberations, tying their hands against breaching certain rights, even in cases where an isolated breach might advance dominion. The fact that it involves a restrictive, rights-respecting form of consequentialism is the fourth key feature of our theory.

The rights-respecting aspect of the theory should be no surprise, given the republican target. Dominion, freedom in the republican sense, requires more than the bare fact of exemption from interference by others: more than the liberal notion of freedom. Although it starts from a negative rather than a positive definition of freedom, it requires equal liberty-prospects with others and the knowledge shared with others of having those prospects; it has a social and a subjective side. If the criminal justice system is to promote a psychologically rich target of this kind, it should be no surprise if agents of the system have to restrict the options they are prepared to consider, eschewing the possibility of ever breaching certain rights.

The fifth key feature of our theory is that not only is it rights-respecting, it is also limits-respecting, invoking a goal for the criminal justice system which is, as we have put it, satiable. If the criminal justice system is designed just to reduce crime then even within the bounds of respecting uncontroversial rights, there seems no end to the extreme measures that may be demanded: extremely harsh punishments, extremely invasive techniques of surveillance, extremely incautious prosecutorial practices. The reason is that these measures may well reduce crime and are not criminal themselves. Our theory is limits-respecting, by contrast, steering us away from the apparatus of a police state, because the recourse to such measures in order to prevent criminal invasions of dominion would itself involve a serious reduction of dominion overall. The point is obvious, given the subjective side to dominion.

The sixth key feature of our theory is its association with the four specific presumptions in favour, respectively, of parsimony, the checking of power, reprobation, and the reintegration of victims and offenders. Parsimony, the presumption in favour of less intervention rather than more, gives the theory a minimalist quality which establishes common ground with both the liberal and libertarian traditions. But it is the other three presumptions that give the theory its republican stamp. They mean that the criminal justice system favoured by republicans will place restraints on, and require accountability of, those who have power within the system; that the system will respond to convicted offenders in a way that brings home to them the community's disapproval rather than having blind recourse to the instruments of punishment; and finally that the system will seek to restore to the enjoyment of full dominion those who have been deprived of it by crime or punishment.

The seventh key feature is that the theory is practical. A common error occurs when criminal justice theorists pluck out of philosophical discourse an idealized view of the right and fail to connect it with the discourses of living and breathing communities. An opposite error occurs when theorists accept at face value the common sense of the masses or of the élite, a common sense that may just reflect a prevailing ideology. Our theory, we hope, steers a constructive course between these errors. It deploys tested philosophical ideas associated with traditions like consequentialism and republicanism. But it takes account, given the very nature of those ideas, of people's psychological sensitivities and capacities, of their traditions of reasoning and honour and shame, and of their dispositions sometimes to want retribution, sometimes to offer forgiveness and compassion. The theory is tuned to '*Realpsychologie*'.

It is also tuned to *Realpolitik*. One of its most distinctive features is the prospect it offers of being introduced, bit by bit, under a strategy of incremental implementation. We do not favour incrementalism for its own sake; if it is unguided by theory we think that it systematically favours the status quo. But we think that any theory which lends itself, like ours, to incremental implementation has a precious advantage over those which do not. Our theory is tuned in other ways too to *Realpolitik*. It connects with many conservative traditions of thinking, such as on denunciation and victim concern, and puts them to work in a progressive framework.

Retributivism: A Negative Perspective

Retributivism is a theory concerned to honour constraints, in particular constraints of desert; it denies that the promotion of suitable consequences is, even at base, what the criminal justice system requires. Yet we have seen that retributivism itself runs often in consequentialist channels. Those who look for the rationale of punishment, as the retributivist conceives of it, often slip into thinking of the allegedly rationalizing factor—say, the balancing of benefits and burdens—as itself a goal to promote;

they become target-retributivists. But, more important than this, even retributivists who remain staunchly committed to certain constraints of desert need to have recourse to consequentialist considerations in order to answer questions of criminal justice other than those related to sentencing. Thus retributivists will need to invoke considerations about consequences to determine what should be criminalized, how the police should exercise their surveillance and investigative functions, what apparent offenders should be prosecuted, and so on. They will need to mix their retributivism with consequentialism. If different consequentialist theories are needed to solve these different problems, then retributivists are driven to an exceedingly complex theory.

Is it possible for retributivists to avoid the focus on sentencing and argue that the doctrine of just deserts for all is able to provide satisfactory guidance on most of the questions of criminal justice? We think not, for a number of reasons, all rehearsed in our text. First, constraints, as distinct from goals, are of no value in evaluating or designing institutions when risk and uncertainty prevail; the point was stressed in Chapter 3. Second, retributivist constraints go with an emphasis on never treating individuals as means, say as the deterrence theorist is said to do, and this sort of ideal, at least when strictly interpreted, is going to block most of the work of police and prosecutors; it even looks hostile to the idea of compelling witnesses to testify. More generally, and third, it is not feasible to require police, prosecutors, and environmental inspectors to honour a constraint of pursuing desert wherever they find it. It simply cannot be done. Finally, an attempt to operationalize retributivism in areas like policing and prosecution would make fiscally impossible demands, and this when retributivism makes no provision for fiscal restraint as a proper moral concern.

The fact that retributivism has to be complemented by a consequentialist theory or theories has provided us at various points in the text with a reason to explore other alternatives. We have laid stress on the need to have a comprehensive theory of criminal justice and on the failure of retributivism to help us meet that need. But this is not the only source of our misgivings about the approach. We have also argued that even in the area of sentencing, the home ground of retributivism, the approach does badly. One of our complaints has been indeed that in this area too, retributivism has to help itself to consequentialist supplements. As many retributivists have recognized, retributivism does not fare well on the 'why punish?' question; as we just mentioned, retributivist attempts to provide a rationale for punishment drift into consequentialist doctrines. Thus they are led to argue that while the general justifying aim of punishment is, say, to prevent crime, the way punishment should be distributed is determined by retributivist constraints (e.g. von Hirsch 1985).

We object to this sort of position, and not just because it is excessively complex in having a retributivist and a consequentialist component. It is a theory of dubious coherence, since it is not made clear why punishment should be imposed according to retributivist constraints in cases where its imposition happens not to advance the general justifying aim of the institution. Equally, it is an uncritical theory, in so far as it assumes without question that punishment in the strict sense—as distinct from non-punitive varieties of reprobation, victim-compensation, and the like—is the proper response to crime.

Retributivism: A Positive Perspective

These critical remarks recall some of the reasons why we prefer our republican theory to a retributivist approach. But it is worth also recalling that our theory has much in common with retributivism, endorsing many of the points made by the new retributivists against traditional consequentialist theories of punishment. Here we wish to emphasize three respects in which the theory converges with retributivist doctrine: in its concern for negative desert constraints; in its backward-looking as well as its forward-looking perspective; and in its focus on reprobation.

The implication of our title 'Not Just Deserts', under one disambiguation, is that we are concerned with deserts in some measure. And so indeed we are. We agree with negative retributivists in holding that only those found guilty should be punished, and then not above a certain degree; we reject the extra constraints endorsed by full retributivists, that all the guilty should be punished and punished not below the relevant degree. But two things distinguish our approach from that of negative retributivists.

The first is that unlike them we do not take the relevant constraints as primitives, incapable of being derived from any goal that their fulfilment promotes. The right of the innocent not to be punished, and the upper limit we put on the punishment of the guilty, are both derived within our theory as measures required for the promotion of dominion. We have tried to show that unless such measures are firmly in place the dominion of people in the society at large will be seriously compromised. Although consequentialist in structure, our theory, as we put it before, is rights- and limits-respecting.

The second way in which we differ from retributivists on their negative deserts is that not only do we go deeper, in search of foundations for these deserts; we also go wider. Specifically we argue for the right of the innocent not to be punished as one among a package of rights that we think our theory would support. And equally we argue for the limit on punishment of the guilty as one among a set of limits, such as limits on police intrusion and prosecutorial initiative, that we would want the criminal justice system to respect.

Retributivists may argue against us that in deriving the right of the innocent not to be punished, and the limit on punishment of the guilty, from our republican goal, we make those rights and those limits too contingent; they cease to be properly moral constraints. We would reply that if a right or a limit is to be honoured generally, it must be made generally intelligible and that the best way to do this is a consequentialist derivation. Such a derivation represents rights and limits as moral constraints, in the only sense of 'moral' that consequentialism countenances: they are constraints grounded in the demands of a desirable goal.

Notice in this connection that it is common ground between republicanism and retributivism that while the law should impose a limit on punishment that the courts cannot breach, the law can be changed to alter the value of the upper limit. Both retributivists and republicans can pursue an incremental search for the morally correct level for that limit. And the morally correct limit can change with new circumstances: for both the retributivist and the republican, the pushing of a drug should attract a higher maximum when a more potent, more addictive brand of the drug becomes available; for both the retributivist and the republican, the air becoming more polluted can justify changes to the maximum for pollution. The more important point of agreement, however, is that the law should announce limits on punishment that cannot be breached by the courts. If this agreement is limited in scope, it is fundamental in nature. In any policy conflicts both retributivists and republicans argue that we must always hold firm to the negative desert constraints in preference to other policies. Neither the republican nor the retributivist could agree to ignore the need for an upper constraint on punishment because this will advance reprobation, or advance anything else.

The second respect in which our theory converges with retributivist doctrine is in having a backward-looking aspect as well as the forward-looking feature which is typical of all consequentialist theories. Retributivists pride themselves on having the criminal justice system focus on the actual offence and the actual victim in determining its response. The issue in deciding punishment is not how useful the punishment will be in deterrence, protection, rehabilitation—considerations that do not concern the actual crime—but how far it will help to put right in some way the offence that has been committed. The criminal justice system is held to give a certain satisfaction to the victim, so far as it looks back at her precise complaint, taking it seriously in its own right and not just as a sign of future danger and threat.

Unusually among consequentialist approaches, our theory maintains this sort of backward-looking focus on the offence and the victim. The primary reason for a backward focus on the victim is that if a victim finds herself unable to activate the criminal justice system in the cause of her complaint, in particular if she finds herself less able to do so than others with similar complaints, then her dominion is seriously affected. She now knows that she does not have the prospect she may have imagined she had of enjoying the sort of liberty that was invaded, or she knows that she does not have the same prospect as others who move in more influential circles. This is an undesirable result from the point of view of republican theory, and hence the theory supports the retributivist focus on the actual offence and the actual victim. The victim's complaint is not just a signal that there is a dangerous criminal at large, that there is a need to deter others who may be tempted to copy the crime, or whatever. It has importance in its own right.

But not only does our republican theory match the backward-looking focus of retributivism in this regard. In one other way it goes much further. A feature of the theory is its concern with the reintegration of the victim: its concern with having the criminal justice system do all it can to restore the victim to the full enjoyment of dominion. This will mean providing aid and comfort in the period of initial distress; establishing contact for the victim with those who may be able to help her overcome any lingering problems; ensuring that compensation is available where appropriate; and, if this is something distinct, extracting where possible an act of recognition by the offender that he has wronged the victim.

The third and final respect in which our republican theory converges with retributivism, at least in some influential recent manifestations of that doctrine, is in the emphasis it places on the reprobation of the offender. Many recent retributivist supporters and sympathisers have laid stress on reprobation: see Nozick (1981); Hampton (1984); Murphy and Hampton (1989); von Hirsch (1985); Oldenquist (1986, 1988); and Duff (1986). We are happy to join them in this emphasis but we would mention two ways in which our approach remains distinct from that which most of them favour. First of all, reprobation is something that we see as suitable for promotion; it is a target for the system, not a constraint. Second, and perhaps even more important, we do not see any presumptive connection between reprobation and punishment as traditionally conceived; we think that often it may best be promoted, for example, by non-punitive means of expressing community disapproval.

To the conclusion then of our conclusion. We think that the new retributivism has sounded the death-knell of traditional, consequentialist approaches to criminal justice. We think furthermore that it is a theory, particularly in its negative variety, which has many commendable features. But we believe, and we hope we have done something to show, that it is just not good enough. We offer our theory as an approach that combines the intellectual strengths of consequentialism with the insights of the retributivist tradition. Like retributivism, our approach supports deserts. But not pure, underived deserts; not all deserts; and not just deserts.

References

Alexander, Christopher (1971), *Notes on the Synthesis of Form*, Cambridge, Mass.: Harvard University Press.

Arblaster, Anthony (1984), *The Rise and Decline of Western Liberalism*, Oxford: Blackwell.

Armstrong, K. G. (1961), 'The Retributivist Hits Back', *Mind*, 70: 486–7.

Ashworth, Andrew (1983), *Sentencing and Penal Policy*, London: Weidenfeld & Nicolson.

—— (1986), 'Criminal Justice, Rights and Sentencing: A Review of Sentencing Policy and Problems', Paper to Australian Institute of Criminology Sentencing Conference, Canberra.

Baldwin, Robert, and Hawkins, Keith (1984), 'Discretionary Justice: Davis Reconsidered', *Public Law*, 1984: 570–99.

Baldwin, Tom (1984), 'MacCallum and the Two Concepts of Freedom', *Ratio*, 26: 125–42.

Bardach, Eugene, and Kagan, Robert A. (1982), *Going By the Book: The Problem of Regulatory Unreasonableness*, Philadelphia: Temple University Press.

Barrett, A. R. (1895), *The Era of Fraud and Embezzlement*, Boston.

Bayley, David H. (1976), *Forces of Order: Police Behavior in Japan and the United States*, Berkeley Calif.: University of California Press.

Bedau, Hugo Adam (1976), 'Concessions to Retribution in Punishment', in J. B. Cederblom and W. L. Blizek (eds.), *Justice and Punishment*, Cambridge, Mass.: Ballinger Publishing Co.

—— (1978), 'Retribution and the Theory of Punishment', *Journal of Philosophy*, 75: 601–20.

Benn, S. I., and Peters, R. S. (1959), *Social Principles and the Democratic State*, London: Allen & Unwin.

—— and Weinstein, W. L. (1971), 'Being Free to Act and Being a Free Man', *Mind*, 80: 194–211.

Bentham, Jeremy (1970 edn.), *An Introduction to the Principles of Morals and Legislation*, J. Burns and H. L. A. Hart (eds.), London: Athlone Press, University of London.

Berlin, I. (1958), *Two Concepts of Liberty*, Oxford: Oxford University Press.

Blanshard, Brand (1968), 'Retribution Revisited', in E. H. Madden, R. Handy, and M. Farber (eds.), *Philosophical Perspectives on Punishment*, Springfield, Ill.: Charles C. Thomas.

Blumstein, A., Cohen, J., and Nagin, D. (eds.), (1978) *Deterrence and Incapacitation: Estimating the Effects of Criminal Sanctions on Crime Rates*, Washington, DC: National Academy of Sciences.

Bottoms, A. E. (1980), 'An Introduction to The Coming Crisis', in A. E. Bottoms and R. H. Preston (eds.), *The Coming Penal Crisis: A Criminological and Theological Exploration*, Edinburgh: Scottish Academic Press.

Braithwaite, John (1978), 'An Exploratory Study of Used Car Fraud', in P. R. Wilson and J. Braithwaite (eds.), *Two Faces of Deviance: Crimes of the Powerless and Powerful*, Brisbane: University of Queensland Press.

—— (1982*a*), 'Challenging Just Deserts: Punishing White-Collar Criminals', *Journal of Criminal Law and Criminology*, 73: 723–63.

—— (1982*b*), 'Paradoxes of Class Bias in Criminal Justice', in H. Pepinsky (ed.), *Rethinking Criminology*, Beverly Hills, Calif.: Sage.

—— (1982*c*), 'Enforced Self-Regulation: A New Strategy for Corporate Crime Control', *Michigan Law Review*, 80: 1466–507.

—— (1984), *Corporate Crime in the Pharmaceutical Industry*, London: Routledge & Kegan Paul.

—— (1985), *To Punish or Persuade: Enforcement of Coal Mine Safety*, Albany, NY: State University of New York Press.

—— (1989), *Crime, Shame and Reintegration*, Cambridge: Cambridge University Press.

—— and Geis, Gilbert (1982), 'On Theory and Action for Corporate Crime Control', *Crime and Delinquency*, 28: 292–314.

—— and Grabosky, Peter (1985), *Occupational Health and Safety Enforcement in Australia*, Canberra: Australian Institute of Criminology.

—— Vale, Susan, and Fisse, Brent (1984), *The Role of Prosecution in Consumer Protection*, Canberra: Australian Federation of Consumer Organizations.

Burgh, Richard W. (1982), 'Do the Guilty Deserve Punishment?' *Journal of Philosophy*, 79: 193–209.

Card, Claudia (1972), 'On Mercy', *The Philosophical Review*, 81: 182–207.

Carson, W. G. (1970), 'White-Collar Crime and the Enforcement of Factory Legislation', *British Journal of Criminology*, 10: 383–98.

Chan, Janet (1986), *The Limits of Sentencing Reform*, Canberra: Paper to National Sentencing Conference (unpublished).

Chilton, R., and DeAmicis, J. (1975), 'Overcriminalization and the Measurement of Consensus', *Sociology and Social Research*, 15: 318–29.

Christie, Nils (1981), *Limits to Pain*, Oxford: Martin Robertson.

Clinard, Marshall, Yeager, Peter C., Brisette, J., Petrashek, D., and Harries, E. (1979), *Illegal Corporate Behavior*, Washington, DC: National Institute of Justice.

Cocozza, J. J., and Steadman, H. J. (1978), 'Prediction in Psychiatry: An

Example of Misplaced Confidence in Experts', *Social Problems*, 25: 265–76.

Cohen, M. L., and Groth, A. N. (1978), 'The Clinical Prediction of Dangerousness', *Crime and Delinquency*, 24: 28–39.

Cohen, Stanley (1985), *Visions of Social Control*, Cambridge: Polity Press.

Conrad, John P., and Dinitz, Simon (eds.) (1977), *In Fear of Each Other: Studies of Dangerousness in America*, Lexington, Mass.: Lexington Books.

Conyers, John (1980), *Dissenting Views: Report of the Judiciary Committee of the House of Representatives on the Criminal Code Revision Act of 1980*, Washington, DC: US Government Printing Office.

Cranston, Ross (1979), *Regulating Business: Law and Consumer Agencies*, London: Macmillan.

Cullen, Francis T., and Gilbert, Karen E. (1982), *Reaffirming Rehabilitation*, Cincinnati, Ohio: Anderson Publishing Co.

—— Link, B. G., Travis, L. F., and Wonziak, J. F. (1985), 'Consensus on Crime Seriousness: Empirical Reality or Methodological Artifact?' *Criminology*, 23: 99–118.

—— Maakestad, William J., and Cavender, Gray (1987), *Corporate Crime Under Attack: The Ford Pinto Case and Beyond*, Cincinnati, Ohio: Anderson Publishing Co.

Daly, Kathleen (1987), 'Structure and Practice of Familial-Based Justice in a Criminal Court', *Law and Society Review*, 21: 267–90.

Davis, Kenneth Culp (1969), *Discretionary Justice: A Preliminary Inquiry*, Champaign, Ill.: University of Illinois Press.

Davis, Michael (1983), 'How to Make the Punishment Fit the Crime', *Ethics*, 93: 726–52.

Denning, Lord (1984), in *Report of the Royal Commission on Capital Punishment*, London: HMSO, s. 53. Cited in Honderich (1984: 50).

Department of Transport (1982), *The Cost of Automobile Safety Regulations*, Washington, DC: National Highway Transport and Safety Administration.

Departmental Committee on Corporal Punishment (1938), Chairman: E. Cardogan, *Command Paper*, London: HMSO, No. 5684.

Dinitz, Simon, and Conrad, John P. (1978), 'Thinking About Dangerous Offenders', *Criminal Justice Abstracts*, 10: 99–130.

Drane, Robert W., and Neal, David J. (1980), 'On Moral Justifications for the Tort/Crime Distinction', *California Law Review*, 68: 398–421.

Duff, R. A. (1986), *Trials and Punishments*, Cambridge: Cambridge University Press.

Durham, Alexis M. (1988) 'Crime Seriousness and Punitive Severity: An Assessment of Social Attitudes', *Justice Quarterly*, 5: 131–54.

Durkheim, Émile (1961 edn.), *Moral Education: A Study in the Theory and Application of the Sociology of Education*, trans. E. K. Wilson and H. Schnurer, New York: Free Press.

Dworkin, Gerald (1982), 'Is More Choice Better than Less?' *Midwest Studies in Philosophy*, 7: 47–61.

—— (1988), *The Theory and Practice of Autonomy*, Cambridge: Cambridge University Press.

Dworkin, Ronald (1981), 'What is Equality? Part 1', *Philosophy and Public Affairs*, 10: 185–246.

Ehrlich, E. (1936), *Fundamental Principles of the Sociology of Law*, Cambridge, Mass.: Harvard University Press.

Elster, Jon (1982), *Sour Grapes*, Cambridge: Cambridge University Press.

Ezorsky, Gertrude (1972), *Philosophical Perspectives on Punishment*, Albany, NY: State University of New York Press.

Falls, M. Margaret (1987), 'Retribution, Reciprocity and Respect for Persons', *Law and Philosophy*, 6: 25–51.

Feeley, Malcolm M. (1979), *The Process is the Punishment*, New York: Russell Sage.

—— (1983), *Court Reform on Trial: Why Simple Solutions Fail*, New York: Basic Books.

Feinberg, Joel (1970), *Doing and Deserving*, Princeton, NJ: Princeton University Press.

—— (1973), *Social Philosophy*, Englewood Cliffs: Prentice Hall.

—— (1986), *Harm to Others*, vol. 1, Oxford: Oxford University Press.

Figlio, R. M. (1975), 'The Seriousness of Offenses: An Evaluation of Offenders and Non-Offenders', *Journal of Criminal Law and Criminology*, 66: 189–200.

Finnis, J. (1980), *Natural Law and Natural Rights*, Oxford: Clarendon Press.

Fisse, Brent, and Braithwaite, John (1983), *The Impact of Publicity on Corporate Offenders*, Albany, NY: State University of New York Press.

Foucault, Michel (1977), *Discipline and Punish: The Birth of the Prison*, New York: Pantheon.

Freiberg, Arie, and Fox, Richard (1986), 'Sentencing Structures and Sanction Hierarchies', Canberra: Paper to seminar on Sentencing, Australian Institute of Criminology.

Galanter, Marc (1975), 'Why the "Haves" Come Out Ahead: Speculations on the Limits of Legal Change', *Law and Society Review*, 9: 95–160.

Galligan, D. J. (1981), 'The Return to Retribution in Penal Theory', in *Crime, Proof and Punishment: Essays in Memory of Sir Rupert Cross*, London: Butterworths.

Garcia, J. L. A. (1986), 'Two Concepts of Desert', *Law and Philosophy*, 5: 219–35.

Gaylin, Willard, and Rothman, David J. (1976), 'Introduction', in Andrew von Hirsch, *Doing Justice: The Choice of Punishments*, New York: Hill and Wang.

Geertz, Clifford (1983), *Local Knowledge*, New York: Basic Books.

Geis, Gilbert (1973), 'Victimization Patterns in White-Collar Crime', in I. Drapkin and E. Viano (eds.), *Victimology: A New Focus*, vol. 5, Lexington, Mass.: Lexington Books.

General Accounting Office (1978), *Federal Agencies Can and Should Do More to Combat Fraud in Government Programs: Report to the Congress by the Comptroller-General of the United States*, Washington, DC: General Accounting Office.

Goodin, Robert E. (1982), *Political Theory and Public Policy*, Chicago, Ill.: University of Chicago Press.

Grabosky, Peter N., and Braithwaite, John (1986), *Of Manners Gentle: Enforcement Strategies of Australian Business Regulatory Agencies*, Melbourne: Oxford University Press.

—— —— and Wilson, Paul R. (1987), 'The Myth of Community Tolerance Toward White-Collar Crime', *Australian and New Zealand Journal of Criminology*, 20: 33–44.

Gray, John (1986), *Liberalism*, Milton Keynes: Open University Press.

Green, T. H. (1889), 'On the Different Senses of "Freedom" as Applied to Will and to the Moral Progress of Man', in R. L. Nettleship (ed.), *Works of T. H. Green*, vol. 2, London: Longman Green and Co.

Greenberg, David, and Humphries, Drew (1980), 'The Cooptation of Fixed Sentencing Reform', *Crime and Delinquency*, 26: 206–25.

Greenwood, Peter W. (1972), *Selective Incapacitation*, Santa Monica, Calif.: Rand.

Griffin, J. (1986), *Well-being*, Oxford: Clarendon Press.

Gross, Hyman (1979), *A Theory of Criminal Justice*, New York: Oxford University Press.

Hager, Robert (1985), 'Lawyers on Trial: An Interview with Robert Hager', *Multinational Monitor*, 31: 6–7.

Hall, A. (1985), *Alleviating Jail Overcrowding: A Systems Perspective*, Washington, DC: US Department of Justice, National Institute of Justice.

Hamilton, V. L., and Rytina, S. (1980), 'Social Consensus on Norms of Justice: Should the Punishment Fit the Crime?' *American Journal of Sociology*, 85: 1117–44.

Hamlin, Alan, and Pettit, P. (1989), 'The Normative Analysis of the State', in A. Hamlin and P. Pettit (eds.), *The Good Polity*, Oxford: Blackwell.

Hampton, Jean (1984), 'The Moral Education Theory of Punishment', *Philosophy and Public Affairs*, 13: 208–30.

Harrington, James (1977 edn.), *The Commonwealth of Oceana*, in J. G. A. Pocock (ed.), *Political Works of James Harrington*, Cambridge: Cambridge University Press, 1977.

Hart, H. L. A. (1968), *Punishment and Responsibility*, Oxford: Clarendon Press.

Hawkins, Keith (1984), *Environment and Enforcement: Regulation and the Social Definition of Pollution*, Oxford: Clarendon Press.

Hegel, G. W. (1942 edn.), *Philosophy of Right*, trans. T. M. Knox, Oxford: Oxford University Press.

Henry, Stuart (1983), *Private Justice: Toward Integrated Theorising in the Sociology of Law*, London: Routledge & Kegan Paul.

Hepburn, John R., and Goodstein, Lynne (1985), 'Organizational Imperatives and Sentencing Reform Implementation: The Impact of Prison Practices and Priorities on the Attainment of the Objectives of Determinate Sentencing', Paper to American Society of Criminology Meeting, San Diego (unpublished).

Hestevold, H. S. (1983), 'Disjunctive Desert', *American Philosophical Quarterly*, 20: 357–62.

Hobbes, Thomas (1968 edn.), *Leviathan*, ed. C. B. Macpherson, Harmondsworth: Penguin, 1968.

Homel, Ross (1988), *Policing and Punishing the Drinking Driver: A Study of General and Specific Deterrence*, New York: Springer-Verlag.

Honderich, Ted (1984), *Punishment: The Supposed Justifications*, Harmondsworth: Penguin.

Hutt, Peter (1973), 'Philosophy of Regulation Under the Federal Food, Drug and Cosmetic Act', *Food, Drug and Cosmetic Law Journal*, 28: 176–9.

Ignatieff, Michael (1984), *The Needs of Strangers*, Harmondsworth: Penguin.

Insurance Institute for Highway Safety (1987), *55 speed limit*, Washington, DC: Insurance Institute for Highway Safety.

Jacobs, James B. (1989), *Drunk Driving: An American Dilemma*, Chicago: University of Chicago Press.

Janus, Michael G. (1985), 'Selective Incapacitation: Have We Tried It? Does It Work?' *Journal of Criminal Justice*, 13: 117–29.

Johnson, J., and Douglas, J. (1978), *Crime at the Top: Deviance in Business and the Professions*, Philadelphia: Lippincott.

Johnson, Samuel (1759), *The Idler*, vol. 1 (quoted in Robert Hughes, *The Fatal Shore*, New York: Knopf, 1987: 615).

Joint Economic Committee of the US Congress (1976), *The Cost of Crime in the U.S.*, Washington, DC: US Government Printing Office.

Kaiser, Gunther (1986), 'Capital Punishment in Criminological Perspective', *Crime Prevention and Criminal Justice Newsletter*, 12–13: 10–18.

Kant, Immanuel (1887 ed.), *The Philosophy of Law*, trans. W. Hastie, Edinburgh: T. T. Clark.

Katz, D., and Kahn, R. L. (1978), *The Social Psychology of Organizations*, New York: Wiley.

Kelling, George L. (1988), 'Police and Communities: The Quiet Revolution', in *Perspectives on Policing*, 1, National Institute of Justice and John F. Kennedy School of Government, Harvard University.

Kesner, Idalene F., Victor, Bart, and Lamont, Bruce T. (1986), 'Board Composition and the Commission of Illegal Acts: An Investigation of Fortune 500 Companies', *Academy of Management Journal*, 29: 794.

Kleinig, John (1973), *Punishment and Desert*, The Hague: Martinus Nijhoff.

—— (1986), 'Criminally Harming Others', *Criminal Justice Ethics*, 1986: 3–10.

Knightley, P., Evans, H., Potter, E., and Wallace, M. (1979), *Suffer the Children: The Story of Thalidomide*, New York: Viking.

Kwasniewski, J. (1984), *Society and Deviance in Communist Poland: Attitudes Towards Social Control*, trans. M. Wilson, Leamington Spa: Berg Publishers.

Lane, Michael P. (1986), 'A Case for Early Release', *Crime and Delinquency*, 32: 399–403.

Lewis, C. S. (1967), *Studies in Words*, Cambridge: Cambridge University Press.

Lewis-Beck, Michael S., and Alford, John R. (1980), 'Can Government Regulate Safety: The Coal Mine Example', *American Political Science Review*, 74: 745–56.

Lind, E. Allan, and Tyler, Tom R. (1988), *The Social Psychology of Procedural Justice*, New York: Plenum Press.

Lindley, Richard (1986), *Autonomy*, London: Macmillan.

Lipson, Albert J., and Peterson, Mark A. (1980), *California Justice Under Determinate Sentencing: A Review and Agenda for Research*, Santa Monica, Calif.: Rand Corporation.

Locke, John (1960 edn.), *Two Treatises of Government*, Cambridge: Cambridge University Press, 1960.

Lovejoy, A. O. (1961), *Reflections on Human Nature*, Baltimore, Md.: Johns Hopkins Press.

Lyons, David (1982), 'Utility and Rights', *Nomos*, 24: 107–38.

MacCallum, Gerald (1967), 'Negative and Positive Freedom', *Philosophical Review*, 76: 312–34.

McCloskey, H. J. (1965), 'A Non-Utilitarian Approach to Punishment', *Inquiry*, 8: 239–55.

Mackie, J. L. (1982), 'Morality and the Retributive Emotions', *Criminal Justice Ethics*, 1982: 3–11.

Magnuson, Warren G., and Carper, Jean (1968), *The Dark Side of the Marketplace*, Englewood Cliffs, NJ: Prentice-Hall.

Mann, Kenneth (1985), *Defending White-Collar Crime: A Portrait of Attorneys at Work*, New Haven, Conn.: Yale University Press.

Marx, Gary T. (1977), 'Undercover Cops: Creative Policing or Constitutional Threat?' *The Civil Liberties Review*, 4: 34–44.

—— (1980), 'The New Police Undercover Work', *Urban Life*, 8: 399–446.

—— (1981), 'Ironies of Social Control: Authorities as Contributors to Deviance Through Escalation, Nonenforcement and Covert Facilitation', *Social Problems*, 28: 221–46.

—— (1982), 'Who Really Gets Stung? Some Issues Raised by the New Police Undercover Work', *Crime and Delinquency*, 28: 165 93.

—— (1985), 'The Iron Fist and the Velvet Glove: Totalitarian Potentials with Democratic Structures', Unpublished Paper, Massachusetts Institute of Technology.

—— (1988), *Undercover: Police Surveillance in America*, Berkeley, Calif.: University of California Press.

Mendeloff, John (1979), *Regulating Safety: An Economic and Political Analysis of Occupational and Health Policy*, Cambridge, Mass.: MIT Press.

Miethe, Terence D. (1982), 'Public Consensus on Crime Seriousness: Normative Structure or Methodological Artifact?', *Criminology*, 20: 515–26.

—— (1984), 'Types of Consensus in Public Evaluations of Crime: An Illustration of Strategies for Measuring "Consensus"', *Journal of Criminal Law and Criminology*, 75: 459–73.

—— (1987), 'Charging and Plea Bargaining Practices Under Determinate Sentencing: An Investigation of the Hydraulic Displacement of Discretion', *Journal of Criminal Law and Criminology*, 78: 155–76.

Mill, John Stuart (1910 edn.), *On Liberty*, Everyman's Edition, London: Dent.

Monahan, John (1981), *The Clinical Prediction of Violent Behavior*, Washington DC: Government Printing Office.

—— (1984), 'The Prediction of Violent Behavior: Toward a Second Generation of Theory and Policy', *American Journal of Psychiatry*, 141: 10–15.

—— Novaco, Ray, and Geis, Gilbert (1979), 'Corporate Violence: Research Strategies for Community Psychology', in T. Sarbin (ed.), *Challenges to the Criminal Justice System: The Perspectives of Community Psychology*, New York: Human Sciences Press.

Montesquieu, Baron de (1977 edn.), *The Spirit of Laws*, abr. and ed. D. W. Carrithers, Berkeley, Calif.: University of California Press, 1977.

Moore, Mark H., Estrich, Susan R., McGillis, Daniel, and Spelman,

William (1984), *Dangerous Offenders: The Elusive Target of Justice*, Cambridge, Mass.: Harvard University Press.

Moore, Sally Falk (1978), *Law as Process: An Anthropological Approach*, London: Routledge & Kegan Paul.

Morris, Herbert (1968), 'Persons and Punishment', *The Monist*, 52: 476–9.

—— (1981), 'A Paternalistic Theory of Punishment', *American Philosophical Quarterly*, 18: 263–71.

Morris, Norval (1981), 'Punishment, Desert and Rehabilitation', in Hyman Gross and Andrew von Hirsch (eds.), *Sentencing*, New York: Oxford University Press.

—— (1983), *Madness and the Criminal Law*, Chicago: University of Chicago Press.

Murphy, Jeffrie G. (1970), *Kant: The Philosophy of Right*, London: Macmillan.

—— (1979), *Retribution, Justice and Therapy*, Boston: Reidel.

—— (1985), 'Retribution, Moral Education and the Liberal State', *Criminal Justice Ethics*, 4: 3–10.

—— and Hampton, Jean (1989), *Forgiveness and Mercy*, New York: Cambridge.

Nagin, David (1978), 'Crime Rates, Sanction Levels and Constraints on Prison Population', *Law and Society Review*, 12: 341–66.

Newman, G. (1976), *Comparative Deviance: Perception and Law in Six Cultures*, New York: Elsevier.

—— (1983), *Just and Painful*, London: Macmillan.

New South Wales Bureau of Crime Statistics and Research (1974), *Crime, Correction and the Public*, Sydney: Statistical Report 17.

Nozick, Robert (1974), *Anarchy, State, and Utopia*, New York: Basic Books.

—— (1981), *Philosophical Explanations*, Oxford: Clarendon Press.

Oldenquist, Andrew (1986), 'The Case for Revenge', *The Public Interest*, 82: 72–80.

—— (1988), 'An Explanation of Retribution', *Journal of Philosophy*, 9: 464–78.

Orland, Leonard (1978), 'From Vengeance to Vengeance: Sentencing Reform and the Demise of Rehabilitation', *Hofstra Law Review*, 7: 29–56.

Pepinsky, Harold E., and Jesilow, Paul (1984), *Myths that Cause Crime*, Cabin John, Maryland: Seven Locks Press.

Pettit, Philip (1980), *Judging Justice*, London: Routledge & Kegan Paul.

—— (1982), 'Habermas on Truth and Justice', in G. H. R. Parkinson (ed.), *Marx and Marxisms*, Cambridge: Cambridge University Press.

—— (1985–6), 'Social Holism and Moral Theory', *Proceedings of the Australia Society*, 86: 173–97.

—— (1986), 'Free Riding and Foul Dealing', *Journal of Philosophy*, 83: 361–79.

—— (1987), 'Rights, Constraints and Trumps', *Analysis*, 47: 8–14.

—— (1988*a*), 'The Consequentialist Can Recognise Rights', *Philosophical Quarterly*, 38: 42–55.

—— (1988*b*), 'The Paradox of Loyalty', *American Philosophical Quarterly*, 25: 163–71.

—— (1988*c*), 'Liberalism and its Defence', in Knud Haakonssen (ed.), *The Liberal Tradition*, Sydney: Centre for Independent Studies.

—— (1989*a*), 'The Freedom of the City: A Republican Ideal', in A. Hamlin and P. Pettit (eds.), *The Good Polity*, Oxford: Blackwell.

—— (1989*b*), 'A Definition of Negative Liberty', *Ratio*, NS 2.

—— (1989*c*), 'Decision Theory, Political Theory and the Hats Hypothesis', in Fred D'Agostino (ed.), *Freedom and Rationality*, Dordrecht: Reidel.

—— (forthcoming *a*), 'Social Holism Without Collectivism', in Edna Ullmann-Margalit (ed.), *The Israel Colloquium in the History, Philosophy and Sociology of Science*, vol. 5, Dordrecht: Reidel.

—— (forthcoming *b*), 'Consequentialism', in Peter Singer (ed.), *A Companion To Ethics*, Oxford: Blackwell.

—— and Geoffrey Brennan (1986), 'Restrictive Consequentialism', *Australasian Journal of Philosophy*, 64: 438–55.

Pocock, J. G. A. (1975), *The Machiavellian Moment*, Princeton, NJ: Princeton University Press.

Pontell, Henry (1978), 'Deterrence: Theory Versus Practice', *Criminology*, 16: 3–22.

—— Keenan, C., Granite, D., and Geis, G. (1983), 'White-Collar Crime Seriousness: Assessments by Police Chiefs and Regulatory Agency Investigators', *American Journal of Police*, 3: 1–16.

Pospisil, Leopold (1971), *Anthropology of Law: A Comparative Theory*, New York: Harper and Row.

Quine, W. V. O., and Ullian, J. S. (1978), *The Web of Belief*, 2nd edn., New York: Random House.

Quinney, Richard (1963), 'Occupational Structure and Criminal Behavior: Prescription Violation by Retail Pharmacists', *Social Problems*, 11: 179–85.

Raphael, D. Daiches (1955), *Moral Judgment*, London: Allen & Unwin.

Rawls, John (1955), 'Two Concepts of Rules', *The Philosophical Review*, 44: 3–13.

—— (1971), *A Theory of Justice*, Oxford: Oxford University Press.

Reiss, Albert J. (1971), *The Police and the Public*, New Haven, Conn.: Yale University Press.

—— (1980), 'Understanding Changes in Crime Rates', in Stephen E. Feinberg and Albert J. Reiss (eds.), *Indicators of Crime and Criminal Justice: Quantitative Studies*, Washington, DC: Government Printing Office.

Reiss, Albert J. (1984), 'Consequences of Compliance and Deterrence Models of Law Enforcement for the Exercise of Police Discretion', *Law and Contemporary Problems*, 47: 84–122.

Richardson, Genevra, Ogus, Anthony, and Burrows, Paul (1982), *Policing Pollution: A Study of Regulation and Enforcement*, Oxford: Clarendon Press.

Riedel, M. (1975), 'Perceived Circumstances, Inferences of Intent and Judgments of Offense Seriousness', *Journal Criminal Law and Criminology*, 66: 201–8.

Rose, A. M., and Prell, A. E. (1955), 'Does the Punishment Fit the Crime? A Study in Social Validation', *American Journal of Sociology*, 61: 247–59.

Rossett, Arthur, and Cressey, Donald R. (1976), *Justice by Consent: Plea Bargains in the American Courthouse*, Philadelphia: J. B. Lippincott.

Rossi, P. H., Simpson, J. E., and Miller, J. L. (1985), 'Beyond Crime Seriousness: Fitting the Punishment to the Crime', *Journal of Quantitative Criminology*, 1: 59–90.

—— Waite, E., Bose, C. E., and Berk, R. E. (1974), 'The Seriousness of Crimes: Normative Structure and Individual Differences', *American Sociological Review*, 39: 224–37.

Rouse, John Jay (1985), 'The Relationship Between Police Presence and Crime Deterrence', *Police Journal*, 58: 118–31.

Rutter, M., and Madge, N. (1976), *Cycles of Disadvantage*, London: Heinemann.

Sadurski, Wojciech (1985), *Giving Desert its Due*, Dordrecht: Reidel.

Sandel, Michael (1984), *Liberalism and its Critics*, Oxford: Blackwell.

Saxon, Miriam (1980), *White Collar Crime: The Problem and the Federal Response*, Washington, DC: Congressional Research Service.

Scanlon, Tim (1982), 'Contractualism and Utilitarianism', in A. Sen and B. Williams (eds.), *Utilitarianism and Beyond*, Cambridge: Cambridge University Press.

Schlesinger, S. E. (1978), 'The Prediction of Dangerousness in Juveniles: A Replication', *Crime and Delinquency*, 24: 40–8.

Scholz, John T. (1984), 'Cooperation, Deterrence and the Ecology of Regulatory Enforcement', *Law and Society Review*, 18: 179–224.

Schrag, Philip G. (1971), 'On Her Majesty's Secret Service: Protecting the Consumer in New York City', *Yale Law Journal*, 80: 1529–603.

Sellin, T., and Wolfgang, M. (1964), *The Measurement of Delinquency*, New York: Wiley.

Sen, Amartya (1979), 'Utilitarianism and Welfarism', *Journal of Philosophy*, 76: 463–89.

—— (1982*a*), *Choice, Welfare and Measurement*, Oxford: Blackwell.

—— (1982*b*), 'Poor, Relatively Speaking', *Oxford Economic Papers*.

Shearing, Clifford D., and Stenning, Philip, C. (eds.) (1987), *Private Policing*, Beverly Hills, Calif. Sage.

Sher, George (1987), *Desert*, Princeton, NJ: Princeton University Press.

Shklar, Judith (1987), *Montesquieu*, Oxford: Oxford University Press.

Shover, Neal, Clelland, D. A., and Lynxwiler, J. (1983), *Developing a Regulatory Bureaucracy: The Office of Surface Mining Reclamation and Enforcement*, Washington, DC: National Institute of Justice.

Singer, Richard G. (1979), *Just Deserts: Sentencing Based on Equality and Desert*, Cambridge, Mass.: Ballinger.

Skinner, Quentin (1983), 'Machiavelli on the Maintenance of Liberty', *Politics*, 18: 3–15.

—— (1984), 'The Idea of Negative Liberty', in R. Rorty, J. B. Schneewind, and Q. Skinner (eds.), *Philosophy in History*, Cambridge: Cambridge University Press.

Smart, Alwynne (1968), 'Mercy', *Philosophy*, 43: 345–59.

Sutherland, Edwin H. (1949), *White-Collar Crime*, New York: Dryden.

Swartz, J. (1975), 'Silent Killers at Work', *Crime and Social Justice*, 3: 15–20.

Ten, C. L. (1987), *Crime, Guilt and Punishment*, Oxford: Oxford University Press.

Thomas, C. W., Cage, R., and Foster, S. (1976), 'Public Opinion on Criminal Law and Legal Sanctions: An Examination of Two Conceptual Models', *Journal of Criminal Law and Criminology*, 67: 110–16.

Twentieth-Century Fund Task Force on Criminal Sentencing (1976), *Fair and Certain Punishment*, New York: McGraw-Hill.

Tyler, Tom R. (1988), 'What is Procedural Justice? Criteria Used by Citizens to Assess the Fairness of Legal Procedures', *Law and Society Review*, 22: 103–35.

Van Dine, Stephen, Conrad, John P., and Dinitz, Simon (1979), *Restraining the Wicked*, Lexington, Mass.: Lexington Books.

Vogel, David (1986), *National Styles of Regulation: Environmental Policy in Great Britain and the United States*, Ithaca, NY: Cornell University Press.

Von Hirsch, Andrew (1976), *Doing Justice: The Choice of Punishments*, New York: Hill and Wang.

—— (1982), 'Desert and White-Collar Criminality: A Response to Dr. Braithwaite', *Journal of Criminal Law and Criminology*, 73: 1164–75.

—— (1985), *Past or Future Crimes: Deservedness and Dangerousness in the Sentencing of Criminals*, New Brunswick, NJ: Rutgers University Press.

Wald, Karen (1980), 'The San Quentin Six Case: Perspective and Analysis', in Tony Platt and Paul Takagi (eds.), *Punishment and Penal Discipline: Essays on the Prison and the Prisoners' Movement*, Berkeley, Calif.: Crime and Social Justice Associates.

Wasik, Martin, and von Hirsch, Andrew (1988), 'Non-Custodial Penalties and the Principles of Desert, *Criminal Law Review*, 1988: 555–72.

Wellford, C. F., and Wiatrowski, M. D. (1975), 'On the Measurement of Delinquency', *Journal of Criminal Law and Criminology*, 66: 175–88.

Welsh, Wayne N., Pontell, Henry N., Leone, Matthew C., and Kintrade, Patrick (1988), *Jail Overcrowding: An Analysis of Policymaker Perceptions*, Program in Social Ecology, Irvine, Calif.: University of California, Irvine.

Wheeler, Stanton, Weisburd, David, Waring, Elin, and Bode, Nancy (1988), 'White Collar Crimes and Criminals', *American Criminal Law Review*, 25: 331–57.

Wilkins, Leslie T. (1984), *Consumerist Criminology*, London: Heinemann.

Wilson, James Q. (1975), *Thinking About Crime*, New York: Random House.

Wilson, Paul R. (1978), 'What is Deviant Language?', in Paul R. Wilson and John Braithwaite (eds.), *Two Faces of Deviance: Crimes of the Powerless and Powerful*, Brisbane: University of Queensland Press.

—— and Brown, J. W. (1973), *Crime and the Community*, Brisbane: University of Queensland Press.

Winter, Gerd (1985), 'Bartering Rationality in Regulation', *Law and Society Review*, 19: 220–50.

Wirszubski, C. (1968), *Libertas as a Political Idea at Rome*, Oxford: Oxford University Press.

Wolfgang, Marvin E., Figlio, Robert M., Tracey, Paul E., and Singer, Simon I. (1985), *The National Survey of Crime Severity*, Washington, DC: US Government Printing Office.

Wright, D., and Cox, E. (1967*a*), 'Religious Belief and Co-education in a Sample of Sixth-form Boys and Girls', *British Journal of Social and Clinical Psychology*, 9: 23–31.

—— —— (1967*b*), 'A Study of the Relationship between Moral Judgment and Religious Belief in a Sample of English Adolescents', *Journal of Social Psychology*, 72: 135–44.

Young, Robert (1986), *Personal Autonomy*, London: St Martin.

Zimring, Franklin E. (1976), 'Making the Punishment Fit the Crime: A Consumer's Guide to Sentencing Reform', *The Hastings Center Report*, 6: 13–17.

—— and Gordon Hawkins (1987), 'Dangerousness and Criminal Justice', *Michigan Law Review*, 85: 481–509.

Index